23445

# Mission to America

• • • • • FIVE ISLAMIC SECTARIAN COMMUNITIES
IN NORTH AMERICA

• • • • • *Yvonne Yazbeck Haddad and Jane Idleman Smith*

*University Press of Florida*

Gainesville • Tallahassee • Tampa • Boca Raton

Pensacola • Orlando • Miami • Jacksonville

Library of Congress Cataloging–in–Publication Data

Haddad, Yvonne Yazbeck, 1935–
    Mission to america: five Islamic sectarian communities in
North America / Yvonne Yazbeck Haddad and Jane Idleman Smith.
        p.    cm.
    Includes bibliographical references (p.   ) and index.
    ISBN 0–8130–1216–3.—ISBN 0–8130–1217–1 (pbk.)
    1. Islamic sects—North America.   I. Smith, Jane I.   II. Title.
BP67.A1H33   1993
297'.8'0973—dc20                                              93–18255

The University Press of Florida is the scholarly publishing agency
for the State University System of Florida, comprised of Florida
A & M University, Florida Atlantic University, Florida International University, Florida State University, University of Central
Florida, University of Florida, University of North Florida, University of South Florida, and University of West Florida.

An earlier version of chapter 2, "The Druze in North America,"
appeared in *Muslim World* 81, no. 2 (April 1991): 111–32. Appendix 2, "United Submitters International Creed," is extracted from
the flyer "Let the World Know, God's Message to the World" (Islamic Productions International, Inc., Tucson, Arizona). Both are
reprinted by permission of the publishers.

Appendix 1, "The Druze Covenant (Al Mithaq)," is a translation
by Abdallah E. Najjar. Reprinted by permission.

University Press of Florida
15 Northwest 15th Street
Gainesville, FL 32611

• • • • • *To Susan and Ramsey, Philip and Leslie*

# Contents

Preface                                                                          ix

*Chapter 1.*  The Sectarian Challenge in Islam                                    1

*Chapter 2.*  The Druze in North America                                         23

*Chapter 3.*  The Ahmadiyya Community of North America                           49

*Chapter 4.*  The Moorish Science Temple of America                              79

*Chapter 5.*  The Ansaru Allah Community                                        105

*Chapter 6.*  United Submitters International                                   137

*Appendix 1.*  The Druze Covenant (Al Mithaq)                                   169

*Appendix 2.*  United Submitters International Creed                            170

Notes                                                                          173

Selected Bibliography                                                          210

Index                                                                          220

# Preface

Events since the 1950s and 1960s have raised interest in the religion of Islam and in the growing community of Muslims in North America representing a broad spectrum of racial-ethnic groups. The general public tends to identify its Muslim neighbors as either immigrants from abroad or indigenous "Black Muslims." Through the depictions of government officials, Washington beltway experts, and the public press, Americans have learned that Muslims come in two basic types, Sunni and Shi'i, and they have been conditioned to think that each group has certain distinguishing characteristics. Shi'ites in particular have been associated with violence, militancy, and terrorism. Most Americans, however, are quite unaware of the range of differences represented among the Muslims in their midst. The Islamic community in the United States is composed of many different kinds of Muslims who have immigrated here as well as Americans who have converted to the faith. They represent not only different national, linguistic, and racial groupings but also a variety of sectarian identifications.

The concern in this volume is not to characterize "mainline Islam," either Sunni or Shi'i. It is, rather, to examine the phenomenon of Islamic sectarianism as it is manifested in five North American communities that consider themselves to be part of the *umma* or community of Islam, or perhaps even the truest spokespersons for the faith. Because of some of the claims made by these groups, however, particularly in relation to their founders, they generally are defined by mainline Muslims as heretical, apostate, or infidel.

The characteristics of these groups vary greatly, but the issues raised by their existence and their claims to valid membership in the community of Islam raise common questions. In general these questions have concerned Muslims since the formative period of the faith: Who can be considered a true Muslim and by what criteria? Who is a valid and acceptable interpreter of the faith of Islam? Who has the right to make that determination? Although Islam has never developed an official clergy, and no formal council has met to agree on "orthodox" doctrine, as has happened in the Christian church, a core of doctrines has come to be associated with the Sunni (those who follow the Sunna, the path or practice of the Prophet) and the Shi'a (the party of 'Ali). The five sectarian groups considered in this study challenge this core of doctrines in a variety of ways.

The first of the sects considered here, the Druze, arose in the twelfth century under the leadership of the Fatimid *caliph* al-Hakim bi-Amr Allah and has flourished over the centuries in Lebanon, Syria, and Palestine. Druze immigrants first arrived in America in the 1870s. Today the American Druze, still a "closed" community made up of emigrants from the Middle East and their descendants, are eager to define their relationship to the Druze community in the Middle East as well as to Islam as a whole. They are debating strategies for survival in a culture that they have appropriated and in which they feel comfortable despite its distance from their heritage and, in some aspects, from the traditional teachings of their sect.

The second group considered here is the Ahmadiyya Community of North America, named for its founder Mirza Ghulam Ahmad. It has been in existence for about a century and has been active in America since the 1920s. Ahmadis, like the Druze, wrestle with issues of foreign identity (in this case Indo-Pakistani) in a Western culture, but unlike the Druze they press hard to mitigate their minority status by attracting converts. Active in the African-American community since their arrival in America, they had a significant early impact on the development of African-American Islam as a reaction to American racism.

One of the groups that the Ahmadis seem both to have influenced and competed with for members in the early decades of the twentieth century is the third group considered here, the Moorish Science Temple of America. Under the direction of their prophet Noble Drew Ali, Moorish Americans, like the Ahmadis, were instrumental in introducing African Americans to Islam. Part of the Moorish-American movement became the Nation of Islam, part was absorbed into Marcus Garvey's Universal Negro Improvement Association, and the remnant continues today.

The Moorish Americans, in some sense precursors of the Nation of Islam, clearly influenced the fourth group considered here, the Ansaru Allah, founded in 1970 by a charismatic African American named Isa Muhammad. The Ansaru Allah share with the Moors a deep concern for affirming their African identity and a strong platform of social and economic advancement for members of the community. But, unlike the Moors, they are increasingly identifying with certain traditional Muslim doctrines while strongly eschewing the Islamic leadership of the Middle East, particularly that of Saudi Arabia. They also espouse overtly racist doctrines that are antithetical to the teachings of Islam.

The fifth group considered here, one that like the Ansaru Allah has participated in a sharp critique of Saudi activities in the name of Islam, now refers to itself as United Submitters International. The Submitters follow the teachings of the late Rashad Khalifa concerning the primacy of submitting to God alone (submission being the literal meaning of *islam*), rejecting what Rashad Khalifa believed to be the idolatrous accretions of the Hadith (sayings by and narratives about the Prophet Muhammad) and the Sunna. Submitters espouse what they consider to be a modernized interpretation of the faith of Islam that is absolutely true to its essential doctrines, based on a numerical system that they insist provides scientific proof of the Qu'ran's miraculousness.

In this study we explore issues of identity as they are raised both by members of these five Islamic communities and by Muslims who consider themselves practitioners of mainline Islam in America and abroad. We examine the sectarian leaders' claims for legitimacy, the theological matters that are of most concern to each group, their distinguishing traits, and the problems that they face as they try to affirm their identities in relation both to the world of Islam and to the American environment. This environment, while not always receptive to their claims or to the ways in which they express their faith, nonetheless provides a context for freedom of religious expression, belief, and practice and offers the potential for each group to propagate and flourish. Despite their conflicts with the main body of Islam and with the often secularizing influence of Western culture, they all enjoy the freedom to grow and develop in a context independent of the authority of official Muslim religious organizations.

We have relied on a diverse set of sources for this study, including the internal documents of the groups themselves, other historical records and accounts, and the texts that provide the descriptions and prescriptions of all of the sects. Whenever possible we have utilized materials prepared by others, Muslim and non-Muslim, in an attempt to characterize each group within the context of Islam as a whole. Perhaps most important, we have tried to view these communities as much as possible from the inside, reading their journals and other writings designed to help their members cope with American life. And, to the extent to which it has been possible, we have personally communicated with members of the communities through correspondence, telephone calls, and private interviews. We have tried to balance scholarly objectivity with a sincere attempt to present the doctrines, worldviews, and concerns of the groups as their own members would affirm them. To this end we are particularly grateful for the cooperation of many of the members themselves, especially Abdallah E. Najjar, Kathy Jaber Stephenson, M. A. Rashid Yahya, Alhaj Ata Ullah Kaleem, Mubasher Ahmad, Sandra Weaver Bey, Sam Khalifa, Edip Yuksul, and Senobar Tofazali.

We offer this study, then, in the hope that it will add to the store of knowledge about the range of perspectives that characterize Islam in America today. We hope to contribute to a better understanding of the struggles that confront members of sectarian groups as they try to live lives of integrity in a secularizing, generally unsympathetic, and sometimes even hostile American environment, and to foster appreciation of the variety of attempts that Muslim Americans are making to appropriate, express, and live in accordance with what they understand to be God's commands for the human community.

# CHAPTER 1

# The Sectarian Challenge in Islam

From its earliest days Islam has been characterized by tension between the dominant body of worshipers, those who for a complex of
often political reasons have identified themselves as "orthodox,"
and opposition groups that have tended to be viewed by the orthodox as sectarian deviations. The general lack of appreciation for the
doctrines of these opposition sects by what emerged as mainline
(Sunni and Shiʿa) Islam, expressed in terms of hostility, rejection,
and charges of heresy, reflects the lengthy history of Islam's struggles to maintain correct belief. Sectarianism generally has been
viewed as a challenge to central political authority as well as to
theological canonicity, and efforts to define sects as existing outside
of the mainline community have a rich history.

According to an Islamic tradition, frequently cited in treatises on
heresiography,[1] the Prophet Muhammad said that the Magians will
be divided into seventy sects, the Jews into seventy-one, the Christians into seventy-two, and the Muslims into seventy-three.[2] In recent years various nationalist and sectarian leaders have used this
tradition to plead for tolerance, claiming that sects are a part of the
mosaic of Islam and that there is room within the faith for a variety
of interpretations and ideas. At other times sectarian leaders have
anathematized those who have not recognized the legitimacy of
their claims. Some Muslims cite a variation on this tradition in
which the Prophet says, "My community will be divided into
seventy-three sects but only one of these will be saved, the others
will perish."[3] When asked which one will be saved, the Prophet says

that it will be the one that follows the Sunna.[4] Advocates of the Sunni tradition take that as an affirmation of their own interpretation of Islam and as evidence that those who would follow other than the Sunna will be condemned.[5]

Some scholars have argued that the term *sect* is an inappropriate translation of the Arabic term *firqa* used in this tradition. Historian Marshall S. G. Hodgson suggests that "school of thought" may be more appropriate. "The elevation of many less well-known viewpoints on one or another issue into full-blown 'sects,' " he writes, "has peopled with strange ghosts the history of Muslim rebellions and urban factions as well as the history of doctrine."[6] Despite the difficulty in comparing orthodox and sectarian doctrine, as well as the problems Western historians and sociologists of religion have had in agreeing on a working definition of *sect*,[7] the term is used here on the assumption that the descriptions provided of the communities in question will give it integrity at least for the purposes of this study.

• • • • • *Traditional Islamic Sects*

During the early centuries of Islamic history many Muslim groups were designated as sectarian. Primarily protest movements dissatisfied with prevailing social and political conditions, they sought to bring about a society that guaranteed justice, equality, and freedom from oppression to all believers. Their aim was to root out corruption and to maintain the piety of their communities according to the standards of the formative period of the faith. While their fortunes have risen and fallen over the years, many have continued as identifiable groups within the larger body of believers. A primary focus of the theological discussions and disputes of these groups has been the issue of legitimate leadership of the Muslim community.

This issue of leadership is one that Muslims have had to face squarely from the moment of the death of the Prophet Muhammad in the year 632. Since he left neither a male heir nor, according to Sunni majority opinion, specific instructions on how to determine his successor, an immediate dispute arose in the community as to how to proceed.[8] In Medina there was confusion; the Ansar (here referring to those citizens of Medina who had been "helpers" and supporters of Muhammad) proposed that leadership should alternate between the Medinians and the immigrants.[9] A further threat to the Islamic coalition surfaced as some of the bedouins who had been giving fealty to Muhammad decided at his death that their treaty obligations were concluded and that they need pay no more alms tax to Medina.

The plea for unity won the day, however, and both the Ansar and the Quraysh (the tribe of the Prophet in Mecca) were persuaded to accept the leadership of Abu Bakr al-Siddiq, with the bedouin tribes soon brought forcibly back into the fold. Abu Bakr, who was elected by acclamation of the leading companions of the Prophet, took the title Khalifat Rasul Allah, successor to the Apostle of God. This line of leadership became known as the caliphate, with 'Umar ibn al-Khattab, 'Uthman ibn 'Affan, and 'Ali ibn Abi Talib, Muhammad's cousin and son-in-law, following in succession. The title Amir al-Mu'minin, leader of the faithful, was first assumed by 'Umar, acknowledging the caliph as commander in chief of the army and the civil administration.

As a political institution the caliphate was developed to serve the current needs of the community. Theologians and jurists later developed political theories either to support the existing order or to affirm the strong central authority of the caliphate when military rulers undermined that authority and turned the caliphs into puppets whose only purpose was to legitimate the rulers' policies. Traditions of the Prophet were quoted supporting the institution of the caliphate, allegiance to which was to be accepted as a matter of faith. The caliphate, therefore, provided the political means of safeguarding palace (orthodox) theology against the opposition, those who interpreted the faith in a fashion different from that propagated by the state and its bureaucracy.

Virtually from the beginning of the Islamic umma, however, the position of the caliphate as the sole authoritative religious leader of the Muslim community sustained major challenges. Supporters of an alternate Islamic leadership known as the Shi'ites or the Shi'a (party) of 'Ali increasingly began to draw their own course away from the main body of Sunni Islam and to develop their own doctrine of religious authority and corpus of prophetic traditions. They came to attribute to 'Ali a kind of special legitimacy that made him not just one in a line of caliphs but the first genuine successor to the leadership role of Muhammad by virtue of a particular knowledge obtained through closeness to the Prophet. The Shi'a

insisted that the leaders of the community must be descendants of
ʿAli, who as *Imams* were to provide religious guidance.

The real impetus for this division in the community was perhaps
less theological than political. The Umayyad caliph Muʿawiya, following ʿAli in the line of caliphal succession, was a strong and ef-
fective ruler in Damascus. His authority, however, was increasingly
challenged by the Muslims of Iraq, who began to look to ʿAli's son
Hussein for leadership. One of the great internal tragedies of Islamic
history occurred in the year 680 when Hussein and his retinue, on
the way to Kufa to meet with a group of supporters, were intercepted
and massacred by Muʿawiya's troops. It was with this event that
Shiʿism really came into its own as a religious and political opposition movement to the Sunni majority. The early struggle between
the caliphate and the followers of ʿAli for legitimate leadership of
the community led al-Shahrastani to say almost a millennium ago,
"No sword has ever been drawn in Islam on a religious question as
it has been drawn at all times on the question of the imamate."[10]
(See table 1 for a listing of Shiʿa Imams.)

The history of Shiʿism is too complicated to sketch in detail
here, but one doctrine in particular has relevance for the self-
understanding of several of the founders of the five groups of this
study. That is their interpretation of the role, function, and identity
of the Imam. The term *imam* is used in a number of different ca-
pacities by Sunni as well as Shiʿi Muslims,[11] but it came to take on
a special meaning as applied to the supporters of ʿAli. In general all
Shiʿites agree that only the blood descendants of ʿAli ibn Abi Talib
are legitimate rulers of the Islamic community. Over the years,
however, the Shiʿa movement split into several branches.

The Zaidis, known also as the "Fivers," acknowledge the legitimacy of Zaid ibn ʿAli as the fifth Imam. Zaidis maintain that the
Imam must be a learned man from the house of the Prophet, although not necessarily through a direct line of heredity. His leadership post is contingent on his religious knowledge as well as his
ability to be a leader in warfare (consequently, he can be neither a
child nor a person in occultation). Followers of Zaid still constitute
an active Muslim group in Yemen, the line of Imams having continued until 1961. Small groups of Zaidis also can be found in Syria,
Lebanon, and the Caspian region of Iran.

Ismaʿilis recognize the legitimacy of leadership of Ismaʿil as the
seventh Imam, and thus are known as "Seveners." In the tenth cen-

tury their appeal increased to the degree that they were able to establish the Fatimid countercaliphate in North Africa, whose hegemony at one time extended into Syria and beyond. At present there are two Isma'ili groups. The Nizari Isma'ilis recognize the legitimacy of Nizar, whose line of Imams has continued from 1095 to today; the Agha Khan is believed to be the current incarnation of God. Nizaris live mainly in Pakistan, India, West Africa, Syria, Bangladesh, Afghanistan, and Tajikistan. The line of leadership of the second Isma'ili branch, the Musta'lians, came to an end in 1130.[12] Another Islamic sect that developed out of the Fatimid caliphate is the community of Druze, one of the groups in this study.

The largest Shi'ite group, known as the Imamis or Ithna 'Asharis ("Twelvers"), traces the lineage of Imams through the eleventh Imam, Hasan al-'Askari, to his son Muhammad al-Muntazar. Still a child when his father died in 873, the twelfth Imam mysteriously disappeared. The doctrine arose that for a variety of political and theological reasons this Imam went into major occultation (*al-ghayba al-kubra*), where he remains on a separate plane of existence managing the affairs of the believers. Imami doctrine teaches that because the Imam serves to guide the inner aspects of human life and action it is not important that he be present physically in the world. It is believed that he will return at the end of time to lead the Muslim community into a state of perfection, ushering in the day of resurrection.[13] Imami Shi'ites constitute most of present-day Iran, over half of Bahrain and Iraq, large minorities in Kuwait, Saudi Arabia, and Dubai, and significant groups in Lebanon, Afghanistan, Bangladesh, Pakistan, India, and the Asian republics of the former Soviet Union.

Some Shi'a groups that continue to have adherents today have been considered extremist (*ghulat*) by both Imami Shi'ites and Sunnis. Two such groups that thrived in Christian areas of the empire appear to have incorporated ideas of a trinity into their esoteric teachings. The 'Alawis, also known as the Nusayris, believe that their founder, Abu Shu'ayb Muhammad ibn Nusayr, was the *bab* (gate) for the eleventh and last legitimate Imam. They have no expectation that a figure will return at some future time. Their teachings have been considered extreme and heretical because of such doctrines as that which calls 'Ali the esoteric essence, Muhammad the exoteric name, and Salman al-Farisi the gate to the essense.[14] A second such syncretistic group considered extremist by both the

Table 1

Legitimate Line of Imams for Shiʿa Groups

| Zaidis (Fivers) | Ismaʿilis (Seveners) | Imamis (Twelvers) |
|---|---|---|
| 1. ʿAli ibn Abi Talib (661) | ʿAli | ʿAli |
| 2. Hasan ibn ʿAli (669) | Hasan | Hasan |
| 3. Husayn ibn ʿAli (680) | Husayn | Husayn |
| 4. ʿAli Zayn al-ʿAbidin (713) | ʿAli Zayn | ʿAli Zayn |
| 5. Zayd ibn ʿAli | Muhammad al-Baqir (732) | Muhammad al-Baqir |
| (followed by an independent line; came to an end in 1961) | Jaʿfar as-Sadiq (765) | Jaʿfar as-Sadiq |
| 6. | Muhammad ibn Ismaʿil | Musa al-Kazim (794) |
| 7. | | |

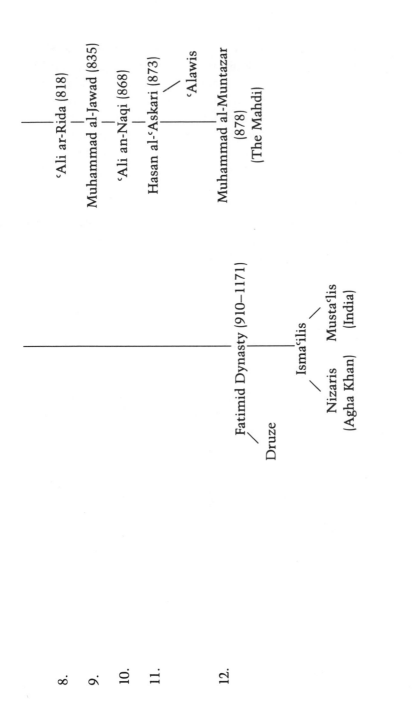

8.  'Ali ar-Rida (818)

9.  Muhammad al-Jawad (835)

10. 'Ali an-Naqi (868)

11. Hasan al-'Askari (873)
    'Alawis

12. Muhammad al-Muntazar (878) (The Mahdi)

Fatimid Dynasty (910–1171)

Druze

Isma'ilis

Nizaris (Agha Khan)

Musta'lis (India)

Sunnis and the Shi'a are the Bektashis, who believe in a trinity of God, Muhammad, and 'Ali.[15]

Another challenge to Sunni authority came from the Kharijites, who refused to accept either Sunni or Shi'i political theory and insisted that the leadership of the community could be assumed by any qualified Muslim and need not be restricted to persons of a certain tribal affiliation (as, for example, the Quraysh, as the Sunnis have insisted) or to the lineage of the family of the Prophet (as the Shi'ites believe). Their only criterion for the legitimacy of the leader of the community is his knowledge in matters of belief. The Kharijite heritage is kept alive today among the Ibadis in Oman, Tanzania, and Algeria.

Between the sixteenth and nineteenth centuries the Ottoman caliphate allowed sectarian groups considerable leeway in matters of belief as long as the groups did not challenge the central authority, did not seek to propagate their beliefs beyond their own adherents, and accepted the rulings of the prevalent legal school. Unlike non-Muslim religious minorities such as Jews and Christians, however, such groups were not recognized as separate religious entities with their own laws pertaining to issues of personal status and leadership of the community.

Real empowerment of the sectarian groups took place under Western colonial rule as the foreign powers used members of minority groups in an attempt to control the majority.[16] The dominance of the West and the control it has exerted on Muslim societies has provided the freedom for the sects to propagate and grow at the same time that reform movements have been suppressed because of their anticolonial stance. Colonial powers both encouraged these sects and used them to their own advantage. Members of the sects were employed in the colonial bureaucracy and given the freedom to practice and propagate their religion. Because of their close association with these foreign powers, sectarian groups have been treated with suspicion, especially in Saudi Arabia and Pakistan, but in general by all Sunni Muslims.

• • • • • *Modern Islamic Sects*

The colonial intrusion into Islamic countries and the domination of the Muslim people by the West provided the context for the rise to prominence of a variety of religious leaders seeking the protection and preservation of their communities. They expressed their opposition to domination in different ways, with a noticeable reinvigoration of religious activity. Opposition to foreign authority ranged from armed struggle, such as that of the *jihads* in India as well as West and North Africa,[17] to reform movements that tried to emulate the values of the conquering West while rejuvenating Islamic teaching to make it relevant for the modern world. Colonialism also gave rise to millenarian groups that attempted to gain relief from subjugation through the hope that a messiah or savior/guide would return to earth to restore justice and equilibrium in a world of turmoil; such groups include the Murids and the Hammalists in West Africa and the Mahdiyya of the Sudan.[18] Among the modern sectarian movements are those that have tried to interpret the faith of Islam as a universal religion, one that is essentially syncretistic in structure, propounding doctrines that in many ways parallel those of the oppressive foreigner at the same time that they struggle to maintain a sense of authenticity and dignity. Such efforts are exemplified by Babism and Baha'ism propagated in Iran,[19] as well as the Ahmadiyya movement, with both its Lahori and Qadiani branches.

Many of the modern sectarian groups that have developed in North America are predominantly African American. They have their roots in the heritage of slavery and emancipation, the urbanization and industrialization of post–Civil War America, and the migration of rural blacks from the South to northern urban centers such as Chicago and Detroit. Important early propagators of Islam in America include immigrants such as Fard Muhammad, American converts such as Russell Webb, and the immigrant missionaries of the Ahmadiyya movement. African Americans have seen in Islam the hope for egalitarian association and a chance for participation in the brotherhood of all believers regardless of race or ethnic background.

The conversion of African Americans to Islam during this century is considered by some to be a return to the religion of their forebears since it is estimated that about one fifth of the slaves brought from Africa were Muslim.[20] As much as a third of the Muslim community in America is made up of persons, mainly African Americans, who have converted to Islam sometime during this century. Many of them are or have been part of the Nation of Islam, which was formed by Elijah Muhammad in the 1930s. Elijah's attempts to provide a firm economic base for the members of his community were reminiscent of the similar efforts of Noble Drew Ali of the Moorish Science Temple. Unlike Ali, however, Elijah based his understanding of the potential of the black man on a doctrine portraying whites as devils, a notion echoed in the early writings of Isa Muhammad of the Ansaru Allah and in the teachings of Clarence Jowars Smith (Clarence 13X) of the Five Percenters (another contemporary sect considered heretical by mainline Muslims).[21] Elijah Muhammad's teachings contrasted sharply with Islamic doctrines of racial equality, a contrast most notably underscored in the later work of Nation member Malcolm X. After Elijah's death in 1975 his son Warith Deen led many of the members of the Nation back to Sunni Islam. A remnant of the Nation of Islam continues to function under the leadership of Louis Farrakhan.

The emphasis on hope for the future of the African-American community based on principles of dignity, hard work, and ethical living has characterized all of the indigenous African-American Islamic groups. Members are called to a transformation of life in which they are challenged to reach their best potential. Salvation lies not in the attainment of a future existence, but in the achievement by individuals and by the community of a sense of self-worth and a place of recognition in the midst of predominantly white American society. Toward this end most of these African-American groups have looked to Asia and Africa, to an original black Islam, for both their identity and their inspiration.

African-American Muslim groups include those who espouse Sunni teachings but appear to have sectarian characteristics, such as exclusive membership with total allegiance to the charismatic leader as well as distinguishing external signs (such as clothing and oaths of allegiance). Darul Islam, at one time the largest African-American Sunni organization, thrived in the 1960s and developed more than twenty mosques. By the early 1980s the membership had come under the influence of Sheikh Jaylani, a Sufi (mystic) of Pakistani origin. A large number of the group defected, and the rest have become the Fuqara (those who accept poverty) under the leadership of Yahya Abdul Karim. Other Sunni groups in the African-American population include the Hanafis under the leadership of Hammas Khalifa Abdul Khalis and the Islamic Party under the leadership of Muzafaruddin Hamid.

Unique among American Muslim sects is the sect known as United Submitters International, a modernist group that arose and to a large extent developed as a result of the pressures of American culture. It is a small movement that was formed from within the immigrant community in America, attracting members from many nations as well as indigenous whites and African Americans. Its adherents affirm the special mission of their founder, Rashad Khalifa, validated by his discovery through the computer that the key to the understanding of the Qur'an is the number nineteen. They seek to focus the faith on rational understanding of the Qur'anic text, which they affirm is the sole source for the revelation and religion of God. For them, adherence to the Sunna of the Prophet is tantamount to the sin of associating the Prophet Muhammad with God.

• • • • • *The Sectarian Challenge*

Islamic revivalist literature claims that in Islam there is no separation of religion and state, a perception agreed upon by Western scholarship on Islam. Regardless of the exceptions that some twentieth-century Muslims have culled from Islamic history to disprove that proposition,[22] it remains true that the issues over which Muslims historically have been divided—those things, to be exact, that have tended to foster sectarianism—have been ones in which definitions of doctrines as well as of the legitimate roles of religious leaders have been inseparable from political issues and concerns. Matters both of doctrine and of leadership have been and continue to be of great importance to the Muslim community as a whole in assessing the legitimacy of the various sectarian movements.

The Qur'an defines *iman*, faith, as the affirmation of the reality of God, of God's messengers, books, and angels, and of the day of judgment.[23] It also suggests a distinction between right practice and right belief. One can fulfill the obligations of right practice— affirmation of faith (in the unicity of God and the prophethood of Muhammad), prayer, fasting, tithing, and going on the pilgrimage—but not necessarily have belief in his or her heart. Thus, one can be a Muslim but not necessarily a believer, as expressed in Sura 49:14.[24] To believe in God is to affirm God's "unicity," that affirmation referred to as *tawhid*. Association of anyone or anything with God, *shirk*, is considered to be heretical. In the medieval period of Islam there were lengthy discussions about whether the affirmation of the attributes of God such as his hearing, seeing, and knowing actually constituted shirk. For many reformist Sunnis shirk has been applied to the adherence to any kind of personality cult, often referred to as "saint worship." At present the influential and conservative Muslim Brotherhood affirms tawhid as its central doctrine. Their literature points to it as the organizing principle of theological and ideological reflection, a holistic Islamic perspective posited in opposition to doctrines such as capitalism or communism.[25]

The Druze have always called their faith "the religion of tawhid" and referred to themselves as *muwahhidun*, unitarians. In the Druze context the reference is not just to the unity of God but to the unity of all being with God, reminiscent of the Sufi doctrine of the unicity of being (*wahdat al-wujud*) that has come under relentless condemnation in the modern world by Wahhabis in Saudi Arabia, by many modernists, and by members of the Muslim Brotherhood and the Jamaati Islami. While the Moorish Americans do not use the language of tawhid, their emphasis on the spirit-man as one with Allah suggests this kind of unity. Rashad Khalifa carries his understanding of tawhid to another extreme. He is so intent on affirming the oneness of God alone that he rejects the second affirmation of the *shahada*, or testimony of faith, that which attests to the prophethood of Muhammad. His concept of tawhid does not deny that prophethood; rather, it denounces what he considers to be Muslim veneration and glorification of Muhammad. Association of the name of God with any human, he says, even the Messenger of God, is tantamount to shirk.

The authority by which individuals have claimed leadership within Islam often has related to the appropriation of particular roles and identities, which the Islamic community has invested considerable time defining. Five specific categories of Islamic religious leadership have been appropriated by founders of the five sects in this study. Most of the leaders have assumed several titles, although none of them has laid claim to all five. These titles are *nabi* (prophet, pl. *anbiya'*), *rasul* (messenger, pl. *rusul*), *mahdi* (guided one), *masih* (messiah), and *mujaddid* (renewer). A brief look at how these designations have been understood historically will help illustrate their importance in elucidating the roles of the leaders of these groups and explain some of the reasons why the appropriation of these roles often has led to responses of outrage on the part of Sunni Muslims.

In Islam, God is understood to have revealed himself through a line of anbiya' (prophets) and rusul (messengers) beginning with Adam and culminating with Muhammad. From this perspective humanity has never been left without guidance; whenever people have strayed from the path of obedience to God's commandments he has sent a prophet to guide them. On the whole the idea of multiple prophets does not signify a multiplicity of messages. Rather, the prophets, according to Sunni belief, were sent by God in a variety of circumstances. Some were reforming prophets who came when the teachings of the previous prophet had disappeared or had been corrupted and there was need for new teachings because members of the community had deviated from the path of righteousness. Some came with a progressive revelation, when the teachings of the previous prophets were no longer sufficient for the needs of humanity, or as prophets confirming the message of another.[26] Others came with a universalizing mission when the teachings of a previous prophet were seen to be restricted to one community and there was a need among other nations for the message. These universalizing prophets were sometimes the bearers of what has been designated as a book, or scripture, the recording of God's divine word. The message that each has brought is basically the same, that of faith in the unity of God. The scriptures considered valid by Muslims in their original form are the Torah (tawrat), the Psalms (zubur), the Gospel (injil), and, finally, the Qur'an, which is a replica of the umm al-kitab, the "mother of the book" or primal revelation eternally preserved with God and currently entrusted to the Muslim community.

A distinction between nabi and rasul (both of which are used in the Qur'an as titles of the Prophet Muhammad) at times has been made by saying that the messenger has a universal revelation or message while the prophet is a particular leader of a particular people. Some have said that it is only the messenger who is sent with a book, while others (in this study, for example, Rashad Khalifa)[27] claim the opposite. That such a clear differentiation of role and audience can easily be made has been challenged by serious critical study of the use of the terms in the Qur'an as explicated by tradi- tional commentators. Willem A. Bijlefeld, for example, concludes that while the words *nabi* and *rasul* do have very different and distinctive connotations, it is impossible on the basis of the Qur'anic text to distinguish clearly between their roles, especially on the matter of bringing a book.[28] We do know that the Qur'an recognizes many more prophets than messengers; the latter are designated specifically as Noah, Lot, Ishmael, Moses, Shu'ayb, Hud, Salih, and Jesus in addition to Muhammad.[29]

Sunni Muslims believe that in the fullness of time the Prophet Muhammad was sent as the final prophet, to be followed by no other. For this he is specifically referred to as the seal of the prophets, *khatm al-nabiyyin*, in Sura 33:40. While the Qur'an does not provide a categorical explanation of this designation, it has been interpreted by Muslims as a direct divine affirmation of the fact that after the revelation of the Qur'an to the Prophet Muhammad there will be no more prophets and, by implication, a cessation of revelation. This is known as the doctrine of *khatm al-anbiya'*, the seal or ending of prophecy. The doctrine as understood particularly by Sunni Muslims affirms the finality of God's communication with humanity, the perfection of Islam, the completeness of the Qur'an, and the understanding of its sufficiency for all human needs for all generations to come.

The importance given to this doctrine explains the strength of the antipathy Sunni Muslims have toward some of the sectarian groups under consideration here, especially insofar as their doctrines might seem to impinge on the belief in the finality of revelation. "No one has received any messages from God since the Prophet Muhammad," says contemporary Muslim writer 'Uthman 'Abd al-Mun'im 'Aysh. "This is a necessary doctrine of the religion and anyone who flaunts it is considered a heretic whose killing is permissible."[30] Islam is a perfect religion, sufficient for all times and places in all situations; thus no new prophet and no new interpretation of religion is needed.[31] Some have felt that it is less clear from the Qur'an whether or not there may be the possibility of more messengers.

The cessation of prophecy, however, has not meant for Muslims a foreclosing of the hope of some assistance for the community in the form of a future deliverer, as the Ithna 'Ashari doctrine of the hidden Imam illustrates. Belief in a messianic figure who will vanquish the forces of evil and bring about a rule of justice and peace is common to many religious traditions. Not prominent at the beginning of Islam when the emphasis was on the establishment of a growing community based on God's revelations, it fairly quickly began to make itself felt and before long had intersected the several major branches of Islam. There is generally no Muslim tradition that expects the return of the Prophet Muhammad himself, aside from a brief flurry of interest in such a possibility several decades after his death.[32] His mission is understood to have been complete and perfect, and when he died it was clear that his task was over. Thus any expectation of a return has been couched in terms of a messiah figure, however that has been interpreted.

D. S. Margoliouth has suggested that the differences in the Christian, Jewish, and Islamic expectations for a messiah are that Jews expect the one who is yet to come and the Christians the return of Jesus or the Second Coming, while at least originally Muslims expected a person who would restore to perfection the present situation of disorder and chaos.[33] From very early times, when the Islamic community began to be rent with internecine struggle, it was clear to the Ithna ʿAsharis that a deliverer was urgent. One title by which such a person came to be known was mahdi, guided one. It was first given to ʿAli's son Muhammad ibn al-Hanafiyya.[34] Even in this context the term began to take on some connotations of esoteric knowledge, especially in matters of Qurʾanic interpretation.

The large corpus of Hadith literature associated with the end of time and the warnings delivered to the community concerning its expectation contains reference to Muhammad's foretelling of the future mahdi. The function of this personage was to "fill the earth with justice even as it has been filled with injustice."[35] Some have attached to the prophesy the expectation that a particular person would come out from the east to prepare the way for the coming of the mahdi, setting the scene for the idea of a "forerunner" that plays a role in the understanding of three of the sects in this study, the Ahmadiyya, the Moorish Americans, and the Ansaru Allah.

The development of the mahdi concept, then, went from that of a deliverer from present chaotic conditions, to someone who would come at a future time, and finally (and gradually) to a figure who is to appear at the end of the world heralding the day of resurrection. The progression suggests foci that are not mutually exclusive, as Abdulaziz Sachedina's summary of the function of the messiah would indicate: "The Islamic messiah, then, embodies the aspirations of his followers in the restoration of the purity of the Faith which will bring true and uncorrupted guidance to all mankind, creating a just social order and a world free from oppression in which the Islamic revelation will be the norm for all nations."[36] This definition certainly seems to fit the self-understanding of those of the founders of the sects under consideration who claim to fulfill the role of mahdi. It is also said in some of the sources that the mahdi will be rejected and persecuted by religious leaders who will regard him as opposed to the Qur'an and the practice of the Prophet. Such persecution has served in the eyes of several of these groups as verification of their founder's role as promised messiah.

The hope for a savior or messiah to come, generally understood as mahdi, characterizes both Sunni and Twelver Shi'i Islam, the latter identifying this figure with the expectation of the reappearance of the twelfth Imam.[37] This promised mahdi of Shi'i hopes is known as the *sahib al-zaman* (Lord of the Age).[38] One of the complications of Islamic eschatological expectations is the lack of clarity between expectation of the mahdi and expectations of the return of 'Isa (Jesus).[39] In the development of the traditions, says D. B. Macdonald, "the roles assigned to Jesus and to the mahdi came to be confusingly alike."[40] Jesus is referred to as the messiah, al-masih, eleven times in the Qur'an, each time in a Medinan Sura. Since there is no clear explanation of just what the appellation means in these references, it is open to a range of understandings. The only verse that might possibly suggest a second coming is 43:61 ("He [Jesus] is a sign for knowing the Hour [of resurrection]"), but that is obscure.[41]

The identification of Jesus with the mahdi in the context of eschatology is understood by some Western scholars to indicate the influence of Judaism and Christianity on early Islam. But it seems clear that for most Muslims the return of Jesus and the coming of the mahdi are seen to be separate events. First the mahdi will arrive to bring in the reign of justice and to strengthen people in the faith, then the Antichrist will make his appearance along with the signs indicating the arrival of the hour of resurrection, then Jesus will come to kill the Antichrist.[42] Regardless of whether the mahdi and Jesus are identified, the general concept of a savior figure has served as a promise for a better time to come and for a release from the oppression of this world for Muslims through the ages. And it is not surprising to find that many figures throughout Islamic history, including several of the founders of the sects under consideration here, have claimed for themselves, or have had claimed for them by their followers, the right to be called the mahdi or messiah of Islam.[43]

It should be noted that some modern Muslim writers reject the notion of a mahdi outright, giving them yet more reason to critique the doctrines propagated by some of the these sects. Extending the idea of the cessation of revelation and prophecy, they say that the concept of mahdi was developed by those who were looking for a justification of their authority. "The idea of the mahdi was developed by the Fatimids, Isma'ilis and Druze," writes al-Nadawi.[44] 'Abd al-Qadir 'Ata agrees, saying that the Druze believe that on the last day Jesus, that is, Hamza, will appear. He rejects the idea of the mahdi outright, saying that those who advocate it believe that the mahdi will bring justice to the earth in a period of seven to nine years. How strange, he says, since no prophet has been able to assure justice in such a short time![45] 'Ata goes on to insist that there is nothing in the Qur'an that points to the appearance of a prophet or a messenger or the return of a mahdi or a reformer as a second coming.

Sunni Islamists not only actively oppose all forms of charismatic leadership, but also reject milleniarian expectations on the grounds that they undermine individual responsibility. Emphasizing a kind of collective communal leadership in which all Muslims are mobilized to assume responsibility for the state of Islam, they decry futuristic hopes in an outside agency as leading to a lessening of personal initiative. The role of the individual Muslim in reshaping this world is emphasized since the recovery of the control of the secular world is at stake. Such control cannot be appropriated by the quietistic political strategy advocated by these sects.

One more traditional Islamic expectation needs to be explained to set the context for the claims of most of these sectarian leaders— that of the mujaddid or renewer of Islam. This concept has to do not with eschatology, but with the periodic renewing of the faith in the face of inevitable departures from the vision and program of the Prophet Muhammad. It is believed that at the beginning of each Islamic century a person will appear who will foster this process of reawakening or revivification, affirmed by reference to a saying of the Prophet Muhammad that "Allah will raise a reformer at the beginning of every century to revive the faith."[46] The function of this person is to identify and purge accretions to the faith and to purify and restore it to its pristine condition. The mujaddid has been conceived as a "rejuvenator of the sciences of each century,"[47] a role for which not many candidates are believed appropriate.

Various groups throughout the history of Islam have produced their own lists of persons whom they consider to have been true mujaddids. The Wahhabis and others who emphasize the importance of Hadith and see themselves as an outgrowth of the Ahl al-Sunna have tended to list the jurisprudents and collectors of Hadith as mujaddids. Sufis ascribe the role to their own leaders. Still others have cited philosophers such as Ibn Rushd (known in the West as Averroës) or Ibn Khaldun. While there is no consensus on a master list of persons who have actually been designated mujaddid in Islamic history, generally those acknowledged by Sunnis have been jurists such as Abu Hanifa or Malik, who established a legal school to organize personal and communal life around the teachings of the Qur'an and the Hadith, or scholars such as Ibn Taymiyya, who reformed Islam and defended it against attempts to incorporate pagan laws. A majority of Muslims in earlier centuries accepted that Abu Hamid al-Ghazzali, author of the twelfth-century *Ihya 'Ulum al-Din* (Revivification of the Sciences of Religion), who developed a creative way to infuse Islamic law with Sufi principles, was in fact the mujaddid for the end of the fifth Muslim century.[48] In the modern period Hassan al-Banna, founder of the Muslim Brotherhood, and Abu al-A'la al-Mawdudi, former leader of the Jamaati Islami, have been given the title of mujaddid by some of their followers for their roles in reshaping Islamic thought to make it relevant for modern life. Most recently the title has been awarded by some Muslims to the Ayatollah Khomeini of Iran.[49]

There is, finally, no consensus as to who qualifies as a mujaddid, what constitutes his role, or who decides whom to place on the list. This teaching, however, has not only justified the development of a variety of sects throughout the history of Islam but has also provided the general framework within which reformers have chosen to operate. It has served, as we shall see, as a highly significant concept in the self-identity of the founders of the majority of the sects under consideration here.

• • • • • *Muslim Sects in the United States*

The immigration of Muslim individuals and communities to the United States for more than a century has brought together people from more than sixty countries providing a mosaic of local customs, traditions, languages, and races. They represent a variety of formulations of religious heritage and identity, sectarian affiliations, and beliefs fashioned by their respective environments. They also have brought with them memories of a heritage of struggle and conflict. Over the centuries they have developed many different ways of survival and have honed their skills at withstanding persecution and villification for their beliefs. They now find themselves in a society that is officially committed to provide religious freedom within the context of democracy, yet one that in very real ways discriminates structurally against those who do not share the perspectives of the majority.

The Islamic population in the United States includes members of a number of traditional sectarian groups that were formed during the early centuries of Islam: Imamis, Druze, Isma'ilis (both Nizari and Musta'li), Ibadis, Alawis (Nusayris), Bektashis, and Zaidis as well as more recent sects such as the Babis, Baha'is, and both the Qadiani and Lahori branches of the Ahmadiyya. It also includes a variety of "American-made" sects that arose within the African-American community during the early decades of this century as a response to American racism and a means of seeking political and economic empowerment, as well as those that came into existence during the 1960s and the 1970s. The sectarian community constitutes a minority among the Muslims in the United States, although the number of sectarians in this country is probably higher in relation to Sunnis than is true elsewhere in the world because so many sectarians have sought haven here.[50]

Most Shi'a Muslims in the United States are Imamis or Ithna 'Asharis. The earliest group to immigrate here came from South Lebanon in the 1880s. Their numbers have dramatically increased during the last two decades as a consequence of American foreign policy in the Middle East. In the 1980s a large number of Iranians, the vast majority of whom were supporters of the Shah's regime, came after the establishment of the Islamic Republic in Iran. In 1982, as a consequence of the devastation in South Lebanon brought about by the Israeli invasion, relatives of those in Shi'a communities such as that in Dearborn, Michigan, intensified their immigration. Unlike the Iranians, who appear to have little interest in organized religion except for attending religious services at funerals and weddings,[51] some of the emigrants from Lebanon are veterans of the sectarian wars in that country and have already established two mosques in Dearborn that are sympathetic to Hizbullah ideology. Some Imami Shi'ites have come from the Indian subcontinent (via Britain or Canada).[52] Those of Indian background who immigrated in the 1960s and 1970s have opened a small seminary in New York, believed to be the first of its kind in North America. Since there are very few Imami religious leaders in the United States, official legal/religious opinion concerning matters of life in this country was sought from the late Imam Khoi of Iraq.

Also among the Shi'a groups in America are the Isma'ilis, most having immigrated to the United States after 1960 as a result of the lifting of U.S. restrictions on the immigration of Asians. The majority are of Indo-Pakistani origin; many were living in Africa during the British colonial period and had to leave after African nations achieved independence and adopted Africanization policies, by which indigenous Africans replaced expatriates in the government bureaucracies.

The Zaidis, mostly from Yemen, were among the first Shi'ites to come to the United States. While a small number settled in Brooklyn, the major concentration of Yemenis in the United States is in the Dearborn area; many came to work at the Ford Rouge factory there. Some have found employment in the steel mills around Buffalo, New York, and a significant group are seasonal agricultural workers in California. There are also very small numbers of other Shi'a groups in America, including 'Alawis, who are mostly from Syria, northern Lebanon, and parts of eastern Turkey, and Ibadis, who are mainly students from Oman. Some of the latter have recently protested to their *mufti* in Oman that Sunni students in America discriminate against them by not allowing them to lead the Friday congregational prayers.[53]

Albanian Bektashis are dispersed in communities in Connecticut, New Jersey, Massachusetts, and Michigan, with a resident leader in the Tekke in Michigan.[54] The first Baha'i group in the United States was formed in 1894. Their center in Wilmette, Illinois, was dedicated in 1953. Baha'is are followers of Mirza Husayn 'Ali Nuri (1817–92). Of Imami background, he taught that religious truth is relative, interpreting the five pillars of Islam in order to spiritualize their meaning.[55]

There is a tendency on the part of immigrant Muslims in America to assume that the truth of Islam as they understand it is so self-evident that sectarian Muslims, once confronted with this truth, will inevitably accept it and forego false interpretations. Since Warith Deen has officially disbanded the American Muslim Mission, immigrant organizations have made special attempts to reach out to African-American Muslims. Many of those who do formally affiliate with immigrant Islam, however, find that the egalitarianism they seek and expect sometimes remains elusive. Tensions between African Americans and immigrants are often acute, as are the tensions within immigrant communities from different countries and cultural areas of the world.

The American context provides new opportunities to propagate the teachings of Islam, both Sunni and sectarian, and to prove that the faith is indeed suitable for life in the West. In the process, however, there is also a tendency on the part of many to insist on a kind of conformist Islam, one that is streamlined and standardized and that can be made marketable. Although there have been a few incidents in which sectarian groups have taken over Sunni mosques, on the whole the different groups operate independently. Yet while the field for propagation is wide open, the competition for members, for recognition by the larger society, and for legitimacy of leadership may provide situations where old tensions and conflicts between mainline Sunnis and sectarians can be replicated.

It is worth noting that mainline Muslims today appear to tolerate the old sectarian groups much more than they do the more recent ones. Controversies that at earlier times were literal matters of life and death are now virtually ignored. Their condemnation of the more newly established groups, however, especially those that are growing in membership and apparently flourishing in the American environment, continues unabated. The elimination in 1924 of the Ottoman caliphate, the center of Islamic Sunni legitimacy, has served in some ways to give different sectarian groups a chance to explore their heritage and to develop their own interpretations of doctrine and guidance. Theoretically the question of the leadership of the Muslim community as a whole, whether that be through an Imam or a caliph, seems to many to be irrelevant. In reality, it has become a paramount issue in many Arab countries, as well as in Pakistan, where Islamist groups are striving to institutionalize an Islamic (Sunni) state governed under the laws of the Shariʿah and with the hope of a reestablished caliphate.

The abolishment of the caliphate has led to renewed vigilance on the part of Sunni Islamic groups seeking to safeguard orthodoxy. In order to erect a dam against erosion of the faith they have placed great emphasis on adherence to the Sunna of the Prophet and on observing the practices that they consider essential for those who call themselves Muslim. True to the heritage of the earliest members of the umma, they feel the heavy burden of maintaining the purity of Islam. Representatives of Sunni orthodoxy speak and write with vigor about the perversions and distortions of Islam that they perceive being perpetuated by the recent sectarian groups. Sectarian leaders, well aware of this critique, counter both with defense of their own doctrines and practices and with offensive attacks against the Sunni majority.

By whose authority and by what standards are persons and groups deemed to be true members of the faith? This question, faced for fourteen centuries by mainline Sunni Muslims as well as by members of all of the sects that have persisted in the name of Islam, still casts its shadow across the face of Muslim America. To the extent to which groups such as the five chosen for this study continue to push at the boundaries of traditional interpretations of faith and practice, the challenges and counterchallenges will remain a part of the picture of Islam in this country. In some cases these challenges, as well as the ones posed by Western secular society itself, will prove too great, and sectarian movements will die out. In other cases they will gain in strength and number, engaging majority Islam in debates over matters of authority and legitimacy. What does seem certain is that new movements in the name of Islam will continue to arise, as they have always done, fostered by creative leaders who provide guidance for their willing followers in the ongoing quest for survival and success.

# CHAPTER 2

# The Druze in North America

Because so much of the Druze faith has been shrouded in mystery, its beliefs and practices kept secret from uninitiated members as well as nonmembers, the movement today is little known and often misunderstood.[1] The Druze by tradition have kept their beliefs hidden from outsiders. This is partly because their doctrine has been considered too esoteric for the uninitiated to understand, and partly because their fear of persecution has led them to invoke the Shi'i practice of *taqiyya*, dissimulation or the right to conceal one's faith if danger is apparent. (Contemporary Druze practice what they call "selective taqiyya," choosing to follow the practices that are conventional to the area in which they are located.)[2] The faith has developed as a closed religion that is passed on only to progeny. Interfaith marriages have been strongly discouraged, and only a person whose father was Druze can be considered a Druze. As members of the community in the West today respond to developments in the Middle East and in America, they are recognizing the importance of understanding who they are, where they come from, and what it means to be Druze. In this process of acknowledging and recovering their self-identity, to a significant extent as part of an attempt to assure that their young people are aware of their heritage, they share many of the concerns of other Arab-American groups, Muslim and non-Muslim.

That the Druze movement grew out of the deep Islamic roots of Isma'ili Shi'ism is undisputed. Whether or not the Druze of today, especially those living in the United States, consider themselves to be Muslim is a matter about which there now seem to be different and sometimes quite strongly held opinions. Some feel that if being Muslim means adhering to the Qur'an and the primacy of the Prophet, facing Mecca during prayer, and following the Shari'a, then the Druze clearly are not Muslim.[3] A spokesperson for the Committee on Religious Affairs of the American Druze Society, however, relayed an opinion held by many when he included this statement in a recently published summary of the tenets of the Druze faith: "Our Tawhid Faith embodies the essence of Islam. It is not a separate religion, independent of Islam. It stemmed from and its roots are firmly anchored in Islam."[4] Abdallah E. Najjar, prominent leader and spokesperson for the Druze community in America, makes this distinction: "We Druze are Islamic but not Muslim. However a concerted effort is being put forth by many prominent Druze to bring us back to the mainstream of Islamic orthodoxy."[5]

This issue has taken on greater significance recently as a result of two important factors. One is the struggle in Lebanon, in which the Druze since the 1980s have reemerged as a distinct community with a particular political objective in the complex mosaic of contemporary confessional Lebanon. The other is the rise of Islamic revivalism, which since the 1970s increasingly has created an atmosphere in which Muslims, who for several decades in the Middle East had been less than stringent in observing the requirements of the faith, are now expected to observe the ritual responsibilities in ways befitting true and pious believers. We will return to these realities below.

• • • • • *Origins and Doctrines*

The Druze came into existence as a religious sect in the eleventh century near the end of the rule of al-Hakim bi-Amr Allah (996–1021), sixth caliph of the Fatimid dynasty. To a great extent the religion developed as a direct result of the personality, and the persona, of al-Hakim himself. Historians have been less than generous in their treatment of this extraordinary ruler, often portraying him as eccentric and cruel.[6] The Druze remember him as a man of unusual spiritual as well as temporal powers, a ruler dedicated to religious, moral, and social justice and reform in ways that sometimes led to acts of violence, yet one who remained in close touch with his people. He was a figure to be reckoned with, one who inspired both awe and fear.[7]

The Fatimids were Ismaili Shi'ites whose leaders claimed descent directly from Husayn ibn 'Ali through Muhammad ibn Isma'il.[8] Their rule in the tenth and eleventh centuries was marked by a highly impressive administrative organization that encouraged territorial expansion and the development of new trade markets, as well as some of the most significant movements in the philosophy and theology of Islam. Under al-Hakim the Dar al-Hikma (House of Wisdom) was founded in Cairo. It was an impressive institution of higher learning dedicated both to the nurture of such sciences as law, mathematics, medicine, astronomy, logic, and grammar and to special training in the doctrines of the faith. The Fatimid aim of universal rule was fostered by a highly developed system of missionary activity, *da'wa*, through which the esoteric and secretive doctrines of Isma'ili belief were transmitted across the Middle East into North Africa and Asia.

The fact that the Fatimids failed to achieve their aim of universal rule, resulting in the disillusionment of many in the Isma'ili community, has been cited as one of the direct causes of the rise of the Druze. One of the major tenets of Isma'ili Shi'ism is the belief that a messianic Imam or mahdi will return to earth in time to usher in the true kingdom of justice. When the "messianic kingdom" did not become a reality, other candidates arose to fulfill the role of the messiah. One of these, it would appear, was the caliph al-Hakim.[9]

In any case, we do know that around the year 1009 al-Hakim underwent some extraordinary changes. Druze tradition makes much of the fact that he renounced outward caliphal trappings and turned to a simple, even austere, life-style. Historians from outside the tradition recall the bizarre public and private actions that have contributed to his reputation of being on the edge of madness. It does seem that whatever else might be said about this ruler, he was a man of mystical orientation and vision. In these later years he turned from the involvements of worldly rule to prayer and contemplation, often in the silence of the desert. For a millennium the Druze have nurtured the story that one night in 1021 he went riding into the Muqattam Hills and never returned. Searches for his body were fruitless. Manuscripts were later discovered, however, that suggest he may have gone to eastern Iran on the Indian border to continue his mystical quest.[10]

It seems to have been the case that al-Hakim's personality was so powerful that many believed him to be the messiah or mahdi of Shi'i expectation. Al-Hakim is understood by the community to have espoused the doctrine of *"nasut wa-lahut,"* or God in man, whereby the purer man is the truer image of the God he reflects. This has led to what some Druze feel is the mistaken interpretation that he thought himself to be God. It is nonetheless clear that the doctrine of his divinity has not been absent from Druze tradition. A nineteenth-century Druze catechism, for example, refers specifically to "our Lord al-Hakim," who was of the seed of Muhammad, and who for specific reasons concealed his divinity.[11] (Responses in the American Druze community to this identification of al-Hakim as God will be discussed later in this chapter.) His missionaries had linked the proclamation of a kind of "unitarian" religion with the expected appearance of the mahdi, and the preaching of this doctrine began publicly in 1017.[12]

It is to al-Hakim's main preacher, Hamza ibn 'Ali, that the Druze owe many of the original texts of Druze belief. Basic to the message is the Islamic doctrine of tawhid, God's oneness; al-Hakim's preachers described the path of oneness, madhhab al-tawhid, whose followers would be called muwahhidun, unitarians. The doctrine contained a highly complex, esoteric, and philosophical understanding of the relationship of the divine to the human and material worlds, clearly influenced by the contemporary currents of Shi'i and Sufi Islam (especially the Ikhwan al-Safa or Brethren of Purity), Neoplatonism, Hermeticism, and even Zoroastrianism. It moved beyond the pale of Islam in its adoption of a doctrine of reincarnation, *tanasukh.* In this understanding there is a finite number of human souls, which will neither increase nor decrease, and at death every soul will experience immediate rebirth in another human body. The condition of the new life is not, as in Hindu thought, determined by the character of one's deeds in the previous life; tanasukh does provide, however, a kind of continuing context for the spiritual realization of truth. This process of birth and rebirth will continue until the end of time.[13]

The sacred texts of the Druze religion are restricted to the initiates. Known as the *al-Hikma al-Sharifa* and in English generally referred to as the Epistles of Wisdom, they are comprised of 107 epistles that were written in the eleventh century by the first, second, and fifth luminaries of the faith[14] and collected into six volumes. On the one hand it is clear that the Druze doctrine is highly complex and incorporates elements of several different strains of philosophy and theology. On the other hand, its unitarianism is also straightforward and direct. It has always eschewed the external trappings of religion, believing that the time has come to approach God directly without the necessity of mediating ritualism, a message that was preached strongly by Hamza ibn ʿAli. As the Druze over the last several decades have sought to understand their faith both to promote their own sense of identity and to be able to inculcate it in their young people, this straightforwardness has been emphasized over the more esoteric doctrines that have been communicated internally over the centuries from one shaykh to another. In the words of one contemporary expositor of the Druze faith, Sami Nasib Makarem, "It is a simple religion with no rituals involved. It heeds only man's constant search for realizing himself in God, the absolute Reality, the only Existent and the only Real, the One Whom no one can realize in himself unless he moves away from his own self that separates and alienates him from the Unity that comprises all existence."[15]

It may be helpful to understand how Makarem describes the pillars of Druze religion. Though not specifically intended as such, his discussion serves as an informative expression of the ways in which Druze faith builds on but differs from the classical Islamic pillars.[16] The student of Islam will note that there are seven pillars, following Shiʿi rather than Sunni articulation. The theme of unitarianism dominates these interpretations.

1. Testimony, *shahada.* Exoterically (*islam*), Muslims have understood that God sent the Prophet Muhammad to humankind with God's word; esoterically (*iman*) the Shiʿa have believed that the Imam is the interpreter of that word.[17] The real meaning, that is, what it means to the Druze, is a kind of combination of islam and iman in the essential purpose of humankind, striving to feel united with the One God.

2. Prayer, *salat.* While Muslims understand prayer as a set of specific rituals performed five times a day, the Druze understand it as a process of drawing one's soul close to God through the realization of the divine unity.

3. Almsgiving, *zakat.* The Islamic understanding of *zakat* as the practice of giving fixed amounts of money to the needy of the community is seen by the Druze as exoteric, while the esoteric or real

meaning as expounded by Hamza ibn ʿAli combines exoteric and esoteric to mean the practice of safeguarding one's fellows through the purification of the soul, which leads to the knowledge of God's unity.[18]

4. Fasting, *sawm*. The external, Islamic meaning of abstinence gives way in the Druze faith to the real or internal significance, which is self-realization, or understanding within oneself the unity of God. *Sawm* becomes a kind of abstinence from anything that detracts one from that purpose.

5. Pilgrimage, *hajj*. While the *hajj* for most Muslims means the physical act of going to Mecca and (for those who favor an allegorical interpretation) adherence to the teachings of the Imam, for the Druze it means "taking oneself" to the place where one understands the knowledge of the unity of God.

6. Striving in the way of God, *jihad*. Striving or giving personal effort means for the Druze not physical fighting through the staging of a holy war, but the effort to come to the knowledge of God's oneness.

7. Allegiance to the Imam, *wilaya*. For the Muslim *wilaya* means paying allegiance to the head of the community, or, more specifically, following the teachings of the Shiʿi Imam. For the Druze, however, it means submitting to "the human embodiments of the luminary cosmic principles,"[19] by which one will see everything in its reality and will see God immanent in all things.[20]

The formal leadership of the Druze religious community lies with the *shaykhs* or elders, the chief of whom is known as the Shaykh al-ʿAql (from the Arabic meaning "to bind"). The title comes from the original teaching of Hamza ibn ʿAli that God's will controls, orders, and binds or encompasses the whole world[21] and emphasizes the bond or connection between all of the Druze religious leaders in the world.[22] Traditionally the shaykhs have been the only ones privy to the secrets of the faith—they undergo a strenuous initiation and are bound to secrecy. It has been their role to lead the faithful and to instruct them in the basics of the religion, but not to reveal the esoteric mysteries contained in its inner teachings. The present Shaykh al-ʿAql of Lebanon was elected in 1949 at the age of thirty-nine. Once he was elected he decided to leave his successful business and dedicate himself completely to the welfare of the community.

The Druze community traditionally has been divided into two groups, the ʿuqqal and the juhhal. The ʿuqqal are those men and women who have undergone formal initiation into the esotericism of the faith and who constitute the elite of the community. They practice the prayer, which is recited every week on Friday evening;[23] by so doing they sustain the religious life of the group as a whole. Those who have not been initiated are called juhhal (plural of the Arabic jahil, which literally means ignorant), and they make up at least four-fifths of the body of Druze. Robert Betts, who has published an extensive study of the Druze community in the Middle East, writes that although there are no statistics on the numbers of male and female ʿuqqal, he estimates that two-thirds to three-quarters of the initiates are men.[24]

While Lebanon historically has served as the worldwide administrative center of the Druze, as a consequence of the French colonial partition of Greater Syria, several other Shaykhs al-ʿAql have been elected in other countries, although they are held accountable to the Lebanese Shaykh.[25] The Shaykh al-ʿAql is elected for life, but should he be unable to fulfill his responsibilities he is relieved, either upon his own order or upon the order of another. His responsibilities include the administration of religious law and other legislative matters, the appointment of judges and the supervision of a staff engaged in the administration of Druze community affairs, and the management of Druze properties. Like other spiritual leaders in sectarian Lebanon, his office is partially funded by the Lebanese treasury.[26]

The authority of the Shaykh al-ʿAql, of course, extends to the Druze community in America. Because the Druze in this country do not have formal structures for holding religious services, in terms either of buildings or of personnel, the Shaykh al-ʿAql has designated several persons, called Mashaykhat al-ʿAql, his honorary representatives in the United States and Canada.[27] These Mashaykhat al-ʿAql function as leaders in the civil concerns of the faith, taking care of issues of personal status law and maintaining records relating to membership, marriages, births, deaths, and wills. (Unlike in Islam, Druze wills are executed at 100 percent; the one in whose name the will is drawn has full control over its disposition.) All Shaykhs preside over funerals and may pray on such occasions,[28] but they do not function "religiously" in terms of communicating

Muhammad Abu
Shakra, Lebanese
Shaykh al-ʿAql as of
the early 1990s.
Courtesy of the
American Druze
Society.

or interpreting doctrines of the faith. There are currently five Shaykhs serving in North America.

Traditionally a distinction has been made between different types of Druze meeting places. The elders, those initiated into the inner secrets of the faith, gather and receive their training in what is called the *khalwa*, a secluded place where they also go for private prayer.[29] The uninitiated meet in a retreat center called a *majlis*. In the United States these strict distinctions are often not maintained, and the term *majlis* is often used to mean a general place of worship. It can also mean any kind of public meeting hall or part of a private home used for that purpose.[30] A new majlis currently being built in Los Angeles will be the first nationally recognized Druze structure with that name.

Women have always enjoyed a position of status and respect in the Druze community. The Druze believe that men and women originated from the same source and that therefore they should in-

teract as partners to maintain the evolution of human life.[31] Druze
women are considered equal to men in both rights and responsibilities, and they have had access to education and to professional opportunities while at the same time enjoying the protection and
support of the males of their families. Therefore, equality does not
necessarily mean identical roles. As is true for Arab women in
general, the Druze woman is seen as a symbol of the honor of her
family, and she is expected to maintain her chastity until marriage
and to remain faithful to her husband.[32] Marriages are not forced,
and the Druze do not permit trial or term marriages or polygamy.
Marriages cannot be dissolved except by a judge, and divorced couples are not allowed to remarry.[33] The Druze woman is expected not
only to be responsible for home and family but also to serve as the
religious and moral guide to her children.[34]

In the United States Druze women have been among the most
Westernized of Arab Americans and have participated fully in Arab
social and political organizations. This has not come without a
price. Nada F. Najjar has expressed some of the concerns facing
women of the Druze community in America as they struggle to be
faithful to their heritage in a context in which the "old ways" are
often difficult to maintain: "Druze women in the West face complex
problems. The society they live in is unfavorable to their faith. The
media misrepresents their religion and their heritage. . . . There are
many materialistic temptations that draw them away from their
faith. A Druze woman in the West fears isolation and wishes to be
accepted in her environment, so she either becomes indifferent to
her ancestral background or she joins some group, not out of belief
in the teachings of that group, but out of lack of knowledge and belief in her own. As a result, she loses contact with her sisters and
brothers of Tawhid and remains marginal in her new circle (she neither walks like a crow nor like a partridge). It is a gloomy picture
indeed, but certainly not hopeless."[35]

• • • • • *The Druze Community in America*

Members of the Druze community in the Middle East today live primarily in Lebanon and Ante-Lebanon, in the vicinity of Damascus
and Mount Hawran in the south of Syria in a region known as Jabal
al-Druz (the mountain of the Druze), and in small communities in

Jordan and Israel. It is difficult to ascertain exact figures, but they probably number around half a million in total.[36] Conflicts in the late nineteenth century precipitated the migration of Druze to North and South America, Australia, and West Africa; today there are also Druze communities in various parts of Latin America, the Philippines, and the West Indies.[37]

Expatriated Druze communities have carried images of their native societies to their new homes, but those images differ. The history of conflict and cooperation, enmity and mutual support among the various religious sects in Lebanon, which at times has been exacerbated by European (and more recently American, Israeli, Libyan, Syrian, Iranian, and Saudi) meddling in the internal affairs of the area, inevitably colors the ways in which the sects interpret history and view each other as communities. Each immigrant generation brings with it its own distinctive experience and tries to project it as the true understanding of reality. Hence there is a tendency simply to replicate what had prevailed in the Middle East—which leads to confusion as it spills over into the American experience.

The Druze clearly have a reputation for secrecy and for great physical courage, the latter sometimes understood as a proclivity for war. For example, while some Lebanese Christians portray the civil war of 1860 as a massacre in which Druze attacked Maronite areas in Lebanon,[38] the Druze recall that atrocities were also committed by the other side and refer to their having been known to visitors and travelers to the Middle East for centuries as a people of exceptional hospitality and of openness to Christians and Jews. They insist that they have permitted Maronites, Greek Orthodox, and Greek Catholics to settle and live peacefully in Druze territory.[39] In the introduction to his book on the Arab-Israeli conflict, Muhammad Said Massoud discusses the plight of the Catholics in Lebanon in the early part of this century who were opposed by the British, the Maronites, the Orthodox, and the Muslims. The Druze leader, hearing of their problem, welcomed them and even gave them land and money to build a church. Massoud notes that the Catholics gave the church the name Church of the Savior to refer not only to the saving act of Christ but also to the Druze leader who had been so helpful.[40] (Copies of letters of Greek Catholic clergy expressing gratitude for Druze help have been given to the authors.) Massoud likens this experience to a similar act of generosity on the part of the Druze toward the Jews in the sixteenth century.[41]

Despite such memories of warm intercommunal relations, it must be mentioned that the Lebanese Druze in the nineteenth century viewed with great concern what they perceived to be the favoritism of French rule toward the Christian community there. Also, the work of Protestant missionaries had the inevitable effect of driving another wedge between the Christians and the Muslims and Druze. The Muslims were greatly concerned about Western Christian influence on their communities and resisted the establishment of missionary schools in their territory.[42] These concerns are part of the cultural baggage that Druze immigrants have brought with them to the United States. Memories of Western intervention in earlier days in the Middle East as well as reactions to current forms of imperialism, especially Western support for Zionism, are important elements in the current attempts of the Druze in this country to determine their own sense of identity.

The immigration of the Druze to the United States from the Middle East began a decade later than that of the Christians from the area. They feared that it would be difficult to maintain their beliefs and practices in a Christian country that seemed clearly to be interested in proselytization. Nonetheless the trickle of immigrants that began in the late nineteenth century increased somewhat in the early part of the twentieth century, when some Druze left Syria and Lebanon to avoid the draft.[43] The first Druze known to have come to the United States was Malhim Salloum Aboulhosn, who arrived in 1881. As a consequence of migration and of procreation, the number of his relatives has grown to the point where there are an estimated twelve hundred Aboulhosns now living in the United States, dispersed over some nineteen different states.

As the number of Druze immigrants increased in America, pockets of settlement began to form in different parts of the country. Druze immigration records indicate that there were Druze communities on the East Coast and in the Pacific Northwest, as well as in numerous places in between. Many of the early immigrants traveled across the Midwest as peddlers, establishing homes in North Carolina, Kentucky, Tennessee, West Virginia, Pennsylvania, Michigan, Iowa, Missouri, and elsewhere. Those who lived through those days describe walking in the heat and the cold, through snow and wind, trying to sell their wares across America. As time passed the Druze began to purchase their own merchandise stores, groceries, import establishments, and other businesses.

In the early days of the immigration period the women of the Druze community in the Middle East were forbidden by the elders to leave, and the men who came to America were without marriage partners or had wives who had been left behind. Some men made frequent trips back to the Middle East just to visit their wives and families. Restrictions against interfaith marriages eventually broke down, and some Druze men married American Christian women.[44] Because there were no clearly defined religious structures in which to raise children, many immigrant Druze who were concerned about the moral upbringing of their youth had to settle for passing on the faith in terms of "heritage" or "tradition" while sending their children to the neighborhood church school or daily vacation Bible school. This has led to identity issues for some today who struggle with whether to see themselves as Druze or Christian.

The first formal Druze society was established by some young men of Seattle, Washington, in 1907. They formed the first of several chapters of an organization they called Albakourat al-Durzeyat (the first fruit of the Druze), which altogether attracted over 350 members, some of whom would come from Oregon to attend the monthly meetings.[45] Their awareness of the new status of the Druze as a people participating in two nations and cultures is shown in the following statement of purpose for the organization: "The aims of the society are twofold. First: Promotion of honorable Druze interests and purposes in their new homes and surroundings. Second: Giving assistance to good causes and praiseworthy movements in the service of their native land insofar as is possible and desirable."[46]

The Seattle Druze community received a sizable influx of members in 1913. Records indicate that some three hundred youths gathered in the Midwest to go by train to Seattle in search of employment and, presumably, to join the already well-established Druze community there. These Druze, some as young as thirteen years of age, came to the United States to avoid serving in the Ottoman army or as a response to what was perceived as "Ottoman tyranny."

Albakourat al-Durzeyat held its first national convention in 1914, and by the late 1930s the organization numbered ten branches. That these branches were formed in various parts of the country is evidence of the quick geographical spread of the immigrants.[47] As of the 1990s the three largest concentrations of Druze in North America were in Los Angeles, Houston, and Edmonton, with another significant group in Dearborn, Michigan.[48]

Albakourat al-Durzeyat was designed to meet the needs of Druze emigrants from the Middle East. Thus its Articles of Incorporation did not make any provision for American-born Druze. A senior member of the Druze community who calls himself "Uncle Nafe" remembers the painful decision that he and others had to make in switching from Arabic to English to record the bylaws and the general proceedings.[49] As the years went by it became apparent that the organization needed to find ways to reach out to the new generation of Druze in this country. On October 15, 1946, on the occasion of a Druze funeral in Charleston, West Virginia, a conversation was held concerning the need to create more fellowship among members of the community in the United States. As an immediate result, the American Druze Convention was founded in Charleston the following year. The organization's name was later changed to the American Druze Society (ADS). The organizers of the convention agreed that in order to maintain the leadership in the younger generation, the elected chairman must not be more than thirty-five years old.[50]

The ADS flourished for several decades. In time, however, its members felt that some new thinking was needed. The year 1970 witnessed a crisis in the society. Some members voiced the feeling that while they knew that the national officers were dedicated, capable, and hardworking, the annual conventions were going nowhere. In particular the conventions were not attracting American-born Druze. Many observed that younger Druze seemed to attend the conventions only to gather with their friends or because their parents wanted them to go.[51]

The search for direction became the agenda of the early 1970s. It took the form of a realization of the need to formulate a sense of Druze identity. "Who are the Druze? What are our beliefs? What is our role in the American society? What are our ties to Lebanon, Syria, Palestine, and the rest of the Arab world?"[52] These and other questions circulated throughout the community, especially in relation to the problem of how to inculcate in the youth an understanding and appreciation of their heritage. Many members wanted to know how they could learn more about the Druze religion. Young people in the community were asked about what they wanted to know concerning their faith and heritage so that materials could be developed to provide answers to those questions.

Because of the fact that the tenets of the faith had always been so closely guarded, many persons of Druze heritage realized that they did not know which to believe of the various and often conflicting stories that their parents had told them. They wondered where they could obtain reliable information in English about the Druze faith. As Druze historian Ajaj N. Andary puts it, "The simple, innocent, naive answers given by the parents in good faith to their children in the Forties and Fifties became no longer acceptable in the American society of many religious beliefs and cultures side by side and freely interwoven."[53]

In 1971 the ADS decided to rewrite its constitution to obtain federal tax-exempt status as a charitable and religious organization. Ten years later the organization began the publication of a magazine, entitled *Our Heritage*,[54] which was charged with forging links between the widely dispersed members of the community. Articles were published concerning the geographical and historical roots of the Druze, their distinctive religious beliefs, founders and heroes of the faith, persecutions that the community has suffered, and other subjects contributing to a sense of ethos and identity. The journal has also published a special tribute issue (volume 1, no. 1, Sept. 1981) in memory of Sultan Pasha al-Atrash of Syria, the great hero of the Arab revolution of 1917–20. While American-born Druze had heard family stories about al-Atrash and about the struggle of the Druze against Ottoman tyranny and French colonial occupation, they and their children had little detailed knowledge of events that were formative in the lives of their parents and grandparents.

Other steps were taken to meet the needs of the American-born generation of Druze. The traditional reticence of the elders to reveal the teachings of the faith came into conflict with the need to inculcate a sense of Druze identity among the young, who were living in an open society where movement from one religion to another was easier than in the Middle East and where there were few cultural barriers or penalties imposed for adopting a different faith. Druze children traditionally had to demonstrate a kind of blind trust in the values and heritage of their parents if they were to remain loyal. A Committee on Religious Affairs was formed in 1970 by Abdallah E. Najjar to compile material for the education of the young. A one hundred–page manuscript entitled "The Tawhid Faith: Lessons,

Stories and Prayers" was prepared, despite the concerns of some of the older immigrants that the basic principles of the faith were going to be revealed.

In 1972 a request was sent to the Lebanese Shaykh al-ʿAql requesting permission not only to translate works about the faith into English but also to provide additional material that would better instruct young American Druze. As a result, Druze scholar Sami Makarem was charged by the American Druze Society and approved by the Shaykh to prepare a text. Makarem, who earned his Ph.D. in Near Eastern studies from the University of Michigan in 1963 and is a professor of Islamic thought and Arabic language at the American University in Beruit, published *The Druze Faith* in 1974. Along with a 1973 volume by Abdallah Najjar entitled *The Druze*, the Makarem volume has been distributed by the American Druze Society as an authoritative articulation of the faith.[55]

At the inaugural session of the 1973 convention of the American Druze Society, which met in Lebanon in July, Abdallah E. Najjar delivered an important address calling for change in the secretive nature of the Druze religion in response to the open religious atmosphere of the United States. He straightforwardly recognized the difficulty of keeping the Druze spiritual heritage intact in a country where ideas are constantly changing and where religious institutions are highly organized and public. America, he said, is a society in which "well-established cults and other 'ways to God' . . . are aggressively and dogmatically pursued by zealous adherents who assume monopoly on the ultimate Truth."[56]

What Najjar clearly was addressing in these painful times of discussion and reflection was that the survival of the community was at stake in a society that prided itself on being a "melting pot." Some Druze have expressed their strong opinion that to be a real Druze one had to live in Lebanon, that it was impossible to maintain any true Druze identity in the American context. During their first century of existence in the United States the Druze were able to maintain coherence as a community by virtue of their ethnic identity. Najjar recognized that ethnicity alone was no longer sufficient to preserve the community, and that greater religious clarity was needed. "For the third, fourth and future generations whose ethnic consciousness differs from ours," he said, "the Druze society must create a fresh atmosphere for spiritual identity and a new sense of history, relevant and meaningful."[57] His plea, therefore, was for a reform of the ways in which the cult was taught, again specifically for the purpose of reaching the young people and maintaining the members in the faith.[58] He even called for a translation of the Epistles of Wisdom.[59]

Part of the traditional understanding of taqiyya has been not just keeping secret the doctrines of the faith for clandestine reasons or out of personal fear, but the strong sense that faith is private and that as a group the Druze pose no threat to the national identities of the countries in which they reside. They wish to live in harmony with their neighbors in Lebanon, Israel, America, and elsewhere. They have, therefore, adhered to an old Arabic saying that runs counter to the theme of Islamic nationalism: that *"al-din li 'llahi wa'l-watan li'l-jami'"* (religion is for God and the nation is for everyone). To expose their teachings in a way that runs counter to this traditional notion of taqiyya is not easy for many in the community, especially for those who have a deep appreciation for the esoteric or mystical teachings of the faith.[60]

It is clear, then, that these concerns about whether or not to make more public the traditional teachings of the faith and about how to maintain a sense of religious identity in a pluralistic and rapidly changing social context will remain with the Druze community for some time to come.[61] What is important to understand, and to recognize as an issue that is not the Druze's alone, is the way in which events at home and abroad have made the questions new and relevant in the latter part of this century.

The problems that the Druze have had to face in America often have had less to do with religion than with the usual difficulties that persons from other cultures encounter when they come to this country. Some of the early immigrants found it difficult to learn the English language and obtain the rudiments of an education while trying to earn a living and provide for their families. Many Druze, as has been the case with other immigrants, have struggled with the question of whether or not to Americanize their names. Some were forced to do so by immigration agents at Ellis Island, and others have decided to do so to help themselves blend in. For example, Jack Hamady, who arrived in America in 1919 at the age of eleven, came to acquire the name Jack when on his first day of summer school he signed an arithmetic paper with the name "Amen Hamady"—his attempt at an English rendition of "Amin." The teacher accused him of not taking summer school seriously, since he had foolishly signed his name "Amen." Hamady was so embarrassed that he decided to give himself an American name. Since Jack Dempsey was then at the height of his popularity, he decided that Jack must be it. His parents agreed, and from then on he was Jack Hamady.[62]

Like other Arab Americans, the Druze have taken pride in their American identity and in the country to which they have come to feel a real sense of belonging. The American Druze Society donated funds to the Centennial Commission for the restoration of the Statue of Liberty, for example, and proudly published the citation it received from the chairman.[63] In a profile published in *Our Heritage,* Fred Massey, one of the early generation of Druze intellectuals who immigrated to the United States, expressed his pride in America as he reflected on the sixty-odd years that he has spent here: "In spite of some drawbacks and social matters and this and that I didn't like very much, still there is freedom here. People can't jump on you for some prejudice or because they don't like you. So, it is a good country—politically speaking, a very good country. America, really, is the greatest country in the world."[64]

This genuine appreciation for America has not weakened the Druze bond with Arab Lebanon. The Shaykh al-ʿAql exhorted his followers in the United States to teach Arabic to their children as part of an effort to maintain a connection with their Arab roots and heritage. He stressed the purity of the Arab descent of the Druze, linking what he called a "moral and linguistic genuineness" that must be affirmed through continued study of the language.[65] Children are urged to learn the Arabic words that signify the American holidays and in so doing to understand distinctive ways in which Arabs might celebrate such occasions. Instead of candy treats at Halloween, for example, raisins and nuts would be more consistent with Lebanese culture. Parents are urged to teach their children how to sing "Happy Birthday" in Arabic rather than in English.[66]

In the last several decades the Druze have also solidified their efforts to affirm their Arab as well as their sectarian identity. Clearly the Arab-Israeli conflict and the civil war in Lebanon have heightened the significance of that identity. Druze communities have been ravaged in the Golan Heights and in Lebanon, and in America Arabs have experienced continued misunderstanding and enhanced prejudice. The Druze-Maronite conflict in Lebanon has brought refugees reporting horror stories of massacres and sectarian wars, to which the members of the Druze community have responded with intensified feelings of sectarian identification. The use of the Arabic language has increased among the Druze as an ingredient in Arab identity and political consciousness. As a consequence of the 1982 Israeli invasion of Lebanon and the one-sided coverage it received in the American media, many in the community have come forward attempting to tell the full story.

Like immigrants to America from other Arab countries, the Druze became active in Arab-American organizations such as the Arab-American Anti-Discrimination Committee, the National Association of Arab Americans, and the Arab-American University Graduates, which were formed in the early 1970s to combat American racism and Zionist campaigns of disinformation about people of Arab heritage. In the 1980s many Druze welcomed the formation of the American Druze Public Affairs Committee (ADPAC). Under the chairmanship of Sam Ackley, ADPAC was structured with the specific aim of countering the falsification of events surrounding the Lebanese and the Arab-Israeli conflicts that was propagated by the "Jewish lobby" and the "Phalangist lobby" and the resulting anti-Druze policies of the American government. The Druze community was particularly pained when the battleship *New Jersey* lobbed huge shells at the Shouf district of Lebanon, whose major population is Druze. This was perceived as a wanton and vindictive attack inspired by Phalangist and Zionist interests because the Phalangist militia was about to lose its grip on the village of Souk el-Gharb. The Druze believed that the United States had abandoned its neutral role and had become another militia in the Lebanese civil war, fighting on the side of the Phalangists and Israelis against the Druze.

ADPAC's stated purpose is to provide information for the media, for public officials, and for the general public concerning the political and human struggles of the Druze people of the Middle East.[67] In a letter to members of the American Druze Society, the leaders of ADPAC described the pressing need for their efforts: "The Druze are in desperate trouble, politically. The frightening fact is that they are misunderstood and seen as a 'secretive, mysterious sect' by the Western world. And nothing will change this fact until we, as American Druze, decide to be active and aggressively involved in American policy-making. Yes, policy-making."[68]

ADPAC wanted what it considered the truth about the situation in Lebanon to be known and was very concerned that other political

Left to right: Jean Kasem, Jesse Jackson, Casey Kasem, and Muhammad Ali at a 1985 dinner honoring Druze Casey Kasem as Man of the Year of the Lebanese-Syrian-American Society of Los Angeles. Courtesy of the American Druze Society.

action groups might be disseminating false information that was leading to the death and suffering of its people in Lebanon. The group also took the position that U.S. foreign policies, influenced by foreign governments with powerful lobby groups in Washington, were actually bringing about the disenchantment of many Arabs with America. Like other Arab-Americans, the Druze have great respect for American ideals and values and fear that current U.S. foreign policy concerning the Middle East is evidence of the country's loss of moral standing in the world.

ADPAC has struggled to find ways in which to convince the U.S. government to listen to the Arab perspective. It has urged Arab Americans in general and the Druze in particular to become part of the mainstream of American politics, on the grounds that the greater the degree of Arab participation the greater the chance that Arab voices will be heard. American politics take time, effort, and money, however, and until Arab Americans are willing to make a greater commitment there will be little chance of making a real difference. In an attempt to have just this kind of impact on the American political process, television and radio personality Casey

Druze Cultural Center, Los Angeles, California. Courtesy of the American Druze Society.

Kasem, a prominent member of ADPAC, hosted a fund-raising party for candidate Jesse Jackson during the 1984 presidential campaign.[69] Kasem was also very involved in the Rainbow Coalition that Jackson formed to support his 1988 bid for the presidency.

Another result of the 1982 Israeli invasion of Lebanon has been the formation of the Druze Foundation for Social Welfare, which concentrates on raising funds for the Druze of war-torn Lebanon. Chaired by Abdallah Najjar, it was a response to an appeal from Lebanon for physical assistance in the attempt to "preserve dignity and honor." Over a period of some fifteen months the organization received $2.1 million and was able to donate food, clothing, blankets, and medical assistance as well as to provide support for orphans and scholarships for needy students.

The 1980s, then, saw a clear increase in Druze involvement in the organizational life of their community. Paid membership in the American Druze Society reached over thirteen hundred by the early part of the decade. By 1984 ADS chapters had been formed in cities in West Virginia, California, Virginia, New York, New Jersey, Connecticut, Massachusetts, Texas, and Georgia; by 1991 there were fifteen chapters. By 1985 community leaders were feeling the need for permanent institutions. They considered it important to be in proximity to the seat of American government because of the influence of American policy on the daily lives of relatives and loved ones overseas. Thus land was acquired in Alexandria, Virginia, in the hope of building national executive offices. Also, to preserve the memory of the achievements and contributions of the early American Druze community, a plan was conceived to establish a national archives of Druze history at the national office. The national office is also to serve as a center for education, public relations, student aid, and community relief, and as a prayer hall.[70]

A cultural center in Los Angeles, acquired in 1990, is being modified to serve the needs of the largest concentration of Druze in the United States. It is expected to serve as a community center where members can gather and socialize informally; as a place to conduct weddings and funerals; as a library and depository of memorabilia; as a majlis for preaching, teaching, and meditation and prayer; and as a school to teach Arabic language and culture and the Druze religion.

• • • • • *Conclusion*

What we see in the modern American Druze community, then, is a series of struggles over the matter of identity. The Druze are challenged both individually and as a group to try to determine simultaneously their relation to their Arab and Islamic heritage and to their American home. They must worry about inculcating in their children a sense of belonging and appreciation for tradition while struggling to clarify what it means to practice their Druze religion when the secrets of the faith are still accessible only to an elite group of men who live in Lebanon. They are forced to cling to memories of another time, country, and culture, stranded in America with no majlis, no shaykh, and no sacred books to read.

For some, the struggle is too much, and it is easier simply to become American. One Druze woman has remembered the personal conflicts she experienced moving back and forth from Christianity to the Druze faith. Having attended a Protestant Christian church as a young girl, she then rejected Christianity in an attempt to reaffirm her Druze heritage. "Finally I was neither a Druze nor a Christian American," she lamented. "I could not say I was a Druze because I did not know what it was. So I came back to Christianity."[71] A young Druze man has commented on the different identities that he feels a Druze is compelled to assume: "Sometimes we want to be more American, sometimes more Druze, sometimes more Lebanese, Palestinian, Syrian, or Jordanian. At times for me, I do not want to identify with any of them. I just want to be a citizen of the world if that's possible."[72]

Thus it is clear that with over a century of existence in the United States the Druze community is in the process of redefining its identity and assessing the possibilities for maintaining and perpetuating the faith outside the focal ritual religious circle in Lebanon. Nurtured within the confines of the Lebanese mountains, a closed society that neither sought nor accepted converts, the community traditionally has thrived in the religious circle of the ʿuqqal. The Druze village provided the social, cultural, political, educational, economic, and religious life of the community. With modernization and urbanization, changes on the periphery of the Druze sphere—in Beirut, Damascus, Amman—have inevitably affected its center. The interest of some members of the community in reforming the faith by making it relevant and meaningful for modern life and by providing a new *ijtihad*, individual interpretation, applicable outside the geographical area that has defined the land of the Druze for nearly a millenium, has inevitably been seen by the central authorities as a threat.

For the Druze who immigrated to North America in the early days, such questions were moot. In their understanding Druze life was possible only within the social context of the homeland, the legitimizing core of the community. The Shaykh al-ʿAql, through his attainment of knowledge of God, assured that all Druze eventually would become part of the progressive reincarnation into perfected being, the union with the deity.

In the 1980s the third and fourth generations of immigrants were faced with the choice of simply dropping any kind of religious affiliation or converting from the Druze religion to become part of the mosaic of American religious communities. The latter did not necessarily mean a dramatic rejection of the identity of their parents and ancestors. It was, rather, the consequence of the slow erosion of the cohesive system nurtured in the mountains of Lebanon, not replicable in the United States, where there was neither the social control necessary to maintain it nor the spiritual center to hold it together. And, most important, there was no prospect of such a center being set up in the United States because of the geographical limitations of the residence of the Shaykh al-ʿAql.

Unhappy with these choices, some in the Druze community have attempted to undertake the role of reformer. They are attempting to provide a context for the survival of the community in the face of relentless pressure to Americanize. Even among those who believe that some kind of change is necessary for survival in America, there are significant differences as to how this should take place. Opposing the reformers are the traditionalists, those who hold to the literal interpretation of the religion. Renouncing all new ijtihad, they see any attempt at reform as representing an abandonment of the faith. The rise of Christian and Muslim (both Sunni and Shiʿi) sectarianism, as well as the sectarian clashes between various militias allied to different religious groups in Lebanon and the resulting suffering of the Druze community there, have enhanced the necessity of holding on to the faith of the fathers, traditionalists believe. Young veterans of the Druze militia who have seen relatives and friends killed simply because they were Druze or were defending Druze villages strongly favor upholding the traditions of the faith to the letter. One of those who has been trained in the Druze teachings, having studied the Epistles of Wisdom and officiated at religious ceremonies in the United States, comments, "I regret to see that our young have not been taught to follow the road of Al-Tawheed. I am proud of the ADS [for having] finally done some translation into our faith and history, but I am against complete 'Kashef' [unveiling] of this faith. . . . Learning is not as important as practice."[73]

One of the matters of faith about which there is little information available to the general public has to do with the divinity of the founder of the Druze, al-Hakim bi-Amr Allah. In the Druze Covenant, composed and recorded in Arabic at the time of Hamza ibn Ali, each time the phrase "Our Lord" is mentioned, the specific identification with al-Hakim is made. (See appendix 1 for a translation of that prayer by Abdallah E. Najjar. The name al-Hakim is added in brackets where it is present in the original Arabic text, although Najjar omitted it.) The fact that such an identification is rarely made in the literature of the American Druze community may signal either a lack of awareness of this "secret" Druze doctrine, a concern for not sharing that perception with the uninitiated, or the feeling that it is the matter of God's unity, tawhid, that is of concern and not whether any individual was ever considered actually to have been God.

In some cases, however, those writing about the faith are quite explicit about their belief in the possibility of human manifestations of the divinity. In the spring 1991 edition of *Our Heritage*, for example, physician Mohamed Khodr Halabi, in writing about his feeling of pride that one thousand years ago he took the oath of the faith upon his soul (a reference that affirms his belief in reincarnation), says this about divine indwelling: "It is about time that those Druze who take it upon themselves to teach religion explain clearly who our God is, and to discuss openly the concept of At-TAJALI [incarnation] of God (AN-NASUUT [humanity])." He then explains that God has actually taken human form at earlier periods in history in order to show to humanity the reality of the divine. Thus the faithful have been able to see with their own eyes the object of their worship. Expressing what the editors of *Our Heritage* refer to as "an orthodox religious view about the Tawhid Faith," he goes on to cite what he calls the prayer of the faithful: "Oh God, help us understand you more and more. Cleanse us of our sins so that one day we may be able to see you. Strenghten our resolve and endurance as we recite Mithaq HAMZA IBN-ALI every day. Help us move forward in our pilgrimage of Tawhid, instead of looking backwards to other faiths. Remove from our hearts fear, doubt, and hypocrisy which are very prevalent in the last days before judgement. Oh God, help us to worship you in our hearts and openly with our brethren. The faithful are looking for the day when you are worshipped openly in every continent. Thou are most merciful and giving. Amen."[74]

Many Druze express the conviction that it is important for the Druze community to explain its own history and doctrines. They are concerned because the secrecy surrounding Druze belief has led to wild speculation by scholars ranging from Godfrey Higgins (who in 1836 traced the Druze to the Druids of Ireland) to the well-known historian Philip Hitti (who in 1933 decided that the "strange dogmas and beliefs" of the Druze were marked by "Neo-Platonic and Manichaean influences" and "traces of Jewish and Christian influences which have trickled thereto through Moslem strata," and that one of the founders of Druzism was a renegade Christian). Many Druze therefore feel that the task of correcting such false records must be undertaken and that the true image of the Druze faith can only be presented with integrity by those within the tradition.[75]

Speaking for the reformers in a revolutionary address to the forty-first convention of the ADS in 1987, American-born Samah HeLal expressed his strong conviction that the secrets so long in the hands of the ʿuqqal must be made accessible not only to members of the Druze community but to all persons of faith in America. It was no longer acceptable, he felt, for most Druze to be considered juhhal. "We know that the term means pagan," he said. "And believe you me! There is no greater spiritual insult you can give a person than to call him/her a pagan. . . . Yet even today that is how many of the Uqqal regard us—as pagan—spiritual barbarians—Juhhal!" He also said that he dreams of the day when Druze children can invite their friends to come to the khalwa and when Dar al-Hikma will be resurrected and built in replica in the United States as "the center for universal movement to unite all monotheistic faiths."[76]

In 1985 an issue arose that serves to illustrate some of the tensions present in the community over the matter of making changes in traditional religious practices. At the annual convention of the ADS that year, a time of devotion and common worship was introduced, using instrumental music and led by Abdallah E. Najjar. That went in the face of tradition in several ways: in traditional Druze society, only the ʿuqqal can lead worship, music is never used, and the community does not worship together.[77] Despite the controversy, the custom has now been established of including a devotional at each annual convention. Women are expected to wear modest clothing and scarves, but the service is open to all participants. Other devotional needs of the community are met by attending churches, mosques, and chapter meetings that include a devotional service.

What has really happened with the institution of the time of common devotions is that the community has been transformed from a loosely affiliated, dispersed group into a congregation. With the provision of a liturgical base for worship, the Druze have assumed a form similar to that of other denominational religious organizations in the United States. It may well be that the only real alternative to total absorption or (dis)integration into the whole is what is really another form of Americanization—the formation of a separate religious entity with creed, scripture, and devotional practice.

Such a compromise, if a compromise it is, appears to some in the community to be not only inevitable but crucial for the survival of the faith and potentially instrumental in its evolution into a religion in which all members have a more vital and meaningful role.[78] As Abdallah E. Najjar said to his colleagues at the 1985 convention, in which the controversial devotions were introduced: "I believe it is incumbent upon us to rise above the national and racial surroundings and emphasize instead our moral and spiritual trust if we are to impact on the life of this society and rejuvenate a Tawhid front in the diaspora. To establish a new Druze reality in this land we must be agents of change in full obedience to the truth. We do not deny our history and native culture as we blend the old and the new into an integrated reality possessing hybrid vigor."[79]

Time will tell if the efforts of the newly structured Druze organization in America, along with the current and often politically motivated mood in this country for ethnic identification, will suffice to allow the Druze to survive as a separate and distinguishable group in the complex fabric of American life.

# CHAPTER 3

# The Ahmadiyya Community of North America

While the majority of Muslims living in North America are either foreign born or members of immigrant families, an estimated one-third are converts to one or another of the Islamic movements in the American context. One of the most active sects in the propagation of its understanding of the faith of Islam has been the Ahmadiyya community, which claims some ten million adherents located in 117 countries, particularly in India, Pakistan, and Indonesia as well as parts of East and West Africa. Most Asian and European countries, including those of Eastern Europe and the former Soviet Union, have some Ahmadiyya presence, and the movement has made its way through Palestine, Syria, Iran, and Egypt in the Middle East and through many parts of North America. Ahmadi Muslims in the United States and Canada number between three and four thousand, including both Pakistani immigrants and native converts, mainly African Americans.[1]

In many places Ahmadiyya mosques were the first, and perhaps are still the only Islamic mosques in the area. As of the early 1990s there were more than five hundred such houses of worship in the world; most of the major cities of Europe have Ahmadiyya mosques. The first mosque to be built in Spain since the end of Muslim rule there over half a millennium ago was the one constructed by the Ahmadiyya in 1982.

Support for the maintenance of the community, the construction of mosques, and the propagation of the faith comes primarily through the contributions of the community's members, who are expected to give one-sixteenth of their income to the movement. When special projects require additional funding the *khalifa* or leader of the movement may issue an appeal for more financial assistance. The contributions of Ahmadi women have been particularly significant and have fully supported the construction of mosques such as those in London, Copenhagen, and The Hague.[2] Another aspect of the Ahmadi mission has been the establishment of hospitals and elementary and secondary schools as well as some institutions of higher learning. Translation of the Qur'an has been one of the projects to which the Ahmadiyya are most dedicated; they have provided the full text in 54 languages and collections of selected verses in 117 languages.[3]

Because of the nature of certain Ahmadiyya doctrines, which will be examined later in this chapter, Sunni Muslims have denounced the movement as a deviation from the true teachings of Islam. Ahmadis themselves, however, are dogmatic in their insistence that theirs is a true interpretation of Islam. One of the most prominent modern spokespersons for Ahmadi Islam, Muhammad Zafrulla Khan, who served as judge and president of the International Court of Justice at The Hague and as president of the seventeenth session of the United Nations General Assembly, contends that "the Movement is established at the very center of Islam and represents the essence of Islam, shorn of all encrustations that have through the centuries gradually been patched upon the body of Islam and have thus defaced and disfigured it. The Movement does not depart from Islam in the very least, nor does it add one iota to the doctrines and teachings of Islam. . . . It is not a new religion nor is it an innovation. It sets forth only that which has been inherent in Islam from the very beginning."[4] Alhaj Ata Ullah Kaleem, *ameer*, missionary in charge, and Imam of the American Fazl Mosque in Washington, D.C., argues, "The Ahmadiyya Movement stands towards Islam in the same relationship which was occupied by Christianity in its early days toward Judaism. One of the claims of Mirza Ghulam Ahmad (on whom be peace) was that he was the Promised Messiah. Keeping this in mind one can easily understand that Ahmadiyyat is Islam itself, and not a mere off-shoot of Islam, as Christianity was not an off-shoot of Judaism, but was pure Judaism in a plain and simple form."[5]

Hazrat Mirza Ghulam Ahmad, founder of the Ahmadiyya movement, was born in 1835 in Qadian, a village in India's Punjab. (Because the movement began in Qadian its followers sometimes are referred to as "Qadianis." This name has been used by opponents of the movement as a derogatory designation.) He is said to have come from a family dedicated to religious learning and pious living, although one that had experienced a great deal of hardship and poverty. He demonstrated a proclivity for religion early in life, to the concern of his father, who worried about his material well-being, and he spent much of his childhood reading and studying the Qur'an. His biographers insist that he was never interested in worldly pursuits, and even when he reached his adult years he resisted his father's efforts to invest him in secular vocations.

The death of his father in 1876 provided the first substantive clue to the special status that his followers believe Ghulam Ahmad to have been accorded by God. Thinking that his ailing father actually was beginning to recover, he slept and experienced what to his understanding was a divine revelation in which he recognized not only that his father would die that day but that God himself was offering condolences. He began to worry that his family would now be without his father's sources of income. He wrote later, "Thereupon I received another revelation [which came in Arabic]: 'Is not Allah sufficient for His servant?' " He inscribed this reassuring word from God on a semiprecious stone and had it set in a ring that he always kept with him. "Nearly 40 years of my life passed under the care of my father," he concluded, "and with his departure from this life I began to receive divine revelation continuously."[6]

These revelations (begun in 1876), which Ghulam Ahmad clearly identified as divine signs, apparently continued throughout his life, increasing in frequency and duration. In his later writings he described a series of visions that he had when he was still a child.[7] When his father died Ghulam Ahmad turned over the management of the estate to his brother and devoted himself to religion. He is said to have engaged in the study of the various Indian faiths. Finally he determined that Islam was the most worthy and true, although he was discouraged at the ignorance and superstition he saw among Muslims and the general lack of understanding of the real values of Islam. As it became clearer to him that Islam was in dire need of reform and revival, he began to understand his role to be that of the mujaddid or renewer of the faith.

Finally in 1889 Ghulam Ahmad proclaimed himself the long-awaited mahdi whose coming was foretold by the Prophet Muhammad. He then received a revelation in which he was assured that he was in fact the messiah whose coming has been foretold in many of the world's great religions. According to Muhammad Zafrulla Khan, in one revelation he was called "Champion of God in the mantles of all the Prophets."[8] Ahmadis generally have argued that they do not, as is sometimes alleged, deny the doctrine claiming that the Prophet Muhammad is *khatm al-anbiya*ʾ, seal of the Prophets.[9] What they do say is that there will be no prophet after Muhammad who will bring a new law or who will not be completely obedient to him. But, they say, Muhammad's advent did not mean that other prophets could not appear "through allegiance to him, by receiving light from his light and as his shadow and reflection."[10] Ghulam Ahmad thus understood his role as the promised reformer as subordinate to Muhammad, as the fulfillment of the Islamic expectation of the second coming of the Messiah. In this understanding, then, and in the understanding of his contemporary followers, he was in no way undermining the doctrine of the final prophethood of Muhammad, but realizing the expectation set forth in the Qurʾan (Sura 61:6): "Jesus son of Mary said: O Children of Israel. Truly I am the messenger of God unto you . . . bringing good tidings of a messenger who will come after me, whose name is Ahmad."[11] By using this reference to Ahmad in the Qurʾan, Ghulam Ahmad left himself open to charges that he actually claimed the status of prophet. His assertion that he received revelations from God when Muslims believe that the Qurʾan is the final revelation has been strongly condemned.

Ghulam Ahmad devoted himself to teaching what he proclaimed to be a purified Islam, a religion that in its most spiritual form is the one by which the world can be transformed. In December 1896 he addressed the Conference of Great Religions in Lahore with a talk entitled "A Grand Piece of News for Seekers After Truth." In this address he declared his message to be "full of the light of truth, wisdom and understanding which will put to shame all other parties."[12] He acknowledged that God had sent a shining light on his heart, the light of the truths of the Holy Qurʾan that would spread around the world and expose the untruths of false religions. With this, his mission to the world began in earnest. He is said to have written more than eighty books, of which most were in the Urdu language and some also in Arabic and Persian. Probably that most cherished by his followers is his four-volume *Barahini-i-Ahmadiyya* (Proofs of the Ahmadiyya).[13]

The Ahmadiyya movement began to spread to provinces beyond the Punjab and gradually to make its way past the borders of India. The name *Ahmadiyya* first appeared in 1901 in a pamphlet in which Ghulam Ahmad instructed his followers to list their religious affiliation as "Ahmadiyya Sect of Muslims."[14] Some of his followers claim that the name was adopted not because it was a part of the founder's name, but because it was one of the two names of the Prophet Muhammad.[15]

When Ghulam Ahmad died in 1908, leadership of the movement passed to Maulawi Nur-ud-Din, elected as the first successor caliph (Khalifatul Masih I). Some of the members of the community felt strongly that the institution of the *khalifat* should be abolished, but they lost to those who maintained that such leadership was in accord with Qur'anic principles. When Nur-ud-Din died in 1914, Ghulam Ahmad's son Bashir-ud-Din Mahmud Ahmad became the second khalifa. At this point a significant number of the more influential and educated followers defected. As of the early 1990s there were still two Ahmadi groups. Those who defected and relocated in Lahore, Punjab, are known as the "Lahore Jamaat"; they believe that Ghulam Ahmad was a mujaddid but not a prophet. The Lahore Jamaat has its own organization in the United States.[16] The "Qadiani Jamaat," those who remained in Qadian (later relocated to Rabwah), not only affirm the prophethood of Ghulam Ahmad but say that those who do not are *kafir*s, unbelievers.[17] The following discussion will focus on the Qadiani Jamaat, particularly the sect's development in the West.

Ghulam Ahmad's son interpreted the defection of some of the members of the group positively, as an opportunity to strengthen the community. In his *Introduction to the Study of the Holy Quran* he commented, "Every day that dawned brought with it fresh factors that contributed to my success and every day that departed left behind elements that hastened the failure of my opponents."[18] The institution of the khalifat has continued, with the khalifa elected for life. The fourth leader of the Ahmadiyya is Hazrat Mirza Tahir Ahmad, elected in 1982 after the death of Hazrat Mirza Nasir Ahmad.

A recent issue of the *Ahmadiyya Gazette,* the official publication of the Ahmadiyya Movement in Islam, Inc., USA, contains an article affirming the importance of the khalifat. It is obviously not within the power of a human being to fulfill all of his prophetic duties in one lifetime, it contends, and thus every prophet has had to have khalifas to continue and bring his work to consummation. "No mere nominated or elected Khalifa can accomplish this mighty task unless he be constantly guided and inspired by God in the discharge of his onerous duties. He must be a rightly guided khalifa." The article goes on to say that the khalifa, although elected by the majority of the people, is divinely sanctioned and therefore cannot be deposed.[19]

As has been said, the Ahmadiyya consider themselves to be clearly within the body of Islam. They see the role of Mirza Ghulam Ahmad to be similar to the role played by Jesus in relation to the teachings of Moses. "Just as by the time of Jesus the teachings of the Jewish religion had ceased to represent the original teachings of Moses owing to the innovations and interpolations which had been introduced into them," writes Bashir-ud-Din Mahmud Ahmad, "so in the time of the Promised Messiah the teachings attributed to Islam had ceased to bear any resemblance to what Islam really taught."[20] So strongly do Ahmadis affirm the legitimacy of Ghulam Ahmad that in some writings they speak harshly of those Muslims who do not accept it. Attributed to Bashir-ud-Din Ahmad are the words "Everyone who believes in Moses, but does not believe in Jesus, or believes in Jesus, but does not believe in Muhammad, or believes in Muhammad, but does not believe in the Promised Messiah, is not only *kafir* but is an inveterate *kafir,* and is outside the pale of Islam."[21] It was under the second khalifa that the separation from Sunni Islam was fully effected. Ahmadis were no longer allowed to pray when a Sunni Imam was leading the prayer. They also were banned from marrying Sunni Muslims and from burying their dead in Muslim graveyards.[22]

The impetus for the development of the Ahmadi movement in Islam must be seen to a significant extent as a defense both against other religious movements in India and against Western opposition to the faith arising from Christian missionary activity in the country. One important element in the development of the Ahmadi message during its formative period was the attempt to counter the powerful Hindu movement Arya Samaj, which claimed that the door of revelation was closed after the revelation of the Vedas.[23] (The Arya Samaj, it has been argued, was itself at least in part a Hindu response to Christian missionary activity.) "The doctrine has wrought another mischief," wrote Ghulam Ahmad, "for it is because of [it] that the Arya Samaj treat the books of all other religions, as fabrications of man. . . . Reason itself revolts against this exclusiveness."[24] Not only is the revelation of Islam a divine revelation, but the "Person of God" has been manifested in different countries among different people (and, of course, most specifically has been manifested in Ghulam Ahmad himself).

More important to the long-term development of the Ahmadiyya movement, however, was its confrontation with Christian missionaries and the various ways in which it sought to counter Christian opposition to Islam. According to Ghulam Ahmad, Christian missionaries used what he characterized as "vile and abusive" language about the Prophet Muhammad, accusing him of being an adulterer and a liar.[25] Perhaps in reaction, Ghulam Ahmad reviled the Jesus of the Gospel as unworthy of being a prophet. Thus, one of the ways he sought to defend Islam was by "appropriating" the figure of Jesus, using the Qur'anic understanding of Jesus as an attack on Christianity. For Ghulam Ahmad the 'Isa (Jesus) of the Holy Qur'an and the Jesus of the Gospels were two different and distinct personalities. He deeply revered 'Isa, the prophet of God, who was loved and chosen by God, but saw the fictitious Christian Jesus portrayed in the "distorted" Gospels as an immoral being, pointing out that Jesus indulged in liquor, that some of his grandmothers were guilty of adultery, and that his mother was charged with adultery by his enemies.[26]

According to an Ahmadi report, this confrontation with the Christian missionaries proved successful. "The Promised Messiah . . . has not in the slightest degree defamed Hazrat Isa. . . . He has only, by way of refutation, condemned the Christians on the basis of the Gospels. In doing this, his only purpose was that the Christian missionaries should refrain from abusing and defaming and uttering false charges against . . . Muhammad Mustafa. . . . It is a fact that his adoption of this method of refutation silenced the Christian missionaries forever."[27] It is reported that Ghulam Ahmad was so convinced of his victory over the missionaries that he called on Queen Victoria on the occasion of her Diamond Jubilee to convert to Islam "to rescue the honour of Jesus from the stain that has been put upon him."[28]

Ghulam Ahmad's interpretation of the events related to the crucifixion and death of Jesus attracted sharp criticism from other Muslims. While traditional Islam claims that Jesus was "gathered" up to God from the cross, Ghulam Ahmad taught about his continuing activity on earth.[29] Sura 3:55 of the Qur'an (Pickthall's translation) reads, "[And remember] when Allah said: 'O Jesus! Lo! I am gathering thee and causing thee to ascend unto Me.' " The Ahmadi translation (3:56) reads, "When Allah said, 'O Jesus, I will cause thee to die a natural death and will exalt thee to Myself.' " Ghulam Ahmad taught that Jesus did not die on the cross but only fainted, that he was not buried but put in a room cut out of rock, and that he did not ascend to heaven but went searching for the lost tribes of Israel. He finally reached Kashmir in India where he died at the age of one hundred twenty and was buried in Srinagar, where his tomb is still popular as a pilgrimage site.[30] In one sense the affirmation of Jesus' post-cross ministry in India could be seen by his followers to have endowed Ghulam Ahmad with special authenticity, since Christians had truncated their understanding of Jesus' mission and confined the report of his activities to Palestine.

Ghulam Ahmad and his followers met with opposition from within the Muslim community itself as well as from the other religious communities to whom his message was addressed. Ghulam Ahmad's son, in listing the criticisms raised against Ahmadis by other Muslims, signaled the belief about Jesus to be high on the list. "The first and the most crucial objection raised against us by our enemies is that we believe that Jesus of Nazareth died a natural death. To believe that Jesus died a natural death is said to be an insult to Jesus, an offense to the Holy Qur'an and dissent from the teaching of the prophet."[31] To defend against the Muslim accusation that Ahmadis were British agents, Ahmadi authors cite the fact that Ghulam Ahmad dubbed Christian missionaries who were supported by the British colonial administration as the Antichrist.

A second way in which the Ahmadiyya countered Christian attacks on Islam and the Prophet was by emulating the methods and strategies utilized by the missionaries in their attempt to bring Christianity to the world. In examining the development of Ahmadi missions and the ways in which Ahmadis propagate their faith, one can see almost a mirror image of the strategies used by Western Christians overseas. The translation and dissemination of the Qur'an parallels the activities of evangelical Christians in making the Bible available in many languages and dialects. The efficacy of these tactics was verified when in the 1970s the Muslim World League approved the translation of the Qur'an into other languages, a practice that had been opposed for centuries.

A third method of contesting with Christians comes in the form of the *mubahala*, which is defined as a means of adjudicating a dispute by asking God's judgment (literally, curse) on someone who is perceived as professing a falsehood. The concept is based on Sura 3:61 of the Qur'an: "And whoso disputeth with thee concerning him, after the knowledge which hath come unto thee, say [unto him]: 'Come! We will summon our sons and your sons, and our women and your women, and ourselves and yourselves, then we will pray humbly (to our Lord) and (solemnly) invoke the curse of Allah upon those who lie.' "[32] In the confrontation with Christian missionaries seen as bent on destroying Islam, the mubahala proved a useful tool and has continued to be a device used to challenge those who disparage the faith or the faithful.[33] The January 1989 issue of the *Review of Religions* (p. 46) gives this definition of mubahala: "That when a person who has been sent by God is outrightly rejected and no further room is left for a meaningful dialogue and argumentation, then both those who believe in him and in his claims and those who reject him should invoke the Curse of Allah on the willful liars."[34]

To many Ahmadis, the very success of their mission to Britain and to North America has served to prove the superiority of the message of Ghulam Ahmad and to vindicate his role as the promised mahdi. In the Hadith of the Prophet Muhammad is the prediction that the messiah to come at the end of time will "break the cross." By "defeating" Christianity he fulfilled that prophesy, by halting the conversion of Muslims, especially the educated, to Christianity and by "breaking the principles on which Christianity was based."[35] Not only did the missionaries fail to convert the Muslims, but, as Ghulam Ahmad himself wrote in 1901, "The foundations of the structure of Christian dogmas have now become hollow. The time is coming when the people of Europe and America will turn away from the Christian worship of a dead person and believe in the true religion of Islam in which they will find their salvation."[36]

One of the ways in which Ahmadis have felt that their movement provided a reform for an Islam gone astray is in their rejection of jihad in its most aggressive interpretation, that of holy war. Jihad was necessary in the early days of the faith, they say, but, in the words of Bashir-ud-Din Mahmud Ahmad, "In the present age that particular form of insanity which sought to propagate or destroy a religion by the sword has almost disappeared, and Islam is no longer under the necessity of defending itself by the sword."[37] Mahmud Ahmad says elsewhere that nothing could be farther from the truth than to say that Islam allows propagation of the faith by the sword. Surely a sword is not needed to convince people of the truth.[38] He specifically clarified, however, that the Ahmadi opposition to jihad was only to jihad as aggression. "I have always wondered how such a false charge [denying jihad] could be made against us," he wrote, "for to say that we deny Jehad is a lie. . . . What we deny and resist vehemently is the view which makes it right to shed blood, to spread disorder and disloyalty, and to disrupt civil peace in the name of Islam."[39]

Ahmad's apologetic concerning jihad influenced many Muslim modernists in the twentieth century. While the writings of Sayyid Qutb of the Muslim Brotherhood and Abu al-A'la al-Mawdudi of the Jama'ati Islami and their followers continue to affirm the understanding of jihad as holy war, a large number of Muslims believe that the greater jihad is the struggle of the self against its tendency to deviate from obedience to God. The lesser jihad is to fight, and that is only sanctioned if the Muslim community is oppressed or not allowed to preach the message of God.[40]

• • • • • *Ahmadi Missions in America*

Missionaries of the Ahmadiyya movement have understood their task to be the propagation of the true Islam, for which purpose they preach the message of the Qur'an and provide copies of the text in the appropriate translation. In the Americas, missions have been established in Argentina, Brazil, Canada, and the United States.[41] The Ahmadiyya have taken seriously the necessity for a Muslim spiritual response to the challenges of Westernism and secularism, preaching a way of life that refutes the wisdom of human achievement and invites humanity to declare its faith in God. Missionary activity in the West, however, is inspired not only by the desire to share a recognized truth with those who have not yet heard or accepted it, it is also driven by the necessity of vindicating the authenticity of the one on whose teachings the movement is predicated. That there are converts to the Ahmadi faith in the Americas thus becomes a kind of verification of the belief that the mission of the founder is of divine origin.

Islamic tradition reports that the Prophet Muhammad said that at the end of time, when the messiah has come, the sun will rise in the west. This has generally been interpreted by Sunni Muslims in a literal fashion, as a version of the predictions of the Hadith that at the end of time the regular order of the universe will alter and the sun will rise in the west rather than the east.[42] Some Sunni Muslims do believe that the end of time is near and thus regard the sun as a metaphor of knowledge and civilization, viewing the current ascendancy of the west as a last burst before the impending doom. While the Ahmadiyya agree that the sun rising in the west will herald the end of time, they interpret it not in terms of the physical sun but as the fulfillment of prophesy. They understand that in the time of the promised messiah people in the West will begin to become interested in Islam, signaling the beginning of the spread of Islam in the West.[43]

Ahmadis pride themselves on their ability to recruit converts. They link the beginning of the Ahmadiyya movement in the United States with the conversion of Alexander Russell Webb to Islam in the 1880s.[44] Disenchanted with Christianity, Webb apparently engaged in the study of several faiths and began to correspond with Ghulam Ahmad. Members of the Ahmadi community feel that it was through this correspondence, as well as a trip he took to India in 1892, that Webb actually converted to Islam and assisted in the spread of the faith in the United States.[45] The fact that many of Ghulam Ahmad's revelations are said to have come in English, although he himself was not fully fluent in that language, has been taken by the believers as a clear indication that the propagation of Islam in English-speaking countries is high on the missionary agenda of the Ahmadi.[46] In 1901 Ghulam Ahmad began a monthly English-language magazine entitled *Review of Religions* for the purpose of making his teachings available to the West.[47]

One account of Ahmadi involvement in the United States describes the virulently anti-Muslim campaign of John A. Dowie, a

Catholic priest in Illinois who is said to have proclaimed himself to be the Prophet Elijah. In the first decade of the twentieth century Dowie devoted himself to preaching the destruction of Islam. "I pray to God that the day of destruction of Islam approach nearer. O God! Do like that, O God, bring destruction to Islam."[48] Hearing of Dowie's attack on Islam, Ghulam Ahmad invoked the mubahala, publishing a formal challenge in which he called on the preacher to stop his diatribe and to enter into a prayer contest. According to the terms of the contest, whoever was a liar would die during the lifetime of the one who was telling the truth. Followers of Ghulam Ahmad believe that their leader won the contest, in which the American press took great interest, since Dowie became paralyzed, went insane, and finally died in March 1907. A local newspaper reported that Ghulam Ahmad regarded "the misfortunes which befell his traducer in America as evidence of divine vengeance coming with divine judgment."[49]

The first moves toward the establishment of an Ahmadi community were made in the United States in 1911, when the *Review of Religions* started to take note of Western intolerance of the religion of Islam. In 1915 the journal began to discuss what kind of approach Ahmadi missions should take as they work in Christian countries, and soon translation of the Qur'an into English was begun.[50] The first Ahmadi missionary to the United States was Mufti Muhammad Sadiq in 1920. It is reported that he initially was refused entry into the country, then he was admitted but confined to the Philadelphia Detention House pending the result of an appeal, on the grounds that he represented a religious group that practiced polygamy. Finally he was released on the condition that he not spread any ideas about polygamy through his preaching.[51]

Sadiq, who was a graduate of the University of London and an articulate spokesperson for Ahmadi Islam, first set up headquarters in New York City. He lectured extensively and late in 1920 decided to move his operation to Chicago. There was already a small but active community of non-Ahmadi Muslims in Illinois, although it appears that there was not much cooperation between that group and the Ahmadis.[52] In the fall of 1920 Sadiq and the editor of an Arabic newspaper entitled *Alserat* formed a society for the preservation of American Islam, and Sadiq also formally moved the central operation of the American Ahmadiyya movement to Highland Park, near Detroit. In 1921 Sadiq started publication of the periodical *Moslem*

*Sunrise.* In 1922 he returned to Chicago, where a sizable community of Muslims was already established.[53] According to a 1926 report on Ahmadi missionary work dissention arose in Michigan after it became clear that Sadiq was not preaching orthodox Islam, and attendance at the Sunni mosque dropped significantly. It was as a result of the bitter quarrels that arose in Michigan that the Ahmadi missionary was forced to go to Chicago, as the author of the report puts it, "rejected of Islam itself, with no American converts to solace him."[54]

In any case, Chicago became the official headquarters of the American Ahmadiyya movement and the site of its first mosque. One of the members of the community recalls Sadiq in the early years: "He began visiting various denominations of churches and the Syrian Restaurants. Sometimes he wore a navy blue suit, but mostly he wore black sheerwani with a green turban which caused him to look quite distinguished. He always carried about one hundred large-size cards in his pockets. His photo appeared on one side and on the other side were the Islamic teachings in condensed form. The cards were always printed in green ink. . . . Since he knew colloquial Arabic language, he made a great hit with the Arabs of Syria, Arabia, Lebanon and Palestine."[55]

From the beginning of the Ahmadi mission in America efforts were made to recruit immigrant Muslims as well as white and black Americans. Some Muslims who had come to this country from overseas and found themselves without Islamic leadership turned to Ahmadi missionaries for assistance in learning about the faith. Ahmadi teachings continued to serve as guidelines for Muslims without ready access to Islamic leadership.[56] Most of the appeal of the Ahmadi preaching in America has been to the black community, and in the early days most of the members of the centers in the eastern and central United States were African-American converts.[57] The Ahmadi missionaries developed a rather adversarial relationship to the media in the United States as they continued to point out the blatant racism of American society, an attack with which many in the African-American community found themselves in agreement.[58]

Published examples of early Ahmadi missionary work among African Americans abound. An article in an early issue of *Moslem Sunrise* entitled "Crescent or Cross? A Negro May Aspire to Any Position under Islam without Discrimination" indicates the tone of efforts to communicate the message to African Americans.[59] In 1924 *Moslem Sunrise* reported that Sadiq believed that Muhammadism was "the solution of America's race problem."[60] A 1927 issue of the *Messenger* carried an article with the title "Moslem Propaganda: The Hand of Islam Stretches Out to Aframerica," which noted that Islam (referring to the Ahmadis) was bidding for African-American converts in the larger cities of America. The article contained several personal stories of converts, such as that of a black man raised as a Catholic in the South who was offended when "niggers" were forced to carry the coffin of a white priest. "If that is Christianity," he said, "then I don't want it." He joined the Chicago mosque where he felt that he gained a sense of his own dignity and could command respect from whites.[61] Of the many pamphlets that have been circulated by the Ahmadis the most popular among African Americans have been those concerning Muslim teachings about racial equality.[62]

In the 1920s, then, Ahmadis were particularly active among African-American populations in Chicago and Detroit, and to some extent in St. Louis and Gary, Indiana. The movement was appealing to members of the African-American community both because of its stance in terms of racial equality and because it offered blacks positions of leadership. Some of the members of Marcus Garvey's Universal Negro Improvement Association were attracted to the Ahmadi movement; the *Moslem Sunrise* reported that Sadiq converted some forty of Garvey's followers to the Ahmadiyya faith.[63] The Ahmadis remained the Muslim group most appealing to African Americans until the rise of the Nation of Islam in the 1930s.[64] The message of black supremacy and white inferiority that became part of the Nation ideology, however, engaged many African Americans and was incompatible with the egalitarian message of Islam preached by the Ahmadiyya.[65]

In 1930 Ahmadiyya headquarters were moved from South Wabash Street in Chicago to East Congress Street in the Chicago Loop, "so that people can find ready access to the headquarters of the mission."[66] Sadiq's efforts to speak about Islam in the American context are reported by the Ahmadiyya to have been appreciated by non-Ahmadi Muslims in America, and it is said that he was visited by Arabs from cities such as Detroit, Chicago, and Pittsburgh. A 1975 issue of *Muslim Sunrise* (the name changed in 1950) noted, "These visits gratified their need for the spiritual sustenance so badly needed by people uprooted from their traditional religious environment."[67] Ahmadis made concerted efforts to assure that while they taught their own interpretation of Islam, new members understood that they were in fact part of an international Muslim community. Converts were expected to sign an agreement called the Bismillah (a shortened form for the Arabic phrase meaning "in the name of God, the Merciful, the Compassionate," with which all but one of the chapters of the Qur'an begins), by which they expressed their commitment to the new religion, and they were also required to adopt Muslim names.[68]

A series of missionaries to the United States succeeded the much-beloved Sadiq, one of the most popular being Mutiur Rahman Bengalee, who was officially appointed in 1928.[69] Bengalee's wife joined him in 1936 and is said to have done much to organize the female members of the community and to encourage their activities.[70] Bengalee returned to Qadian in 1948; his children and their families now reside in the United States. Working with Bengalee were Khalid Nasir, Ghulam Yasin, and Mirza Monawar Ahmad; by 1933 they had extended the major centers of the Ahmadiyya community from Chicago to New York, Pittsburgh, Cincinnati, Indianapolis, Detroit, and Kansas City. Like other Ahmadi missionaries, Bengalee based much of his message on an analysis of both religious and racial prejudice in the West and the hope of Islam as an antidote: "Appalling ignorance exists in the Western countries regarding non-Christian faiths. An important cause of religious prejudice is deeply rooted in the ignorance which is to be found among followers of all faiths regarding the faiths of other peoples. . . . Closely related to religious prejudice is the race and color prejudice. The contribution of Islam in this respect is unparalleled. . . . I claim a distinction and the superiority of Islam in this repect."[71]

By 1940 Ahmadiyya membership in the United States had grown to between five thousand and ten thousand. At this time the Ahmadis' most important mission centers were in Chicago, Cleveland, Kansas City, Washington, D.C., and Pittsburgh.[72] After World War II the American mission made some structural changes and divided the various branches of the community into "circles," located in Chicago, New York, Pittsburgh, and St. Louis. Annual conventions were instituted so that members could support each other and discuss mutual concerns. At the first Ahmadiyya annual convention in 1948 national secretaries were elected to administer matters of education, social work, and propagation of the faith. The community was divided into five associations according to the ages of the association members: the *Majlis Ansaarullah* (men over forty years of age), the *Majlis Khuddamul Ahmadiyya* (young men between fourteen and forty), the *Majlis Atfal-ul-Ahmadiyya* (boys under fifteen), the *Nasraatul Ahmadiyya* (girls under fifteen), and the *Lajna Ima' Ullah* (women fifteen and over). Each of these groups is designed to serve the spiritual, cultural, moral, and social needs of its members. Efforts were strengthened to arrange for American Ahmadi youth to visit the movement's headquarters in Rabwah, Pakistan, for concentrated training in the faith.

The Ahmadiyya Movement in Islam was registered officially as an incorporated body under the management of a Board of Directors consisting of twelve members from various parts of the country. Local centers report to the director general of the Ahmadiyya Muslim Foreign Missions in Rabwah. Approval of national, regional, and local officers is given by the International Headquarters in Rabwah, which runs under the instruction of the khalafat.[73]

In 1950, under the leadership of Mutiur Rahman Bengalee's successor, Khalil Nasir, Ahmadi headquarters moved to Washington, D.C. The new headquarters building, known as the American Fazl Mosque, is located on Leroy Place in the northwest section of the city. The large house, which served as mosque, office, and residence for the mission leadership, continued to be the administrative center for the community and the locus of its educational and propaganda mission through the early 1990's. Publications of the American Fazl Mosque are distributed worldwide, with copies sent to members of the U.S. Congress, officials of the executive branch of government, leading newspapers, foreign diplomats, and so on.[74]

With the increased migration of Asians to America in the 1960s, new immigrants swelled the number of Ahmadis. Canadian Ahmadi branches were opened in Toronto, Ottowa, Montreal, and Brantford.[75] Efforts at publication increased, and representatives of the Ahmadiyya made frequent appearances at national and international conferences on religion to present the Ahmadi Muslim perspective. New missions were founded; as of 1990 there were Ahmadiyya centers located in some thirty-five U.S. cities, mainly in the Northeast and the Midwest, with over twenty branch Jamaats in Canada.[76]

Hazrat Khalifat-ul-Masih IV (in white turban) praying at the foundation stone laying ceremony for the Ahmadiyya mosque and mission house in Detroit, Michigan. Courtesy of the Ahmadiyya Community of North America.

In the 1960s the Ahmadiyya movement also reaffirmed its long-standing concern over American racism and remained abreast of the racial struggles that were taking place in the United States. *Review of Religions* featured several articles on the subject. Ahmadis cited the deep racism of white Americans as the reason for the resistance to integration and looked for a solution not only through legislation but in the belief in a common faith in God on the part of all races. Christianity, Ahmadis observed, had certainly not succeeded in providing this common base, and they pointed to Islam as the religion capable of destroying the barriers of race and color.[77]

In 1973, while speaking to the annual convention of the Ahmadiyya at Rabwah, Pakistan, Hazrat Khalifat-ul-Masih announced that in recognition of upcoming centennial celebrations additional steps would be taken to enhance the program of the Ahmadiyyat. Among these steps were to be the opening of more missionary centers around the world, the translation of the Qur'an into one hundred major languages, the publication of Islamic literature in all major languages, the installation of printing presses in Pakistan and elsewhere and of a broadcasting station for the propagation of Islam, and the promotion of enhanced intercommunication among Ahmadis in different countries.[78]

The intensive publication of materials about Ahmadi Islam, so much a visible part of the activities of the modern community, came into full swing in the middle of the twentieth century. The first major English-language volume on Ahmadi doctrine to be published was *The Ahmadiyya Movement in Islam*, by Bashir-ud-Din Mahmud Ahmad. Many of the publications that come from the Ahmadi press are not specifically about the Ahmadiyya but about Islam in general. Booklets such as Muhammad Zafrullah Khan's *Message of Islam* are intended to instruct readers in the basics of the Islamic faith and not to propagate an Ahmadi interpretation. The introduction by the Imam of the Fazl Mosque in his foreword to the Khan booklet talks not about Ghulam Ahmad but about how instruction in "the origin, spirit and teachings of Islam" may help interested Westerners become better informed about Islam and, by implication, less likely to identify Muslims with the "Moslem terrorists" of whom he says one invariably hears in connection with the problems of the Middle East.

Despite their claims that they are teaching and preaching true Islam, the Ahmadis have long been the target of severe Muslim critiques. Writing before the partition of India, for example, Pakistani poet and philosopher Muhammad Iqbal expressed his concern over what he identified as the threat the "Qadiani" movement posed to Islam, which he felt could actually lead to the disintegration of the Muslim community if allowed to go unchecked. "Since the phenomenon of the kind of heresy which affects the boundaries of Islam has been rare in the history of Islam," he contended, "that is why the feeling of the Indian Muslims is so intense against the Qadianis."[79] Writing several decades later, S. Abul al-Aʿla al-Maududi stated his strong support for the unanimous expulsion from the Muslim community of the "Qadianis," whom he likened to "a cancer eating up and gradually consuming the vitals" of Muslim society. He accused missionary Muhammad Zafrulla Khan of misusing his position for the purposes of spreading Qadiani influence.[80]

In recent years Ahmadis have come under particular fire from the Jamaʿati Islami in India and Pakistan as well as the Muslim World League of Saudi Arabia. Official repression of the Ahmadi community in Pakistan has been severe. In 1974 there was renewed anti-

Ahmadiyya violence, and under Pakistani president Zulfikar Ali Bhutto the legislature for the first time declared Ahmadis "Not Muslims for the sake of Law and Constitution." Pakistan's Zia ul-Haqq regime, which fostered Islamic revivalism and the Islamization of Pakistani society, saw fit to crack down on Ahmadis through Martial Law Ordinance XX, issued on April 26, 1984, in an effort to regain Islamic "purity." Ahmadis were denied the right to profess, practice, or preach their doctrines either verbally or in writing, on pain of fine and/or imprisonment.[81] On June 10, 1988, Mirza Taher Ahmad, Imam of the Worldwide Ahmadiyya Movement, issued a mubahala on all who deny and reject the founder of the movement.[82]

Recent restrictions have banned further publication of the English-language Ahmadi translation of the Qur'an, and existing copies are confiscated and destroyed. The Muslim World League, whose founders included anti-Ahmadi Pakistani leaders such as Abu al-Aʿla al-Mawdudi and Hassan al-Nadwi, warns against "the prodigal Qadiani sect which is considered a germ in the body of the Islamic umma." Its publications insist that some Muslims have been deceived into believing that they are Muslims because their names are Muslim and they use Muslim terminology. They are, however, apostates because of the claim of their founder to be a prophet, because of their belief in the Second Coming of Jesus, because they say Qadian is a pilgrimage site, and because they declare jihad to be null and void to please the imperialists. Members are to be boycotted economically, socially, and culturally, treated as *kuffar*, unbelievers, and their activities and false teachings are to be exposed. "Qadianis" are not to marry Muslims, nor to be buried in Muslim cemeteries.[83] The league calls on all Muslims to watch for subversive "Qadiani" teachings that might be infiltrating Muslim schools, mosques, and literature. The Ahmadiyya are, in short, accorded the kind of treatment that is specified for all those considered to be the enemies of Islam.[84] In the United States the Council of Masajid of North America organized by the Muslim World League and the Islamic Society of North America have strongly encouraged the leadership of mosques and Islamic centers to register properties under the name of one of those umbrella organizations in order to safeguard them against Ahmadi infiltration.

Ahmadi missionary Mubasher Ahmad contends that "the persecution of Ahmadis has been escalated into the Pakistani government's repression of basic human rights and freedom of expression of the Ahmadiyya Muslim community. The anti-Ahmadiyya machinery, which is not confined to Jama'ati Islaami alone, has a history of receiving increasing Pakistan government support." He insists that criticism of the Ahmadiyya movement usually contains misrepresentations of Ahmadi beliefs as well as character assassinations of the founder and his successors. Members of the Ahmadi community try to counter this criticism both by posing polemic challenges to scholars of other Muslim sects and by continuing their production of literature explaining true and accurate Ahmadi beliefs and practices.[85]

## • • • • • The Ahmadiyya Community in America Today

As of the early 1990s there were six Ahmadiyya missionaries in the United States, with the national leader attached to the Washington, D.C., mosque. Additional missionaries are said to be on the way from Pakistan, and frequent visits are made by Pakistani scholars and leaders of the movement to lecture and to consult with the members of regional Ahmadi groups. Local administration of the mosques[86] generally is left to locally elected officials, both immigrants and converts. Religious leaders are trained at the international headquarters in Pakistan, where potential missionaries from all over the world are recruited. The training course is a four-year program if the candidate has a high school degree. Some locally elected officials are provided with such on-site training as is required in order to communicate the message of the faith.

The very concept of leadership among the Ahmadis may be a bit different from the usual Western understanding of that term. Leaders are expected to follow their best understanding of the will of God for them and for those whom they "lead" rather than to underscore their own importance or their own powers of decision making. As missionary Mubasher Ahmad states, "The profound wisdom in a Hadith of the holy Prophet Muhammad (s.a.w.s.)—'The true leader of a people is the one who serves them the most'—has always played a guiding role for the development of leadership concept in the Ahmadiyya community."[87] The motivating factor for all of

Ahmadiyya Community mosque, Tucson, Arizona. Photograph by
Yvonne Yazbeck Haddad.

those in leadership positions has been understood to be service, as
the names of the men's, women's, and children's groups signify.

Ahmadis never lose sight of the goal of propagation of the faith as
the overriding mission of the community. One of their most effec-
tive organs of propaganda since the beginning of the community has
been publication of *Moslem Sunrise*, which for many years actually
pictured on its cover the sun (of Ahmadi Islam) rising over a map of
North America. While at first it was issued somewhat irregularly (it
ceased publication completely from 1924 to 1930, probably for financial reasons)[88] it has continued as the strong voice of the community with content and general layout fairly consistent over the
years. Usually included are Qurʾan selections and commentary, passages from the writings of Ghulam Ahmad or his successors, and
articles about specific issues concerning members of the community. There is always ample notice of available literature devoted
specifically to the spread of the movement. Christian missionary
Charles Braden has observed that the United States, which has so
long dedicated itself to the propagation of the gospel around the
world, now finds itself the object of missionary activity on the part

of other religions such as the Ahmadiyya.[89] "It is this Movement," he writes, "which has become the most aggressive missionary arm of Islam. They have taken over almost bodily the methods and techniques of the Christian missionary enterprise."[90]

Although few American Ahmadis, either immigrant or convert occupy prominent positions on the American scene, many have achieved recognition. The community, which in its early days in America appealed largely to lower income and less well educated urbanites, now includes a significant number of highly trained professionals. Their representation on boards of educational institutions is interpreted by Ahmadis as a sign of their growing influence. Education is stressed throughout all levels of the community, and part of the outreach program is the distribution of books both by sale and by donation to libraries and other institutions. Women converts often are more highly educated than the men; literacy among Ahmadi women is reported to be extremely high and has even been estimated at 100 percent.

Pakistani immigrants who represent the Ahmadiyya faith generally do not interact closely with other Pakistanis. In both the United States and Canada, however, efforts are made to invite non-Ahmadi Muslims to their mosques, mission houses, and meeting places to engage in dialogue and discussion. Ahmadis welcome religious dialogue and interfaith activities, and non-Ahmadi speakers are invited to address special gatherings and functions. Such meetings are regularly held at least once every year in major cities such as New York, Chicago, Los Angeles, Dayton, St. Louis, Miami, and Washington, D.C. Leaders of other religious communities are also invited to make presentations about the life and mission of their respective religious leaders during annually held meetings such as All Religious Founders Day.[91] Jews, Christians, Sikhs, Hindus, and Buddhists have taken part in these meetings, which clearly are intended as part of the missionary outreach of the community and as occasions for informing visitors about the meaning of Ahmadiyya Islam. Part of the community's educational program often includes particular attention to the history of religions, presented in such a way that Ghulam Ahmad and Ahmadiyya Islam are seen as the culmination of the line of prophetic revelation. A letter from Mirza Tahir Ahmad, leader of the Ahmadiyya Community in Islam in Pakistan, to the American branch of the movement commended the participation of Ahmadi women in the January 1986 March for Life. It is clear that the support is not so much for the Islamic stance on abortion, although that is highlighted, as because of the opportunity to convert America to Islam.

In general Ahmadis try to promote peaceful relations among all religious groups, though there have been some efforts among Ahmadi immigrants to protest the repression that members of the Ahmadiyya community experience in Pakistan.[92] For the most part their public defense has been of Islam as such and not of specific Ahmadi doctrines. They speak out in protest when they perceive that Islam is being attacked. Responding to a disparaging remark by William Safire in the *New York Times* in 1984 that Lebanon "will be tilted toward Moslem dominance," for example, an editorial in *Muslim Sunrise* accused Safire of being "blinded by prejudice" and of spreading "malicious and misleading generalizations" about Islam.[93] Throughout the 1991 Gulf crisis the Ahmadiyya community called for strict adherence to universal standards of justice. While Ahmadis have never condoned Iraqi leader Saddam Hussein's actions against his own people or against the Kuwaitis, they have not been able to understand how America could have been a staunch supporter of Saddam throughout the Iran-Iraq War and then turn so ruthlessly and uncompromisingly on both him and the Iraqi people. They find it inconsistent with American relationships to other dictators they see as equally ruthless.[94]

Some African Americans in the Ahmadi community are taking it upon themselves to assume leadership in preaching the faith of Ahmadi Islam and perpetuating an accurate understanding of its history and doctrines. "We must have the courage to preach Islam and have no fear of what our new found peers may think," said one. "African Americans: We must be the vanguard of this preaching effort. We have not yet reached our potential. . . . Night after night, on the news we see the destruction that drugs, violence, teen pregnancy, unemployment, poor housing and crime infested neighborhoods are bringing to our people. . . . The ice has been broken. . . . [African-American] Ahmadis must begin to address this arena."[95]

The educational needs of the children of the community generally are met through the efforts of Sunday schools that are organized by the local mosques. Summer schools are operated on a regional basis offering additional instruction for the youth. The curriculum in Ahmadiyya schools normally includes the following: (1) Holy Qur'an: text, translation, and commentary; (2) Hadith of the Holy

Prophet; (3) elementary Islamic jurisprudence; (4) history of Islam with special emphasis on the life of the Prophet and the four rightly guided caliphs; (5) books by the founder of the Ahmadiyya movement, Hazrat Mirza Ghulam Ahmad;[96] (6) history of the Ahmadiyya Muslim community; (7) comparative religious studies with reference to Christianity, Judaism, and other contemporary religions; and (8) Arabic and Urdu language study. Instruction for converts consists of a grounding in elementary Islamic teachings and practices, including the pillars of the faith, ritual ablutions, and recitation of the Qur'an. Books and cassettes have been prepared to aid in the process of education.

Women play an extremely important role in the American Ahmadi mission. During the early years of the movement, when the United States was trying to fight its way out of the Great Depression, many members were extremely poor. Ahmadi women were instrumental in raising funds for the maintenance of community facilities, and they have continued to provide moral, spiritual, and financial support over the years. Women participate in all sorts of religious activities, including taking part in congregational prayers in the mosque. As part of their activities in the community, women are expected to memorize prayers and Hadiths, donate monies and special services,[97] and otherwise enhance their own understanding of the faith and their contribution to the work of the group. They receive points for these various activities (one for delivering a speech, five for learning a new prayer, twenty for instituting a special project, etc.); awards for outstanding work are given at the national convention.[98]

The aforementioned organizations for women and for girls, the Lajna Ima' Ullah and Nasraatul Ahmadiyya, publish their own journals entitled *Ayesha, Lajna News,* and *Nasraat News.*[99] Lajna members are encouraged to be modest in their dress, to hold functions to expose non-Ahmadi members of their local communities to Islam, to raise money for mosques, and in other ways to support the community. It is part of their national propagational program "to disseminate the message of Islam as a complete way of life to the masses" and "to reach non-Muslims and non-Ahmadi Muslims with True Islam."[100] Efforts have been made to establish local lajnas in all cities in which Ahmadi missions exist.[101] The strong support that women must offer each other in the pursuit of the faith is apparent in this statement from the 1982 National Program of the

Lajna: "It is entirely possible for every sister in every city to espouse Ahmadiyya accurately without sacrificing her personality. Islamic concepts *demand* to be practiced collectively. Innovations in the practical application of Ahmadiyyat promote mass ignorance and moral decay. There is ample room in our religion for individuality *and* uniformity. Lajna Imaillah, USA must function as a cohesive unit. One Ahmadi *must* mirror another so as to preserve Islam in its pristine purity. Let us now make a smooth transition from ritual and form to absolute submission to the Will of Allah. Let us now begin at the beginning, Inshallah. May Allah, in His Infinite Wisdom, forever cradle us in the earthly paradise known as Ahmadiyyat/True Islam. Amin. Amin. Amin."[102]

One of the defining characteristics of the Ahmadi community is its emphasis on *purdah* for women. Purdah has two dimensions: one involves wearing modest dress, specifically a head covering and face veil, *niqab*, and the other refers to the physical segregation of women from men in public places. Women are encouraged to attend Friday prayers but to sit in places with microphone facilities segregated from the men. Ahmadis feel that universal observation of the rules of sexual segregation could greatly assist in solving some of the problems experienced today in American culture when young men and women interact too freely. "If I were superintendent of the Philadelphia school system," said Selma Ghani, president of the Ahmadiyya Women of America, "I would separate the sexes at the age of puberty." Ghani was in charge of educational development for the Philadelphia Board of Education as of 1987.[103] "If we reflect on the real cause of the present day teenage problems," writes Amatul Hakim in an article entitled "Islamic Solution to Teenage Problems,"[104] "we find that the main reasons are the lack of training of children by the parents and elders and the free intermingling of both sexes, particularly when they enter the teenage years of their lives."[105] Ahmadis insist that purdah does not mean that women are unable to avail themselves of proper education or to advance in the workplace, and cite the fact that Ahmadi women are active in all professions.

It is probably the veiling aspect of purdah that has attracted the greatest attention both inside and outside of the Ahmadi community. "Muslim ladies are expected to observe the true Islamic purdah which includes the covering of their head," said Shaikh Mubarak Ahmad in 1987. "However, in their homes or when they are relaxing in the company of the close relatives, or they are obligated by the nature of their jobs, they may observe appropriate discretion to veil themselves."[106] In the early and mid 1980s several articles in *Ayesha* were devoted to the experiences that Ahmadi women have had in school and in public places while wearing purdah. In a piece entitled "Personal Experience Attending American Schools in Purdah," for example, one woman described what she encountered in the seven years she had been veiled. While it was clear that she had met with some painful responses, she also indicated that she had used those occasions to inform people about Islam: "Once I had a teacher ask me, 'Why are you in school? I thought that Muslim women are supposed to be uneducated.' I soon set her thinking straight. . . . When I was in the 10th, 11th, and 12th grades, the human relations teacher at my school would ask me to speak to her classes about the Muslim religion. I was always very glad to have this opportunity, for through it, many, many misconceptions were cleared up. . . . I realized . . . that people condemn things they have no knowledge about. They stare and whisper out of curiosity or just plain ignorance. This knowledge helped when I finally entered purdah. If I noticed people staring, I would simply ask them why. This I found was an excellent way to propagate my religion."[107]

Another woman discussed her struggle to decide whether or not to put on the veil. First she did, and then she took it off. Then she decided to wear it only while at the mosque, but she soon realized that this was a "cop-out" and that she was ashamed both to be seen in public with a veil and to be seen at the mosque by her fellow Ahmadis without it. "Alhamdu Lillah [Praise be to God]," she lamented, "I despise hypocrisy!" Finally she decided to veil all the time and to accept experiences such as the time just before Halloween when a girl told her that she had on a really sharp costume or when a group of teenaged boys laughed at her green *burqa* (a Pakistani-style outer garment and veil) and said that she looked like a Christmas tree. She felt that those and other experiences helped her to realize that the problem was not the derogatory laughs, gestures, and comments but her own fear, weakness, and lack of understanding. "Alhamdu Lillah, Allah has now revealed to me that each *niqab* is a mantle of freedom and a prize (the spoils) of war!"[108]

For some women the issue is not so much the question of dress in general, but the specific matter of whether or not to cover the face with a veil. One York, Pennsylvania, convert who accepted Ahmadiyya Islam in 1975 has remembered the confusion she felt over taking that final step: "In November of 1982 I joined the ranks of Ahmadi ladies who had cast aside their last arguments and donned the veil. Spiritually and mentally I felt triumphant, even exhilarated." She candidly admitted that the spiritual and mental joys were accompanied by real physical frustrations as she learned how to become accustomed to having a piece of cloth over her face. Gradually she came to feel so comfortable that when she encountered the stares and giggles of others she was able to giggle herself behind her veil. She assured her readers that veiling provided both greater respect for women in the public domain and an enhanced opportunity for women to profess their pride in being Ahmadi Muslims. "I thank God everyday that I am an Ahmadi lady who has been blessed with the privilege of helping to carry the banner of Islam," she concluded.[109]

It is clear that the Ahmadis are deeply concerned with the experiences their children are having in secular American schools, in terms of both education and socialization. Some of the issues relating to female dress carry over to the school situation. In a brief article entitled "Purdah in a Public Junior High," a young Pakistani girl described her transition from jeans and shirts to the traditional *shalwar* and *camise* to the burqa or full covering. When questioned by her classmates she turned the opportunity into a full class discussion of Ahmadi Islam and of the wisdom of sexual segregation.[110] Although there are some variations in the accounts in *Ayesha* about the experiences of purdah both in school and in public, they all seem to follow a general pattern in which writers describe their own decision to adopt this dress, the various forms of derision that they have had to face, and the wonderful opportunity they insist has been theirs to propagate the faith because of being in purdah.[111]

There is considerable discussion in the Ahmadi community about the advisability of sending young Ahmadis, especially girls, to American public schools. While attending a public school can have obvious advantages—proximity to home, well-trained teachers, good facilities, often a multicultural atmosphere—there are, of course, concerns. An Ahmadi woman who taught in the public schools for many years has written about these concerns, which she identifies as aggression, hostility and verbal or physical abuse against Ahmadi students, ethnocentrism and a failure to appreciate the culture of others, overemphasis on the importance of materialism and profitmaking, the Christian-Jewish domination of holidays, teacher and administrative burnout, and political power struggles. Ahmadi children, she says, can still survive and learn successfully in the public school if parents remain alert to what is happening in the classroom and inculcate proper values at home. Children should be taught to obey Allah and their families, to reject anything that sets races and classes against one another, to plan time for prayer, to dress modestly, to study diligently, to choose their companions wisely, and to set goals in accord with the teachings of the Qur'an.[112]

Such ways of protecting Ahmadi children are not possible in all situations, however. One young African-American convert has written with pathos about the intense hope she had that a Muslim school would be established in or near her community before the first of her three boys reached school age. "As I thought of the task of instilling these [Ahmadi] values and beliefs in the hostile immoral society in which they were born, I began to pray for a Muslim school . . . to save my sons from the ill effects of this society that are so difficult to avoid." When her hopes were not fulfilled, she took the drastic step of immigrating with her family to Ghana, where her children attended Ahmadi elementary schools until the family was forced to return to the United States for reasons of political safety.[113] She reflected that the experiences her children had in Muslim schools and that she and her family had in Ghana were invaluable.

The problem of choosing an appropriate Islamic name when one has converted to the Ahmadi faith has concerned the community since the mission began in America. Early issues of *Moslem Sunrise* listed new converts both by their American and by their newly selected Muslim names. The summer 1988 issue of *Ayesha* suggests names that are appropriate for women, recommending to the faithful that instead of calling newborn children after members of the family, they should select the names of prophets, attributes of God, or lofty virtues.[114]

In a somewhat lighter vein than that which often characterizes the articles in *Ayesha*, the section "Muslim Life in the U.S.A." in the winter 1987 issue featured an article entitled "Arabic in the Land of the Beautiful" in which the author described some of the ways in which Arabic names have been misunderstood—accidentally and on purpose—by Americans. Her own name, Zainab, was first mispronounced as Zainabee by her neighbors and then shortened to Zambee, to which she continued to answer. She also heard someone named Amtul Karim called Krem, someone named Farida called Frito Lay by her school friends, and the last name Qureshi shortened to Fresh. She heard the name Azmat pronounced as Oz Mat (or changed to Ozzie Osbourne) and Nudrat unkindly rendered as Nude Rat. The author found all of this at least partially amusing and could even laugh upon hearing her greeting "Assalamo Alaikum" (may peace be upon you) returned as "Slimy Lake, Zainab." She gamely concluded that "perhaps it's just the American way of adapting to change."[115]


• • • • • *Conclusion*


Problems facing the Ahmadiyya community in America are clearly not insignificant. Ahmadis struggle, as do other Muslims in this country, to raise their children to understand and appreciate the religion of Islam and to live according to its customs and values in a pluralistic and predominantly secular society. Ahmadi parents are encouraged to do their best to implement Islamic practices in their homes so as to impart Islamic values to their children. Members of the community look with great concern at what appears to be increasing sexual promiscuity and other moral and health hazards in the American environment and worry about how to keep their children safe from these dangers. They strive to create a suitable way in which to ensure opportunities for arranging marriages for their youth and instilling the values of sound family life, and to do so in the difficult situation of a community that must bridge the gap between Pakistani culture and American life-styles.[116]

On the one hand the rise of Islamic consciousness, and the increase in the incidence of Islamic dress in the Muslim community at large, may make it easier for members of the community to maintain their standards. Ahmadi girls and women are not the only Muslims to identify themselves by wearing the burqa and even the niqab. It is clear, of course, that they are still subject to the curious and sometimes cruel responses of many non-Muslim Americans. On the other hand, as Sunni Muslims in general increase their vigilance in "purifying the faith" of what are perceived to be unIslamic or heretical elements, the Ahmadiyya doubtless will continue to be under the kind of scrutiny and attack that has characterized their existence over the past century.

Prejudice and misunderstanding are the burdens of many religio-ethnic groups in the United States, and the Ahmadiyya certainly experience their share. Unfortunately for them, the burden is made heavier by their exclusion from the very body of Islam to whose purification they themselves profess to be dedicated. It will be interesting to see whether they will be able to survive the critique of other Muslims as well as of skeptics in American society, and whether, through the activities of Pakistani missionaries and zealous members of the faith, they will be able to maintain and even increase their resident American membership.[117]

# CHAPTER 4

# The Moorish Science Temple of America

During the early decades of the twentieth century Americans of African descent who migrated to the urban areas of the North, having been stripped of their ancestral connections, began a quest for identity and roots. Over the years of their enslavement their African names had been changed, many had been forced to convert to Christianity, and they had been given new identities determined by their slave masters. Emancipation brought freedom in a technical sense but ushered in a host of new problems, including a lack of economic opportunity for most of those trying to find their way in an often begrudging society. Historian Oliver Jones, Jr., has called this period in African-American history "an era of little hope and significant human misery," when a variety of efforts were put forth to reclaim this lost identity.[1] One of the most prominent was the Moorish Science Temple of America, founded by Noble Drew Ali as a way of recalling for African Americans the Asiatic origins of much of African culture.

At a time when Marcus Garvey was preaching a return to Liberia in the motherland of Africa, Noble Drew Ali was discussing how important it was for African Americans to discover their roots while remaining in their new home. Undoubtedly he would have felt sympathy for the statement made some years later by Malcolm X (who may in fact be said to have obtained his inspiration from Noble Drew Ali) that "just as a tree without roots is dead, a people without history or cultural roots becomes a dead people."[2] A physical return to a motherland was not important to Noble Drew Ali; members of the Moorish Science Temple of America understand their Moorish heritage to reflect an affinity with those who originally came out of Asia into Africa. Some who were affiliated with Noble Drew Ali in the early days of his movement, or who were influenced by him, found other bases for ethnic identity. Elijah Muhammad claimed that the black man was the original man and the white man merely a derivation; Malcolm X found his roots in postcolonial Africa; and Isa Muhammad of the Ansaru Allah community located African-American identity in the Sudan.

Noble Drew Ali was perhaps the first African-American Islamic sectarian leader to invoke basic Islamic symbols to unite Americans of African descent (the term preferred by members of the Moorish Science Temple). He understood that in order for a people to have any sense of its own worth, it was necessary for it to have an identity, a name, a land. This identity must be distinct from any designation ascribed to it by the majority culture. Noble Drew Ali's intention was to unite an oppressed people, to give its members a source of pride and an opportunity to contribute individually and collectively to society. He did that by claiming that Americans of African descent were Asiatic, or Moorish, in heritage, and that in his role as the final Muslim prophet "in these days" he was to establish a community based on the five principles of love, truth, peace, freedom and justice. The community, still very much in existence in the early 1990s, was originally known as the Moorish National and Divine Movement, but the name was soon changed to Moorish Science Temple of America. The goals and purposes of the movement as articulated by Noble Drew Ali are "to dispense charity and provide for the mutual assistance of its members in times of distress; aid in the improvement of health and encourage the ownership of better homes; find employment for its members; teach those fundamental principles which are desired for our civilization, such as obedience to law, loyalty to government, tolerance and unity."[3]

• • • • • *Genesis and Development*

The founder of the Moorish Science Temple, originally named Timothy Drew, was born in North Carolina in 1886. At some point he

Noble Drew Ali.
Courtesy of the
Moorish Science
Temple of America.

migrated to the Northeast and worked as a railway expressman in
New Jersey.[4] We know little of his early history, except that although he apparently was self taught, he was aware of the dominant
thinking current in the African-American community at the time
(Garvey's Back to Africa movement), and that somewhere in his experience he became exposed to Eastern philosophies and to some of
the basic teachings of Islam. The scripture he provided for the Moorish American community, entitled *The Holy Koran of the Moorish
Science Temple of America,* makes no pretense at being a replica or
even an approximation of the Qur'an, which Muslims believe was
revealed to the Prophet Muhammad; instead it includes wisdom
reminiscent of the thought of many of the world's religious teachers.

It is part of Moorish-American lore that Drew traveled around the world before the age of twenty-seven in an effort to discover all he could about the heritage of his people and the tenets of the Islamic faith. On one of his trips it is said that he was made a noble by the queen of England and was given the name Ali from Sultan Abdul Aziz Ibn Saud of Mecca.[5] It is because of these acknowledgements that he has been recognized as Noble Drew Ali. According to Moorish-American belief he also visited North Africa, where he received a mandate from the king of Morocco to instruct Americans of African descent in the Islamic faith.[6] Clifton Marsh reports an interview with a member of the community who indicated that Drew's test of authenticity was to be shut inside the pyramids of Egypt and successfully find his way out; he was able to pass. From Egypt he is said to have returned in 1913 to New Jersey.[7]

That year, at the age of twenty-seven, Drew founded the Moorish National and Divine Movement in Newark, New Jersey, "to uplift fallen humanity by returning the nationality, divine creed and culture to persons of Moorish descent in the Western Hemisphere."[8] Convinced of his own role as a prophet of Allah, and now known formally as Noble Drew Ali, he began teaching his understanding of the true identity of Americans of African descent to anyone who would listen. A charismatic leader, he spoke persuasively of his passionate conviction that salvation for the so-called Negro could come about only if blacks discarded the various identities cast upon them by the dominant white race in America—those of Negro, black man, colored person, Ethiopian—and of his understanding that the true origin of Americans of African descent was Asiatic.[9] "The fallen sons and daughters of the Asiatic Nation of North America," reads Ali's *Holy Koran* (XLV:1), "need to learn to love instead of hate; and to know of their higher self and lower self. This is the uniting of the Holy Koran of Mecca, for teaching and instructing all Moorish Americans." Ali taught his followers that they had descended from the ancient Canaanites, Ethiopians, and Moabites who came out of Asia and went first into eastern and then into western Africa.[10] He argued that Asiatics were not black but had olive-colored skin and that Islam was the religion of the Asiatics, not Christianity, which belonged to the white man.

The message was designed to give members of the Moorish community a sense of heritage and belonging in a context that affirmed their ancestral contribution to human civilization. The very terms that Americans used for Americans of African descent, Noble Drew Ali argued, names given to slaves in the eighteenth century and never discarded, served to perpetuate their subjugation in America: "Through sin and disobedience every nation has suffered slavery, due to the fact that they honored not the creed and principles of their forefathers. That is why the nationality of the Moors was taken away from them in 1774 and the word negro, black and colored, was given to the Asiatics of America who were of Moorish descent, because they honored not the principles of their mother and father, and strayed after the gods of Europe of whom they knew nothing" (*The Holy Koran*, XLVII: 16–17).[11] To locate Moorish-American identity in a land and a people distant from America and heirs to a proud and noble heritage would be to allow Moorish Americans to take on a new pride and to have the confidence to assume their proper and rightful place in the larger context of American society: "Come all ye Asiatics of America and hear the truth about your nationality and birthrights, because you are not negroes. Learn of your forefathers' ancient and divine Creed. That you will learn to love instead of hate."[12]

Whatever the basis for Noble Drew Ali's understanding of his role vis-à-vis the African-American community, he recognized that he was a prophet sent by Allah to warn the Asiatics of America.[13] "These holy and divine laws [contained in *The Holy Koran*] are from the Prophet, Noble Drew Ali, the founder of the uniting of the Moorish Science Temple of America"; "The last Prophet in these days is Noble Drew Ali, who was prepared divinely in due time by Allah to redeem men from their sinful ways; and to warn them of the great wrath which is sure to come upon the earth."[14] The phrase "in these days" is an important one in Moorish-American thinking; for some members of the community it suggests that another prophetic appearance might be immanent as the days change, while for others the coming of another prophet is possible but not actively anticipated.

In many ways Noble Drew Ali's teachings are patterned more on a combination of Eastern philosophies than on normative Islam. His *Holy Koran* acknowledges that Allah has been known by many names. "You Brahmans call Him Parabrahm, in Egypt He is Thoth, and Zeus is His name in Greece, Jehovah is His Hebrew name, but everywhere His is the causeless cause, the rootless root from which all things have grown" (X:19). He clearly believed that Moorish

Americans should be considered a part of the heritage of Islam, and he acknowledged the Prophet Muhammad as "the founder of the re-uniting of Islam." All prophets came with basically the same message, and Islam was the original faith of the Asiatics to which Muhammad called people back as the prophet of his time.

Noble Drew Ali's message of pride in an ancient civilization that contributed significantly to the history of the world was appealing to those who were uneducated and economically disadvantaged and who were having a difficult time surviving in the environment of a large city. It also attracted young people who were disenchanted with what they were experiencing in American society and who were looking for an alternative system of belief that would help them deal with what Gayraud Wilmore has called "the tragic realities of color prejudice in a supposedly free and democratic society."[15]

This theme of the special identity of American blacks has continued to be the central focus of the Moorish Science Temple of America. In 1985, for example, the community petitioned the U.S. Congress for the type of recognition that had been accorded to American Indians. Sovereignty has been granted to the native tribes of Indians in the United States, it said, without corrupting their creeds, their tribal heritages, or their integrity; the same should be accorded to the community of Moorish Americans: "Moorish-Americans are erroneously classified as Negroes, Blacks or Colored Folks by institutions within the United States Government and this is discriminatory according to the Constitution. The Congress is reminded that Moorish-Americans, who are sovereign nationals of the United States, and enduring features of American Society and its constitutional institutions of government, are no less entitled to equal treatment from the Congress than those known as Native American Indians."[16]

At the time the Moorish Science Temple was founded by Noble Drew Ali, a similar philosophy espoused by Marcus Garvey was gaining support in the African-American community. Garvey's Universal Negro Improvement Association (UNIA) was not formally founded until about 1917, but his plans for African-American self-identification were well-known during the early years of Noble Drew Ali's mission. Like Noble Drew Ali, Garvey, a Jamaican, preached that so-called Negroes had been deeply subjugated and needed to set themselves apart from the dominant white culture. Garvey was an extremely controversial figure, scorned by many in the African-American community, but he claimed a large and enthusiastic following, especially among lower-income groups; the UNIA eventually enrolled significantly larger numbers than did the Moorish Science Temple.[17]

Although historians often lump the teachings of Noble Drew Ali and Garvey together, there were significant differences. While both founded movements aiming to recover an authentic identity for African Americans, the UNIA attempted concrete political action while the Moors remained focused on religion, with affinities to both Islam and Christianity and drawing on the teachings of both traditions as well as on Asian philosophies. Furthermore, Garvey considered the problems faced by African Americans to be closely associated with colonialism in Africa. One of his main themes, therefore, was the liberation of Africa. He hoped to organize the American community into a kind of vanguard for African freedom and eventually to take all African Americans back to their homeland in Africa.[18] While Ali considered Moorish Americans Africans, this Africanism was identified specifically with the country of Morocco. Ali preached a message of equality for Americans of African descent in the context of the culture of the United States, but despite the reports of some historians that his views were "separatist"[19] he did not advocate a radical separatist position or a return to the "homeland." On the contrary, he strongly encouraged members to see themselves as responsible and enfranchised citizens of the United States. Community members today do not view their reclamation of African identity as a separation from American culture; rather, they want to function like any other ethnic group within the American mosaic. As a member of the Hartford, Connecticut, Moorish community puts it, "We have a history of which we are proud; it is bound in nationality as well as in religion. We recognize our ancestry."[20]

Whether there was strong competition for membership between the Garvey and Ali communities is unclear, although it seems unlikely not to have been the case. Certainly many Americans of African descent considered themselves to be both Moors and Garveyites. What we do know is that Noble Drew Ali encouraged Moorish Americans to think of Garvey as a kind of harbinger, the "John the Baptist" of the Moorish Science Temple, as his *Holy Koran* makes clear: "John the Baptist was the forerunner of Jesus in those days, to warn and stir up the nation and prepare them to receive the divine creed which was to be taught by Jesus. In these modern days there came a forerunner, who was divinely prepared to meet the great God-Allah and his name is Marcus Garvey, who did teach and warn the nations of the earth to prepare to meet the coming Prophet; who was to bring the true and divine Creed of Islam, and his name is Noble Drew Ali: who was prepared and sent to this earth by Allah, to teach the old time religion and the everlasting gospel to the sons of men."[21] By acknowledging Garvey as his forerunner, it was possible for Noble Drew Ali to establish his movement as the fulfillment of prophesy and himself as the natural inheritor of a mantle that he affirmed was laid on him by Garvey.[22]

While Noble Drew Ali's teachings certainly encourage members of the Moorish Science Temple to understand that the white community has tried to keep them in a position of servitude, they also emphasize virtues that Noble Drew Ali felt would contribute to American peace, freedom, and justice. Noble Drew Ali called on his followers to be loyal to the American flag and to acknowledge that Moorish Americans had two homelands—the United States and Morocco.[23] A pamphlet prepared for the centennial celebration of the Moorish Science Temple in 1986 has on its cover a photograph of Noble Drew Ali and on the inside cover a full-page photograph of King Hassan II of Morocco (followed by a statement by the king on the spirit of the country of Morocco). As part of the celebration Moroccan ambassador to the United States Maati Jorio issued a proclamation in which he stated that he had been made "well aware of your devotion to strengthening the ties linking the Moorish American community to Morocco. Morocco, for its part, welcomes your interest, and your work for a better understanding between us. . . . Your initiative is to be both respected and encouraged. As to us, we in turn have every intention of doing all possible to make our relationship a vibrant and a special one."[24]

The official Moorish-American flag, considered an acknowledgement of identity and displayed along with the American flag, is the flag of Morocco, red with a five-pointed green star in the center. Each point of the star is said to represent one of the five cardinal virtues extolled by Moorish Americans.[25] Members believe that the flag is at least ten thousand years old and that their adoption of it kept·it alive during the time of the French occupation of Morocco, when it was not allowed to fly.

Noble Drew Ali's initial teaching, much like Garvey's, took place in informal as well as formal settings, wherever he found people gathered. Noble Drew Ali has been described as small in stature, wearing a bright red fez such as those worn by Turks, and presenting himself with eloquence, persuasion, and a keen native shrewdness.[26] He would talk to anyone who would listen, engaging people with the challenge to recognize their own position of subjugation and then offering them the truth of their own identity as Moors and as Muslims. Those who acknowledged their Moorish-American heritage and became members were asked to pay dues of one dollar. (This is still all that is asked of new members as of the early 1990s. Members are also assessed by their individual temples, with each temple setting its own rates.) Members were given nationality cards (sometimes incorrectly called identity cards)[27] on which were replicas of the star and crescent of Islam, clasped hands representing unity, and a circled 7 with the message that the holder of the card honored all divine prophets including Jesus, Muhammad, Buddha, and Confucius. When the members received their cards it was understood that they were reuniting themselves with their Moorish heritage. Members have continued to carry nationality cards. (When asked how she fills out application forms that inquire about racial/ethnic identity, one member answered that she checks "other," then identifies herself as of the human race, Asiatic division, Moorish American.)[28]

After the establishment of the first Moorish temple in Newark, Noble Drew Ali's following increased, and by 1925 temples had been set up in Pittsburgh and Detroit. While some southern cities had small Moorish-American communities, the movement for the most part had its greatest success in the major cities of the North. Ali provided the religious leadership for the community and also encouraged the establishment of collectively owned small businesses and other means of strengthening the economic base of the Moorish Americans.

In 1926 Noble Drew Ali incorporated a Moorish civic organization in Illinois, and in 1928 the Moorish Science Temple of America was registered as a religious corporation in Illinois. The purpose and goals of the movement were articulated by Noble Drew Ali in the September 14, 1928, edition of the *Moorish Guide*, a national weekly publication. The community, he said, was "building on human needs" to dispense charity and provide for the mutual assistance of its members in times of distress; aid in the improvement of health and encourage the ownership of better homes; find employment for members; and teach those fundamental principles that are desired for our civilization, such as obedience to law, loyalty to government, tolerance, and unity.[29]

Expressing his hope that Moorish Americans could serve as friends and servants of humanity, Noble Drew Ali stressed elevating the moral, social and economic status of his people through a comprehensive program embodying the five cardinal principles. At the first Moorish National Convention, held in Chicago in October 1928 and attended by a group of black dignitaries from the Chicago area, the Moroccan and American flags were flown as reminders of the dual heritage of the community.

A significant aspect of Noble Drew Ali's work involved helping Moorish Americans to achieve economic independence and the sense of self-worth necessary to overcome racist employment patterns. He advocated building up an economic infrastructure owned and operated by Americans of African descent to provide for the welfare of the community and to establish its constituents as full contributing members of society. The Moors in Chicago set up business establishments such as grocery stores, restaurants, and variety stores. The Moorish Manufacturing Cooperation was in full swing there, and on September 14, 1928, Ali commented in the *Moorish Guide* that additional workers were being added to this establishment organized for the explicit purpose of providing employment to Moorish Americans. "We shall be secure in nothing until we have economic power," said Noble Drew Ali. "A beggar people cannot develop the highest in them, nor can they attain to a genuine enjoyment of the spiritualities of life."[30]

Noble Drew Ali recognized that political participation was an important means of assuring full citizenship for Moorish Americans. During the opening session of the Moorish Convention he endorsed the candidacy of Chicago committeeman Oscar DePriest for the U.S. House. DePriest became the first person of African descent to serve in the House. The victory celebration on November 3, 1928, in which Noble Drew Ali took part, was perhaps one of the most successful days in the history of the movement: "Thousands of automobiles formed an impressive caravan of citizens joining forces in unity and love."[31]

In addition to fostering the growth of economic enterprises to help members get on their feet financially, Noble Drew Ali stressed the importance of working carefully with the youth of the community to keep them involved in meaningful activities and away from the temptations of the street. He encouraged the development of a Young People's Moorish League and the construction of athletic facilities for children. "It takes sympathy, patience, interest and the trained eyes of men well versed in the training and handling of your men," he said of the South Side Boys' Club Foundation in Chicago, "to see the hidden beauty beneath the rough exterior."[32] Better boys make better men, he believed, and better men would be better husbands for our daughters.

Moors point with pride to the fact that Noble Drew Ali was the first American Muslim to ensure that something of the faith and tradition and missionary impetus of Islam was properly acknowledged within the official records of the U.S. government. In the corporate information contained in the July 20, 1928, Affidavit of Organization filed in Cook County, Illinois, Noble Drew Ali stated that "the Moorish Science Temple of America . . . [derives] its power and authority from the Great Koran of Mohammed to propagate the faith and extend the learning and truth of the Great Prophet of ALI in America. (It is) to appoint and consecrate missionaries of the prophet to establish the faith of Mohammad in America."[33]

Despite these advances, however, soon after the establishment of the Chicago community things took a turn for the worse within the Moorish-American community. As pride of identity was enhanced, tensions between the members and the white community increased. Moorish Americans carrying nationality cards were convinced that the cards would deter any white person bent on doing them harm. Some Moorish Americans antagonized whites by flashing their cards, praising Noble Drew Ali for freeing them from the slavery perpetuated on them by the white nation, and predicting whites' imminent destruction. Not surprisingly, whites perceived such incidents as threats, and in some cases they led to public disturbances.[34] Noble Drew Ali warned members to cease activities that could be interpreted as reverse racism and to stop staging counterproductive scenes.[35]

Even more ominous for the community in Chicago was the move by Noble Drew Ali to bring in "experts" to assist in the management of temple affairs. As the economic base of the community grew and projects launched by the community expanded, Noble Drew Ali felt it necessary to turn the responsibility over to others more knowledgeable about the affairs of business. Unfortunately, however, some of these persons apparently were less than scrupulous, and they brought into the organization certain practices that were not up to Noble Drew Ali's standards. Members were exploited in various ways, including through the sale of spurious herbs and charms,[36] pictures and relics, and cult literature. Some members thus grew rich through exploiting other members.[37]

These signs of trouble in the Chicago temple led to challenges to Noble Drew Ali's leadership. Some members have contended that there were plots to do away with him by those who wanted to take over the small businesses of the movement.[38] One of the most serious threats came from Sheik Claude Green, identified as "a small-time politician and former butler of the philanthropist Julius Rosenwald."[39] Green removed all of the furniture from Noble Drew Ali's office one day, declaring himself the Grand Sheikh of the movement. Temples from other cities were called upon to support one side or the other, and on May 15, 1929, Green was stabbed and shot to death.[40] The fact that Noble Drew Ali was away from Chicago at the time of the assassination did not deter police (who may have grown weary of dealing with the Moorish Americans and perhaps hoped to put an end to the movement) from arresting him and putting him in prison when he returned. While incarcerated Noble Drew Ali wrote these words to his followers: "To the Heads of All Temples, Islam: I your prophet do hereby and now write you a letter as a warning and appeal to your good judgment for the present and the future. Though I am now in custody for you and the cause, it is all right and is well for all who believe in me and my father, God. I have redeemed all of you and you shall be saved, all of you, even with me. . . . Love and truth and my peace I leave you all. Peace from your Prophet, Noble Drew Ali."[41]

Noble Drew Ali mysteriously died a few weeks after being released on bond. Some have accused the police of abusing him during his incarceration, while others say that he was beaten to death by disaffected Moors or partisans of Green after being released. Other members of the community disagree with both arguments and believe that his health simply gave way.[42] Whatever the case, the death of Noble Drew Ali dealt a serious blow to the Moorish American Science Temple, although not a mortal one. Noble Drew Ali was beloved by those in his community, who often commented that they or some member of their family had been helped by Noble Drew Ali to overcome mental, physical, or financial problems.[43] Over the decades his followers have continued to keep his memory alive and his words in mind, and to believe that each successive leader of the community carries on the teachings of the founder and his concerns for the spiritual and the material betterment of Moorish Americans.[44]

As happens in religious communities when the founder and guiding light is no longer present, various claimants immediately arose to assume Noble Drew Ali's mantle. His attorney, Aaron Payne, attempted with little success to keep the movement unified while disciples such as Ira Johnson Bey, Mealy El, and Kirkman Bey contested each other's claims to leadership. For some members of the community the concept of succession implies that Noble Drew Ali himself is incarnated into the new leader. More than one person has claimed to be the new embodiment of the founder. Noble Drew Ali's chauffeur, John Givens El, for example, fainted soon after Noble Drew Ali's death while he was working on the leader's car and seems to have become convinced that he was the designated successor.[45] Those who believe that John Givens El was the reincarnated Prophet have considered him to be the legitimate head of the Moorish-American community.[46] Others do not feel that every leader is a reincarnation of Noble Drew Ali. Since the first Moorish Science Temple convention in 1928 there have been conventions every year. In 1934 some members present at the convention decided to break from the main body, primarily over the incarnation issue. Thus, in the modern Moorish-American community there are some "incarnationist" temples and other temples whose members do not hold such a belief.[47]

The question of whether the leader of the Moorish Science Temple is a reincarnation of Noble Drew Ali has continued to concern the community. An article in the September 7, 1934, issue of the *Newark Evening News* told the story of the controversy between William Gravitt-El of Temple No. 10 in Chicago and the grand governess of the Moorish Science Temple in New Jersey, Sister R. Jones Bey. Gravitt-El was accused of preaching to his followers that the reincarnation of Noble Drew Ali was living in Chicago. Bey disagreed, declaring that since Noble Drew Ali died in 1929, "his return to earth is impossible in that short space of time, according to the recognized conceptions of the Moorish Science Temple of America." How this matter was resolved is unknown, but that is of less concern than the fact that the doctrine of incarnation continued to be discussed (the article also reported that there were at that time more than 100,000 members of the national order in the United States).[48]

Despite the problems stemming from the leadership crisis, the Moorish-American movement continued in many of the urban areas of the eastern and midwestern United States. It was attractive to disaffected black Christians, such as those in the Holiness and Sanctified churches, as were the movement of Marcus Garvey, Father Divine's Peace Mission, and other nationalist cults that appeared after World War I. W. D. Fard, who established the Temple of Islam in Detroit around 1930, is reported to have been a member of the Moorish Science Temple, as was Elijah Muhammad, who in 1934 assumed from Fard the leadership of what became the Nation of Islam.

Regulations concerning diet, dress, worship days, name changes, and the like have long been popular ways for African Americans to affirm identities separate from that of traditional American Christianity.[49] A 1947 article in *Muslim World* notes that when a Moorish Science Temple was opened on Main Street in Hartford in 1936 many Americans of African descent were attracted to the movement, some because they were not satisfied with their Christian churches and others because the temple offered health benefits, a chance to wear different and interesting clothes, and unusual worship services. "The Negroes who have joined the cult believe they have found the real religion because it provides for spiritual needs and their emotional expression, and for racial advancement through communal rather than individual business enterprises."[50] The movement continued to spread through the 1940s, to Charleston, W. Va.; Milwaukee, Wis.; Richmond, Va.; Cleveland, Ohio; Flint, Mich.; Chattanooga, Tenn.; Indianapolis, Ind.; Toledo and Stubenville, Ohio; Indiana Harbor, Ind.; and Brooklyn, N.Y.[51]

• • • • • *Scripture and Teachings*

Every religious community employs some kind of text, written or oral, to which it can turn for devotional direction and for the spiritual guidance of the community. This serves both to legitimate the founder and to help the followers maintain a sense of unity in times of turmoil.

Noble Drew Ali took the designation of prophet, which he substantiated by reference to his authorization by persons in the Middle East, with the specific mission to bring to Americans of African descent a new sense of their identity as Moorish Americans. It is interesting to note that in modern acknowledgments of the achievements of Ali his followers seem less concerned about his role as divinely sanctioned prophet (although he is always referred to as "Prophet Noble Drew Ali") than about his achievements as a man of vision, purpose, and love, and as a statesman who did much for the Moorish-American people and for American society at large.

Nonetheless, as part of Noble Drew Ali's understanding of himself as a prophet, as another in the line of persons chosen to bring God's message to humanity, he provided a "scripture" for the use of his community. One of the reasons it is difficult to secure information about the inner workings of the Moorish Science Temple is that much of its lore and practice is accessible only to members and initiates. Members say that this is because instruction is needed before one can properly understand the teachings. The grand sheikh or leader of the local community is the facilitator in that understanding. Moors believe that teachings taken without instruction might be misinterpreted.

Noble Drew Ali's *Holy Koran*, the sacred scripture of the community (first published in 1927), is generally not shared with persons who are not community members for fear of misunderstanding or misappropriation. ("Dear readers, do not falsely use these lessons," *The Holy Koran* admonishes.)[52] Even most scholars who have been given some access to Moorish-American teachings have not been allowed to see this volume, although, as is inevitably the case, on occasion it has come into the hands of persons who are not members of the community and it is now available (although it is rare) in a few libraries.

*The Holy Koran* is sixty-four pages long (including the index) and is intended specifically for the Moorish community in America.[53] The opening pages admonish the reader to "know Yourself and Your Father God-Allah that you may learn to love instead of hate." Affirming Noble Drew Ali's special role as the one who has come to teach the African-American community, the first page cites an injunction repeated frequently throughout the scripture, that "every man needs to worship under his own vine and fig tree." On the next page is a large number 7 in a circle with four breaks in it, under which there is a declaration that the book was "divinely prepared by the Noble Prophet Drew Ali by the guiding of his father God, Allah; the great God of the Universe." The purpose of the work is to elevate man from the sinful and fallen stage of humanity to "the highest place of life with his father God, Allah." Before the beginning of the teachings is a photograph of Noble Drew Ali.

While the forty-eight chapters follow successively without being set into separate categories or divisions, the tone and content change quite clearly, suggesting three parts. The first part is made up of chapters 1 through 19, dealing primarily with the life of Jesus, the great teacher of the wisdom that Noble Drew Ali wanted to impart. Before treating the birth of Jesus, the writings discuss the creation and fall of man. The human soul is not destined for failure, however, because of Allah's guidance: "Man cannot die; the spirit-man is one with Allah, and while Allah lives man cannot die. When man has conquered every foe upon the plane of soul the seed will have fully opened out, will have unfolded in the Holy Breath. The garb of soul will then have served its purpose well, and man will need it never more, and it will pass and be no more and man will then attain unto the blessedness of perfectness and be at one with Allah" (p. 5).

Descriptions of the lives and experiences of Mary and Elizabeth are woven around a series of teachings about the lower or carnal self and the higher self clothed with soul and made in the form of Allah (III:5–7). The only devil that man must face is himself: "If man would find his saviour he must look within; and when the demon self has been dethroned the saviour, love, will be entitled to the throne of power. The David of the light is purity, who slays the strong Goliath of the dark, and seats the saviour, love, upon the throne" (III:22–23).

Jesus is said to have journeyed at age twelve to India, where he studied with a wise and rich man named Ravanna. Much of the material of the early chapters is devoted to the message of human equality, truth, love, and peace that Jesus taught in India and in other parts of the East. (It is important to note that about this time the Ahmadiyya movement began its mission in America, preaching that Jesus had been taken down from the cross and had gone to India to teach until the end of his life.) Noble Drew Ali attributes such words as these to Jesus: "If you would serve Allah who speaks within the heart, just serve your near of kin, and those who are no kin, the stranger at your gates, the foe who seeks to do you harm. Assist the poor, and help the weak: do harm to none and covet not what is not yours. Then, with your tongue the Holy One will speak; and he will smile behind your tears, will light your countenance with joy, and fill your hearts with peace" (VIII:14–15).

Jesus also teaches a message of the immediacy of heaven to those who "properly understand." Heaven is not a place of "metes and bounds," not a country to be reached, but a state of mind, a condition of boundless joy that men can create on earth (XII:8,12). John the Baptist, with whom Marcus Garvey is later compared, is described in detail as the one who prepared the way for the message of Jesus. Finally, Jesus is crucified by the Jews, then, after his resurrection ("You men of Rome, I am the resurrection and the life. They that are dead shall live, and many that shall live will never die" [XVII:22]), he continues his preaching to sages in many lands.

The second part of *The Holy Koran* is made up of chapters 20 to 44, which deal primarily with ethical teachings on a range of topics. Jesus is no longer the purveyor of the message; most of the chapters are specifically designated as instructions from the prophet. Included among these teachings, which are reminiscent of what one might read in the Book of Proverbs of the Judeo-Christian Old Testament, are instructions for marriage, the duties of husbands and children, social responsibilities, and the like. Virtues such as justice, charity, gratitude, and sincerity are extolled: "The peace of society dependeth on justice; the happiness of individuals on the safe enjoyment of all their possessions. Keep the desires of thy heart, therefore, within the bounds of moderation; let the hands of justice lead them aright. . . . Happy is the man who hath sown in his breast the seeds of benevolence: the produce thereof shall be charity and love. . . . As the branches of a tree return their sap to the root, from whence it arose; as a river poureth its streams to the sea, whence the spring was supplied; so the heart of a grateful man delighteth in returning a benefit received. . . . The tongue of the sincere is rooted in heart; hypocrisy and deceit have no place in his words" (XXXI:1–2; XXXII:1; XXXIII:1; XXXIV:2).

In the third part of the book, chapters 45 to 47, the historical and racial foundation of the Moorish-American faith is recorded. In this part one finds an explanation of the rehabilitation of Americans of African descent and the adoption of the new names Asiatic, Moorish, and Moslem. Great detail is provided in relation to the divine origin of the Asiatic nations, leading up to the identity of the Moorish-American community in the direct line of the ancient Moabites. The importance of maintaining the purity of the race and of the faith is stressed: "We, as a clean and pure nation descended from the inhabitants of Africa, do not desire to amalgamate or marry into the families of the pale skin nations of Europe. Neither serve the gods of their religion, because our forefathers are the true and divine founders of the first religious creed, for the redemption and salvation of mankind on earth. Therefore we are returning the Church and Christianity back to the European Nations, as it was prepared by their forefathers for their earthly salvation. While we, the Moorish Americans are returning to Islam, which was founded by our forefathers for our earthly and divine salvation" (LXVIII:68).

*The Holy Koran* concludes with a call to Asiatics of America to hear and heed the truth of their nationality and birthright, to learn to love rather than to hate, and to join in the family of nations that is trying to uplift fallen humanity and that honors all true and divine prophets.[54]

While *The Holy Koran* is generally unavailable to persons who are not members of the Moorish-American community, another document, "Koran Questions for Moorish Children" or the "Moorish Temple Questionnaire" (published in 1942 in *Muslim World*), serves as a valuable source of the teachings of the Moorish Science Temple.[55] Some, but not all, of these instructions come directly from *The Holy Koran*. The 101 teachings contained in that questionnaire follow the standard catechismal format.

The questionnaire teaches such doctrines as the following (in paraphrase): God, the creator and father of the Universe, can be seen only in the heart. A Prophet (such as Noble Drew Ali) is a Thought of Allah in fleshy form, whose duty is to save nations from Allah's wrath. Moorish Americans are descendants of Moroccans (the Moroccan empire is in Northwest Amexem) born in America; the Moroccan flag is more than ten thousand years old. The Moorish Science Temple was founded for the uplifting of fallen humanity through the teaching of the "old time religion" of Islam. The Moorish Holy Day is Friday because that is the day on which the first man was formed in flesh and departed out of flesh. Jesus (whose name means justice) was a Prophet of Allah sent by Allah to earth to save the Israelites "from the iron-hand oppression of the pale-skin nations of Europe." Angels, who are also Thoughts of Allah manifested in human flesh, carry messages to all nations. Noble Drew Ali is an Angel of Allah, sent to bring the saving power of the everlasting Gospel of Allah. The Covenant of Allah is to honor thy father and thy mother that thy days may be long upon the earth. Jesus, who taught in India, Africa, and Europe for eighteen years, said the TRUTH will make us free, and TRUTH is Aught, and Aught is ALLAH. TRUTH is HOLY BREATH, great, good and evermore.

The questionnaire (in paraphrase) continues: The Garden of Eden is in Mecca. The first physical man's name can only be used by the Adept Chamber of the Moorish Science Temple of America. Adam and Eve, first mother and father of the human family, went to Asia. Angels, called Asiatics, are guarding the Holy City of MECCA from unbelievers. Moorish Americans have the same father and mother as those angels. There are two human selves, the higher (represented by the angels protecting Mecca) and the lower (those cast out of the holy city). The higher self contains the virtues of justice, mercy, love and right and cannot pass away because it is ALLAH in MAN; the lower self breeds hatred, slander, lewdness, murder, theft, and things harmful. When Jesus said, "It is finished," it was in reference to the end of Satan. The name of the person into whom Jesus was first reincarnated was Prophet MOHAMMED the Conqueror, who took off Satan's head in 1453 (it should be noted that the catechism never states that there was any other reincarnation of Jesus, even in Noble Drew Ali). European nations put into the MOORS the marks of Negro (a West African river containing black water), Black (meaning death), Colored (painted, stained, varnished or dyed), Ethiopian (something divided). Man can be none of these because he is made in the image and likeness of God, Allah.

The questionnaire, which has continued to be used in the Moorish-American community in essentially the same form since its inception, is learned by children at a young age. Exercises are memorized and questions are asked and answered in a spirit of enjoyment and fun. The questionnaire is viewed as a way of introducing young people and new members to the concepts that they will encounter as they continue their study of *The Holy Koran* and the teachings of the prophets.

Sheikh Randy Bey, founder of the Moorish Institute, standing before the Zorayda Castle, a replica of the Alhambra, a Moorish palace. Courtesy of the Moorish Science Temple of America.

Noble Drew Ali has continued to be deeply revered as the prophet of the age to the Moorish-American nation. As a member of the Hartford community expressed in an interview with the authors: "He is a messenger that brought us back to Allah. People talk about Muhammad as founder of Islam. We don't believe that he was; Islam is the natural faith. It has always been in the world. There have been many instances when it was necessary for a person to come and clarify the teachings of God to the people. These include the Buddha and Confucius. Noble Drew Ali was in the same line; he had a divine mission."[56]

• • • • • *Community Structures and Practices*

The Moorish Science Temple of America is open to all who consider themselves to be Asiatic, although as of the early 1990s all members have been African American. The national office is located in Chicago.[57] Some local temples operate independently. Annual meetings are held both regionally and on the national level. The bureaucratic structure of the organization is democratic; grand sheikhs in local temples are elected locally rather than appointed by the central office. The grand sheikhs work with the regular members, who are known as brothers and sisters, and confer the name El or Bey on members. A grand sheikh can be either male or female (the latter is known as a sheikhess). Grand governors, who operate on the state level, are elected by the national body in Chicago. They coordinate the work of the local temples, overseeing necessary legal documents, visiting temples, and solving problems. Members of the Board of Directors are elected to the national body by delegates from all over the country. Directors work with the national leader on policy and problems facing the community.

Governors generally assume the name Bey. Only a few have taken the name Ali, which as the highest honor is supposed to be used only in very exceptional instances. After the death of Noble Drew Ali in 1929 the mainline leadership of the community passed to C. Kirkman Bey (1929–59), F. Nelson Bey (1959–67), J. Blakely Bey (1967–71), and Robert Love El (1971–).[58]

Moorish temples generally have a local Moorish Sisters Auxiliary which focuses on instructing members on the proper upbringing of children, sharing of recipes for wholesome food, and organizing for fund-raising projects. The auxiliaries also provide aid to the needy in the community. Annual meetings are held by the National Moorish Sisters Auxiliary in September and are attended by members from all over the country.

Moorish youth are organized into the Young People's Moorish National League, known on the local level as the Young Moorish League or the Young Moslem League. The programs generally are cultural and educational in content, including activities such as plays, fund-raising, travel, and study. Opportunities are available for the youth to meet each other from temples across the nation at the national league meetings. These young people acknowledge the democratic principles of the Moorish-American community by electing their chairpersons and their officers. The youth are provided regular instruction, generally on Saturdays.[59] The Moorish Science Temple worship service is composed of readings by a sheikh or sheikhess, the singing of some hymns (generally Christian hymns from the black tradition whose words have been changed to fit the Moorish message), and a time of open discussion where members talk with the permission of the presiding officer. There is an offering, readings from *The Holy Koran,* and a communal recitation of the Moorish-American prayer acknowledging the fatherhood of Allah, the prophethood of Noble Drew Ali, and the importance of the five cardinal ideals.

In a number of ways Moorish-American worship services offer specific points of contrast with those of traditional African-American Christians. They are held on Fridays rather than Sundays. In some temples men and women are segregated when attending temple services,[60] although often this is not the case and apparently was not practiced during the time of Noble Drew Ali. The tone of Moorish-American services is low-key; neither speaking nor singing is done loudly or exuberantly. Members are expected to pray at times that seem appropriate to them[61] as distinct from the Muslim injunction for five daily prayers. They face toward Mecca but do not practice prostration. Moorish Americans are encouraged to go on the pilgrimage to Mecca if they are able.

Moorish-American religious life is characterized by the use of many symbols. Since *The Holy Koran* is available only for the use of members of the community, many of the things that Moors say and do are understood only by those who have received full instruction. The primary symbols are the crescent (which symbolizes salvation), the all-seeing eye (which stands for Allah), and the clasped hands (signifying equality and unity of all people under Allah). The number 7 inside a circle with four breaks in it (pictured in *The Holy Koran*), is a perfect number representing the seven days of creation and the seven days of the week and signifying life itself. The circle shows the continuity of life, with the four openings to the four cardinal directions representing free movement in or out of the community. Members of the Moorish Science Temple do not consider themselves to be agents of propagation; it is up to individuals to acknowledge for themselves whether or not they want to join and hear the message of Allah who alone knows what is in their hearts.

Moorish Americans always assume either "El" or "Bey" after their given names, acknowledging that this signifies their true heritage as Asiatics. While the grand sheikh assists in the decision as to which form of identity to use, some members have a sense of which is their true designation and can share that with the sheikh. Members of the group use special greetings that identify them as Moorish American Science Temple members. Sometimes they say *assalaamu alaykum,* peace be with you, which is the traditional Muslim greeting. Their own special salutation, more commonly used, is to say *islam*, peace, when first meeting someone and then to say "peace" in English when leaving. Sometimes this greeting will be accompanied by lifting the right hand up to eye level with the fingers spread apart.[62]

Moorish Americans practice monogamy. The marriage union is performed by the grand sheikh in what is called "a ceremony of obligation"; Allah is the one who truly binds together two souls.[63] Rarely is divorce sanctioned. Husbands are expected to treat their wives with kindness ("O cherish her as a blessing sent to thee from Heaven. Let the kindness of thy behaviour endear thee to her heart" [*The Holy Koran*, XXII:5]) and to support their wives and children, although economic circumstances often make it necessary for women to find employment. Children are extremely important in the community ("Consider, thou art a parent, the importance of thy trust; the being thou hast produced it is thy duty to support [*The Holy Koran*, XXIII:1]), and much effort is put into raising them and educating them in the principles and beliefs of Moorish Americans. Child/parent seminars are sponsored in various parts of the country to help parents understand how to provide a good home environment for their children and give them the best possible support in their growing years.[64] Citations are given to men and women who make exceptional contributions to the educational development of the youth.[65] A very attractive book for children, entitled *When I Grow Up*, through sketches of Americans of African descent who have been prominent on the American scene or who represent different professions, illustrates the possibilities open to Moorish-American children.

Cleanliness is emphasized as an important requisite for Moorish Americans, as is appropriate dress. Traditionally men have worn fezzes and women turbans[66] and long dresses, particularly in the temple. Headcoverings are worn by many (but not all) women in the community, in reverence to Allah and as a protection for the head. Some feel that the eating of meat and eggs is forbidden (particularly those in "reincarnationist" temples), although others think that what is more important is to try to understand how to implement Noble Drew Ali's teachings about taking the best possible care of one's body. Members of the community are specifically enjoined not to use alcohol or drugs; some choose not to drink anything with caffeine in it. Many community members are involved in professions that relate to the physical appearance of the community, including dress shops and designer boutiques, stores specializing in Moroccan wear such as caftans and dashikis, and beauty parlors and jewelry stores. The impetus to provide a solid economic base for the community has continued since the days of Noble Drew Ali[67] and is carried out as members work to maintain their own professional establishments.

It is part of Moorish-American teaching and belief that the physical and the spiritual well-being of the individual are closely integrated, just as the Moorish Science Temple of America is understood to be both national and divine. Islam is a fully integrated way of life. Humans are composed of three interrelated elements: the physical body; the soul, which is individualized and personalized; and the spirit which is not individualized, has no gender and never changes and is part of the spirit of Allah in which all humans share. Moors believe that everything that is done in life should be toward the ultimate progress of the soul to realize its spiritual nature as one with Allah. When one passes out of the physical form one assesses what has gone on in one's life, particularly those things that are now seen to be harmful or stunting to one's growth. Once that assessment is made time is spent on what is called "the plane of soul," the bridge between the physical and the spiritual, where one learns a variety of lessons. When it is ready the soul is reborn in another physical form (which is called "coming back into form"). This process continues until the soul is no longer needed, and the individual is a fully realized spirit at one with Allah.[68] Heaven and hell are human creations, states of mind. The purpose of life is ultimate unity with Allah.

• • • • • *Conclusion*

The Moorish Science Temple and its community have received considerable recognition for their achievements in promoting the social, economic, and moral advancement of Americans of African descent. Proclamations from governors of a variety of states on the occasion of the 1986 centennial testify to the respect in which Noble Drew Ali, with his dreams for the spiritual and ethical uplifting of the Moorish Americans and their promotion as better citizens of this country, is held. As the community moves into its second century (the first beginning with the birth of its prophet), it faces many of the same kinds of identity issues that confront Islamic movements in America in general.

One of those issues may well be its relationship to other ethnic groups and sects, Muslim and African American, in the context of a society that is undergoing significant demographic changes. Relations with other Muslims and especially Arabs appear to be cordial, particularly with Morocco and its king. Nonetheless, it is clear that Sunni Muslims will not accept the Moorish Science Temple as part of the community of Islam, because of the claims of Noble Drew Ali to be a prophet inspired of God, because the Moorish scripture is completely unrelated to the Qur'an of Muslim veneration, and because nowhere in Noble Drew Ali's teachings are there any references at all to the "real" Qur'an. Because of the community's size and the fact that Moorish Americans do not actively propagate (except for some proselytizing in the penal system), however, the community is not considered a threat to Sunni orthodoxy. African-American converts have tended to gravitate toward Sunni Islam once they realize that Noble Drew Ali's *Holy Koran* is not the Qur'an that they expected.

The relationship of the Moorish Science Temple to the Nation of Islam has always been ambiguous. As has been noted, there has been an interchange of members between the two communities.[69] Many of the older Nation members are former members of the Moorish Science movement or of Garvey's UNIA, and Nation members since Elijah Muhammad have tended to see their prophet as the successor to Noble Drew Ali.[70] It is interesting to note in the children's book *When I Grow Up* that while the Honorable Elijah Muhammad is pictured across from the caption "I can be anything great that I make up my mind to be,"[71] there are no sketches of other Nation leaders such as Louis Farrakhan or of Warith Deen Muhammad. There are, however, pictures of African-American Christian figures of national prominence such as Dr. Martin Luther King, Jr., and Rev. Jesse Jackson. The appreciation that Moorish Americans have for the contributions of Christian blacks in the building of America and their identification with those contributions is expressed in Hartford mayor Thirman L. Milner's 1986 proclamation in honor of the Moorish Science Temple Centennial: "The Moorish American Movement exemplifies the successful struggle of Blacks In America, the spirit of the Sojourner Truths and the Dr. Martin Luther Kings, and serves as an inspiration and helpmate to our younger brothers and sisters throughout this nation."

In whatever way the community determines its relationship to the larger body of Islam and to those movements working for African-American advancement, it seems clear that it will probably continue to be fairly small in terms of membership. It is also clear that those who remain members of the Moorish Science Temple will continue to espouse its ideals of love, truth, peace, freedom, and justice. The community provides an important context for the betterment of African Americans with its emphasis on economic and political empowerment to help members move into full participation in American society. In that way it remains true to the goals and ideals of its founder, Noble Drew Ali, who continues to be remembered, in the words of Hartford community member Sandra Weaver Bey, as "a Moorish leader, humanitarian and statesman of distinguished character and everlasting appeal."[72]

# CHAPTER 5

# The Ansaru Allah Community

*Oh Allah! Who is the Breath in my body, the blood in my veins, the light in my day. Please help me in my love of those who do not understand me, and hate me, not knowing that you sent me to them with the light. . . . I see the sirat of my father, I want to teach them to walk in it, love you and not fear. Help me, help me, help me. . . . Even help the Pale, cursed people, for they too need my help.*
                                    —Isa Muhammad, *"What and Where Is Hell?" (p. 39)*

• • • • •

The Ansaru Allah community is a black religious sect that has undergone profound changes in its teachings, increasingly incorporating Muslim traditions, customs, and beliefs into what was initially a segregationist worldview.[1] It was founded in 1970 by Isa Muhammad,[2] who was well acquainted with its teachings as well as with those of the Moorish Science Temple.[3] He was deeply influenced by the 1960s Black Power movements in the New York area and, like other former Nation members, was dissatisfied with the leadership of Elijah Muhammad and Malcolm X.[4] As a result he struck out on his own, initially making use of many of Elijah's teachings.

While Isa Muhammad appreciates the fact that Noble Drew Ali as well as Elijah Muhammad taught the black man that he was not lazy or stupid or inferior as the white man had labeled him,[5] he has rejected their claim to prophethood and clearly considers his message to supersede theirs. He has critiqued Noble Drew Ali's Moorish Science Temple for teaching a version of the Qur'an that he considers "neither divine inspiration nor an original writing," but a hodge-

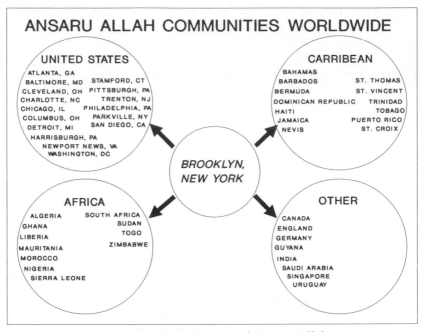

Diagram of the geographical distribution of Ansaru Allah communities.

podge of plagiarized material, its only virtue apparently being its substitution of the word Allah for God.[6] But Isa Muhammad does consider Noble Drew Ali and Elijah Muhammad to have served a purpose insofar as they urged the black community to be economically, socially, and mentally independent from whites. Isa Muhammad also attacks other black leaders as false, although he gives them some credit for serving as forerunners to the Ansar movement. Among them are Christians such as Sweet Daddy and Father Divine as well as so-called Muslim preachers whom he accuses of raising false hopes inspired by the devil and of encouraging economic dependency on whites.[7]

An examination of two decades of Isa Muhammad's writings would seem to indicate a movement from racist doctrines in his early publications to an increasing interest in presenting the Ansaru Allah as the group that follows the teachings of the Qur'an more closely than any other, and himself as the divinely inspired interpreter of the true Qur'anic message. The name of his sect, sometimes spelled Ansaaru Allah, is taken from the Qur'an, Sura 61:14, first translated, "O you who believe, be helpers of Allah." Later translations in the 1980s substitute the word "aiders" for "helpers." Isa Muhammad's choice of Ansar as the name for the community appears to be deliberate because of the Qur'anic reference (Sura 3:52) to Christians, the supporters of God.[8]

• • • • • *Founding of the Community*

Exactly who Isa Muhammad is, and was, is somewhat difficult to determine. His depiction of himself appears to be deliberately wrapped in mystery. It has evolved steadily with what, at times, seem to be dramatic changes in his definition of his own identity. That he is a prolific interpreter of his version of Islam can scarcely be argued; there seems to be no reason to dispute his recent claim that he has written more than 365 books and pamphlets and prepared more than two hundred "True Light" cassette recordings.[9] This productivity, he modestly protests, does not come about because he is capable of such a prodigious effort by himself but because Allah speaks through him.[10] He insists on using the term *Allah* (the Arabic word for God) to designate the divinity and is sharply critical of Muslims who translate the Qur'anic Allah as *God*.[11] He even cites "God" as the last of fifty names of Satan.[12] It is difficult to avoid the conclusion that the development of his doctrines over the two decades of his mission, and especially his understanding of his own role, is directly related both to his awareness of other movements in the African-American community and the claims to leadership being made by other African-American leaders and in the last decade to his attempts to locate himself in the wider Islamic context. He appropriates a variety of titles to himself, some seemingly determined at least in part by the appeal the concepts convey to certain segments of the African-American population. He is also an eclectic who gives evidence of having read and incorporated material on Islam available in English, including ideas put forward by the Ahmadiyya and Rashad Khalifa of United Submitters International.

Isa Muhammad's followers attest to the fact that he was born in 1945 in Omdurman, Sudan, and was given the name Isa at birth. They also report that he has an American birth certificate under the name York. Ansar texts point out that he was born exactly one hundred years after the Sudanese Muhammad Ahmad Ibn Abdullah, whom he recognizes as the true mahdi.[13] In assuming this lineage Isa Muhammad has created an image of an authentic African Muslim background, fusing his American identity with the myth of a divinely sanctioned Islamic heritage. According to Isa, after his return from the Sudan he lived in Massachusetts until he was seven, then he was taken by a guardian to Aswan in Egypt and back to the Sudan, where his "grandfather," As Sayyid Abdur Rahman al-Mahdi, recognized him as the one who would possess "the light."

Isa attended high school in Teaneck, New Jersey, and began to visit the State Street Mosque in Brooklyn. After high school he claims to have attended universities in Egypt and the Sudan, where he met his future wife. Responding to charges that during this period he served time in prison, he protests that while he did get into a few "squabbles," as kids will do, his only incarceration was in a rehabilitation center for children and not in an adult prison.

Isa became acquainted with Elijah Muhammad's Nation of Islam in the 1960s and was introduced to Noble Drew Ali's movement by a friend who took him to the Moorish Science Temple in Queens in the early 1970s. He says that at that time he also saw a lot of Five Percenters (another Islamic sect that split from the Nation of Islam) up and down 125th Street.[14]

Isa changed his name several times. As a teenager he adopted the name Isa Abd'ALLAH ibn Abu Bakr Muhammad (he claims that according to his mentor, Shaikh Daoud of the State Street Mosque,[15] he would have been in mortal danger had he continued using his Sudanese name Isa al Haadi al-Mahdi). He never denies being Dwight York, although he insists that Dwight was his nickname and York his mother's family name. In the late 1970s he even took the role of lead singer in a musical group called "Passion" (cited by his Sunni detractors as evidence of "the licentious nature of this so-called Muslim" leader), and assumed the name Dr. York.[16] His earlier writings are all in the name of Isa Muhammad or As Sayyid al Imam Isa al-Mahdi, although in the early 1990s he returned to what he insists is his exact birth name, and many of his publications read "by the pen of As Sayyid Isa al Haadi al-Mahdi." He will be referred to here as Isa Muhammad.

In 1988 a Jamaican convert to Sunni Islam named Abu Ameenah Bilal Philips, who as of the early 1990s worked with the Muslim World League in Saudi Arabia, published an exposé of Isa Muhammad's movement entitled *The Ansaar Cult*, in which he analyzed

Ansar doctrine and tried to show how it is a perversion of orthodox Islam.[17] It was in refutation of that work that Isa Muhammad published *The Ansaar Cult: Rebuttal to the Slanderers*, (under the name Sayyid Isa al Haadi al-Mahdi), in which he simultaneously attacked Sunni Islam, especially as propagated by the Saudi Arabs, and defended the Ansaru Allah community in America as living out the true interpretation of Islam.[18] While Isa takes serious issue with Philips's interpretations, he does not deny that the changes Philips identified did in fact take place as he solidified his group into its present form.

Isa Muhammad first organized a group of followers that he called the "Ansar Pure Sufi" around 1967, adopting the Star of David inside a crescent[19] with an Egyptian ankh inside the star as a distinctive symbol for the group. He asked members to wear green and black. While Philips argues that the Star of David was adopted so that the group would appeal specifically to black Jews, Isa insists that the six points of the star represent the six major prophets (Adam, Noah, Abraham, Ismael, Moses, and Jesus, all of whom, along with other prophets, he pictures in *The Ansaar Cult* as being black). He also says that the five-pointed star on the symbol of the "Islamic Chamber of Commerce" of New York (part of Daru'l Ifta of the Wahhabi Sect of Saudi Arabia) is really an inverted symbol for Satan.[20]

Before long Isa changed the name of his group to the "Nubians," asking them to wear long African robes, and began to elaborate a theory about the different origins of whites (whom he still calls Canaanites or Amorites) and blacks (referred to as Nubians). In 1969 the name of the group became the "Nubian Islamic Hebrews," and the mahdist crescent and spear were added to the symbol.[21] At that time followers were asked to wear a small bone in their left ear; proper dress was a dashiki and a black fez.

The official founding of the Ansar sect came in 1970. Isa instituted communal living for his followers, with males and females (including married couples) separated and housed in segregated dormitories. In the early 1970s he purchased a building on Bushwick Avenue in Brooklyn, which still functions as the sect's national headquarters. Regular publishing of a newspaper and journals began. In 1973 Isa went to Trinidad in the West Indies, where he formed a branch of the community. An important step in his understanding of his own identity took place in 1973, when he visited

Egypt and the Sudan. He had pictures taken of himself at the junction of the White Nile and Blue Nile rivers and in front of the Steppe Pyramid at Saqqara. A somewhat fuzzy reproduction of the latter suggests light emanating from around his head, which he identifies as an aura, "the manifestation of the light which resides within me."[22] It was by the Nile that he says he met the teacher of the Prophet Moses, who has been known in Islamic mystical thought as al-Khidr or the "green one."[23] Khidr figures quite prominently in Isa Muhammad's writings and is cited as the one whose direct teachings aid Isa in the propagation of his understanding of the Qur'anic message. "With the hand of Allah Subhana Wa Ta'ala over me and the teachings of Shaykh Khidr (SRA)," he writes, "I will continually strive until the end."[24]

In 1975, upon the death of Elijah Muhammad, in an apparent bid for leadership of the Nation of Islam, Isa Muhammad adopted some of the racist teachings of the Nation. He wrote that while he was in the Sudan his picture was also taken with members of the Mahdi family. Upon his return, the name "Nubian Islamic Hebrews" was dropped and the official title "Ansaru Allah Community" was adopted. From this time on Isa Muhammad began publicly to identify himself as the great-grandson of Muhammad Ahmad, the mahdi of the Sudan.[25] Perhaps in an attempt to gain credibility in the face of the criticisms voiced by many in the greater Muslim community to the Ansaru Allah, Isa Muhammad in 1977 invited one of the mahdi's grandsons to visit the Bushwick Avenue mosque, and in 1978 another grandson, Saadiq al-Mahdi (later prime minister of the Sudan), visited the community and promised help in the form of Arabic language instruction. Several Sudanese students in the United States became self-assigned missionaries who provided assistance in Qur'an instruction and interpretation and in translating material from Arabic. The Ansar published a special issue of their newspaper that they entitled "The Final Link," solidifying the identification of the Ansar with the mahdist movement in the Sudan and attempting to provide themselves full legitimacy. A very complex genealogical tree was produced illustrating Isa's alleged relation to the Sudanese mahdi.

The changing developments in the identification of the group and of himself as leader have proceeded methodically. In 1980 Isa Muhammad proclaimed, "The Savior has returned," a slogan that his detractors saw as a claim to be the promised messiah. In 1981 he temporarily referred to the community as the "United Muslims in Exile." By 1985, with interest in Sufi Islam in Brooklyn growing, he spawned a Sufi group called "Sons of the Green Light" that operated as an independent organization to which some of his membership belonged and to which people outside the community were able to become members if approved by application. And by 1988 his genealogical tree traced his descent through Husayn, the Prophet Muhammad's grandson, to the Prophet himself.[26]

• • • • • *Ansaru Allah Doctrine*

The writings of Isa Muhammad display a continual effort to ground his teachings in the black experience. Although he claims to propound true Islam, his teachings originally had much in common with the basic doctrines of the Nation of Islam in regard to the centrality, importance, and election of "the original," or black man. The official "Muslim Pledge of the Ansaru Allah Community" reads: "We pledge allegiance to Islam for the unity of all Black people; and to the Scriptures, for which it (Islam) stands; one people, under Allah, indivisible, with equality and love for all." This affirmation of blackness is set in the context of a constant attack on whites, the "pale-skinned" race. Isa's early teachings on race issues, outlined in such pamphlets as "The Dog," "The Paleman," and "Sons of Canaan," reflect the influence of Elijah Muhammad's teachings on the topic.[27]

Isa Muhammad's early view of the relationship of black people to white people regarded the pale man, born albino, as subject to the curse of leprosy meted out onto Canaan. Canaan fled into the Caucasus mountains with his sister, shunned and persecuted because of the leprosy. His offspring had sexual intercourse with dogs, jackals, and other animals, and also were lepers. It is because dogs would help clean the infected leprous sores by licking them that we have the expression about dogs being man's best friends. The stinking, dead carcasses of these creatures, filled with disease, were eaten by hogs or swine.[28] That Amorites had sexual intercourse with dogs and jackals was just one of many examples of ways in which the pale man participated in bestiality because of his low moral character and nature. White dependency on blacks is illustrated again in this story; the pale man must have the black man's blood and semen so as to be able to regenerate himself through his offspring, since the curse of Canaan has doomed him to ultimate extinction. Since the blood of albinos lacks the necessary factors for clotting and reproducing, whites must have constant blood transfusions, which is why the Amorites have so many blood banks.[29] Despite later moderation of these racist affirmations, Isa asserts clearly in *The Ansaar Cult* that the Nubian race and the pale race are not equal in the eyes of Allah and entitles one section of the book "The Nubian Creed: White People Not Human."[30]

Lest there be any misunderstanding, Isa Muhammad makes it very clear that he considers the pale man actually to be the physical devil. That message, somewhat more subtle in his later writings, is repeated with frequency in the works of the 1970s and early 1980s. "The Nubian does not realize that Canaan and his descendants are the physical manifestations of the devil," he says. "This is what is meant when it is said that they are cursed. . . . The Devil was first cursed spiritually, Ragiim, which caused him to be cast out of the heavens to the physical plane (earth) and was granted respite till the year 2000 A.D." This announcement in one of his popular publications is enhanced by headlines asking "Who is the Devil?" with the response "The Devil is the Paleman," accompanied by sketches of Satan with horns and pointed ears fading into pictures of Caucasian men.[31]

In later writings Isa views the white man, the Amorite or pale man, as conspiring to keep the black man enslaved and ignorant of his great and glorious past cultural achievements. In their attempts to keep blacks ignorant of their heritage whites have even distorted the use of music. One way was to take the songs sung by the slaves and to call them "spirituals." That form of music should rightly be called blues, since blues is the expression of a deepfelt emotion. All musical artistry has originally come from blacks; the white man has emulated it and called it his own.[32] The pale man has also misinterpreted the scriptures in order to oppress the Nubians. If the Amorites were to let the blacks know the truth about their ancestors or their heritage, he says, they themselves would have to bow down to the black man all over the world in the same way that Iblis (Satan) was made to bow down to Adam who was created of dust and black mud. Isa Muhammad's later works graphically portray the blackness of Adam in illustrations. In *The Ansaar Cult*, for example, a very dark Adam is shown with the notation that he lived from 4016 to 3096 B.C.[33]

Isa is clear that mixing the races is to be avoided because it will pollute blackness. "Muslims should marry within their race and not mix their sexes," he declares in a pamphlet on Muslim marriage. "When ALLAH SUBHANA WA TA'ALA, created tribes and families, he meant for them to remain that way and not mix and intermingle to the point that the distinctive race could not be distinguished."[34] Roses should grow with roses, he declares elsewhere, tulips with tulips and violets with violets. If you mix a rose and a tulip you only get something like a "rulip," which would not do justice to either.[35] The pale man will tolerate the mixing of the races and even promote it as what he wanted all the time, but that is because pale people know that they need black genes (specifially melanin for pigmentation) to protect their weak skin from the sun.[36] Pale people need good genes so badly, he notes elsewhere, that they have developed a new science called genetic engineering. They are constantly thinking of new ways to mix the precious seed of the black race with their own cursed blood, and by such mixing the off-spring of the Nubians will surely suffer.[37]

In the late 1980s, on rare occasions, Isa does seem to moderate his attacks against whites in light of the higher teachings of Islam. In a special publication for the month of Sha'baan, for example, he offers these words of encouragement for his community: "Don't hate, it's alright to be hated, but don't be the hater. Don't dislike, it's alright to be disliked, but don't be the one that dislikes. And you people who have the prejudice complex, when you see a person, whether his skin is white, black, purple, green, or aqua marine, and that person tells you 'I believe in Allahu Subhaanahu wa Ta'ala, and the Last Day, and I believe in His Prophet Mustafa Muhammad al Amin (PBUH)' embrace that person and squeeze him into yourself. Hold him close and squeeze him and call him your brother. I say this to you because I know that there is a race problem in America, everybody seems to hate each other. Well, the race problem is over. Now the race is toward 'jannah' (Paradise). The most righteous will be the first ones to get there."[38]

Isa Muhammad claims that he has been given a special gift from Allah, with which he is attending to the task of raising up a chosen body of people. These people are the sole surviving members of the tribe of Israel, whom he identifies as the stem of Jesse of the House of David. His own role is as the Lamb of Sacrifice, suffering persecution from those who reject the truth for the sake of those who accept it.[39] Isa's knowledge of the Hebrew Bible and New Testament is extensive, and during the initial phase of his teaching he utilized Christian concepts extensively in providing his own particular interpretations.

The Americans of African origin are referred to in his literature as Sudanese (from the Arabic word for black, which is also the medieval Arabic name for Africans), or Nubians, those who come from Nubia in the south of Egypt.[40] "We don't refer to ourselves as negroes. We are Nubians. The word Nubia, Nubala means black, the original Egyptians were and are the Nubians. . . . The real Sudanese are the Nubians in our community."[41] Like Noble Drew Ali, Isa is keen on rediscovering the preslavery roots of the African-American community. While Ali saw the link with Morocco, Isa sees it in the Sudan. The quest is for a national origin that not only provides the African-American community with an ethnic heritage and a noble lineage, but also implies a complete rejection of American identification of African Americans by color as "Negroes." Nubian lineage serves as denial of "negro-ness" for Isa in the way Asiatic heritage did for Noble Drew Ali. In later writings Isa grounds African Americans in an ancient civilization whose monuments stand as a witness to its contribution to the world.

During Isa's 1981 visit to Egypt he went to great lengths to study the ancient pharaonic temples and monuments and on his return assured the Ansar community that the ancient Egyptians were black and Muslim and that the Ansar were directly related to them: "We refer to ourselves as Nubians, knowing our origin comes from across the pyramids. . . . The ancient Mizraimites [Egyptians] did not worship many gods—they were Muslims! The devil has also interpreted the hieroglyphics to be a language. Hieroglyphics is an art form, not a spoken language. They are the means by which we are able to understand the customs of this great Muslim society."[42]

One of Isa Muhammad's favorite themes, suggesting some of the eschatological literature of the Jehovah's Witnesses and World Vision, is that of the four horsemen of the apocalypse and the opening of the seven seals. The Book of Revelation in the New Testament is used to explain Surat al-Adiyat of the Qur'an by reference to the four beasts. The first beast is the lion, the symbol of the Babylonian empire; the second the calf, symbol of the Persian empire; the third is man, symbol of the Roman empire; and the fourth is the flying eagle which refers to the European empire (including the United States). In one of his newsprint publications, entitled "Four Horsemen of the Apocalypse: Can the Holy Qur'an Solve It?" he identifies the horsemen, whom he sees as symbolic of the four empires who from the beginning opposed Allah. The first chariot pulled by red horses contained Phillip, Alexander, Cyrus, and Darius and went east; the second pulled by black horses contained Hamilcar Barca, Hasdrubal, and Hannibal and went north; the third pulled by white horses contained Nimrud, Nebuchadnezzar, and Hammurabi and went west; the fourth pulled by bay horses contained the Anglo-Saxon kings and U.S. presidents and went south.[43] "The Amorite, on account of his leprosy," he observes, "is pale and deteriorating [exemplified by bay horses] with blue eyes and blond hair." The might of the fourth empire is doomed to destruction. "The International Trade Center, Wall Street and the Empire State Building are going to be the first to be overturned. They are the heart, capital and economy of NEW BABYLON . . . America. All are located in New York City: THE EMPIRE STATE."[44]

America's identification with this beast is further illustrated through its manufacture and sale of arms, through its control of food prices so that millions of Americans starve while farmers are paid to destroy grain, poultry, fish, and other supplies, and through its methods of mass destruction including birth control, germ warfare, drugs, and other means of brutality. The world is depicted as crying for Allah's vengeance because of the great oppression in America. But Allah's plan is to save the world through Islam. The believers are told that they will be persecuted for their faith but that they will persevere through this tribulation. Then the end will come. "Vengeance is the Lord's when the Beast, America becomes powerless and crumbles to the ground. It will be humbled and broken into pieces by the GREATEST KINGDOM, the KINGDOM of ALLAH."[45] More recent teachings indicate that America's identification with the beast is illustrated through its manufacture and sale of arms as well as its use of computers, microchips, electronic scan bars and electronic eyes.

Isa envisions himself as the opener of the seventh seal at the end of time. In the "Goals and Purposes of the Ansaru Allah Community" the aim of the members, identified as believers in Allah, is to "re-establish Islam in its purest form," which means that under the guidance of Al Hajj Al Imam Isa Abd'Allah Muhammad Al Mahdi they will raise the 144,000 that will ascend Mt. Zion. "This is the Opening of the Seventh Seal and the time for raising a gifted people."[46] Reference to the 144,000 to be saved appears early in African-American Islamic cults. It was first mentioned by Elijah Muhammad and is also taken up in the Ansaru Allah and the Five Percenters. It shows the influence of the teachings of the Jehovah's Witnesses on these groups.[47]

According to Isa Muhammad the saints that will be saved are ones who have labored to liberate the black people, regardless of religious affiliation. In "Christ Is the Answer" Isa interprets what he sees as a scriptural reference to a silence of thirty minutes as actually a period of thirty years. This is to account for the fact that although he opened the seals proclaiming the truth in 1970, the world was not ready for the end of time because in all of its history it has not produced the 144,000 elect saints that will be saved from Allah's wrath. The thirty-year wait is necessary for the saving of additional souls. The end will therefore come in the year 2000.[48]

Nonetheless it is clear that the apocalypse is upon the world. Evident for all who wish to see are such signs as prevalent immorality, homosexuality, and the fact that women are dressing like men. The Ansaru Allah is the elect community, the saints who are destined to be saved, the dedicated minority that will prosper under the guidance of Isa Muhammad. "They will blossom into a great multitude that will propagate the words of Allah" while the "Babylonian Empire" is swiftly declining.[49] With the establishment of the Ansar community, falsehood that has spread across the world like a dread disease is annihilated. The Ansar are those who walk in Allah's light, those on whom the hopes of all people rest, the real teachers (rabbis) and maintainers of the sacred scriptures. "The Ansar are the Lords of host, the Salahudiyn (defenders of the faith), the people of the right hand and the army of Allah."[50]

The question of Isa Muhammad's understanding of his relationship to Jesus the Messiah (Isa Al Masih) in his Second Coming is complex. Philips levies the accusation that it was to boost his own claim to be the awaited Christ that Isa adopted the tale fabricated by the founder of the Ahmadiyya Movement in Islam, Ghulam Ahmad, that Jesus lived out his life on earth after escaping the crucifixion.[51] It is also possible that it was an effort to incorporate part of Ahmadi doctrine precisely because the Ahmadiyya have been successful contenders for converts in the African-American community. Isa Muhammad does agree that Jesus lived to an old age, although he goes to great pains to dissociate himself from Ghulam Ahmad, whom he says made absurd claims.[52] It is also clear that it is Jesus who will be the one who is to usher in the end of time. "Isa Al Masih is the Lamb. His followers, those who believe as he, will be the soldiers of his army that will help in the executing of the Word and Will of ALLAH."[53] The real question comes in the way in which Isa does or does not see himself as identified with Jesus. In "Christ Is the Answer" he says, "Thus is He [Al Hajj Al Imam Isa Abd'Allah Muhammad Al Mahdi]. . . . He teaches the law of the Scriptures and the Sunna of the Prophets. His role is that of the Lamb of Sacrifice."[54] And yet several pages later in the same work he says that he must bear much persecution "*like* the 'Lamb of Sacrifice' [italics ours]." It seems hazy as to whether or not he can be said specifically to equate himself with the Lamb. He does say in a piece entitled "The Proclamation of Redemption"[55] that "I am the first begotten of those who were mentally dead, the resurrection, the light, the truth. . . . I am your Savior. Come and follow me." This claim is repeated in "Four Horsemen of the Apocalypse," when Isa states clearly that "the Messiah Isa is here. The signs of war, famine, drought, and earthquakes are evidence of his presence. Even though there have been earthquakes, famines and wars before, never have they all come at the same time."[56] He adds a chart indicating the increasing frequency of earthquakes in the 1970s.

By the end of the 1980s, when Isa Muhammad was writing in defense of the Ansaru Allah against the attack of Philips, he was extremely careful to deny that anywhere in his writings had he made any identification of himself with Isa Al Masih. In the long series of interviews with members of the community at the end of the Philips volume, one of the set questions Philips asks reads, "Have you heard As Sayyid Isa Al Haadi Al Mahdi declare himself the 'Messiah' or 'the Messiah Jesus'?" No member of the community interviewed ever heard Isa make such a claim. Isa insists that through a careful reading of his works "any fool can see that I didn't say 'I am the Christ.' "[57] In fact, he goes on, the truth is that the spirit of Al Masih will be in the spirit and the flesh of all of his followers, all of the body of people who will be known as the purified ones. He cites John I, 4:3 as proof that the spirit of Jesus will "descend into a person and then after that disperse itself amongst his followers. They would be of him and like him. They would live Islaam, dress in the garb of righteousness and purity, and speak his words."[58] Is this an artful dodge, or a more sophisticated interpretation of a subtle doctrine for a people now better prepared to understand it?

Regardless of how Isa or his followers see this connection between himself and Isa Al Masih, the dominant message in Isa's writings is that he has been chosen to proclaim the truth of which he alone is in sole possession. His truth will prevail over all lies perpetuated by other leaders. His special assignment is to be the translator of the Holy Qur'an. Thus far he has not rendered the entire Qur'an into English, but he has made many passages from different Suras accessible to his English speaking audience in the volume entitled *Al-Qur'an al-Muqaddasa* [The Holy Qur'an] *Al-Wasiyya Al-Akhirah* [The Last Testament]. Each Arabic word is presented in very large print inside a rectangular block, with the English translation just below it. Isa provides an introduction to each Sura from which he takes material, as well as a detailed exegesis of the passage presented. These volumes serve as Arabic primers as well as translations of passages of the Qur'an. Sunni Muslims, of course, decry his translations as well as his interpretations, and claim that he is keeping his followers from having access to correct and full translations of the Qur'an by providing these selected verses. "Thus," writes Philips, "it is only the few among them who dare to think for themselves and read the Qur'aan and Hadeeth, who eventually discover Isa's web of falsehood and leave the cult to join real Islam."[59]

Much of what Isa Muhammad has taught, especially about himself, is directly connected to his changing relationship with the Nation of Islam, and to his perception of the changes that have taken place within that community. He claims that before Elijah Muhammad died he prophesied Isa Muhammad's coming: "The Honourable Elijah Muhammad told his followers that one would come after him who had the wisdom and the understanding of the letter *L* (LAAM), he did not understand the meaning of this himself, but he told his followers that this would be as a sign for them, and to follow whoever possessed this knowledge. This man who he spoke of was the reformer (Mujaddid) . . . who would properly restore Islam as our way of life."[60]

It was in 1979 that Isa actually did claim for himself the title *mujaddid*, or reformer of the faith,[61] next in the line of reformers after

Imam Muhammad Ahmad al-Mahdi of the Sudan.[62] It is clearly not coincidental that this followed quite soon after Elijah Muhammad's son Warith Deen made the same claim for himself. Warith Deen was concerned with reforming what he saw as his father's erroneous teachings and restoring the followers of the Nation of Islam to the Sunni faith. According to Philips[63] Isa Muhammad's assertion of his own role as mujaddid was made to try to attract Nation followers to the Ansar cult by adopting Elijah's "white devil" doctrine. The fact that *The Book of Lam* was written after the death of Elijah Muhammad and the claim of Warith Deen to be the mujaddid would seem to confirm this. In many places Isa professes great respect for Elijah Muhammad and for those teachings that give stature and dignity to blacks. As he states in the introduction to *The Book of Lam*, "The Honorable Elijah Muhammad (HWON) was the 'Greatest Black Man Ever to Be Born in America!! ' He accomplished what no other Black Man during his time or before had ever accomplished." According to Isa, Elijah awakened in blacks ideas of love and respect and set the goals of justice, freedom, and equality. The affinity of the two groups is depicted in a full-page drawing of the Nubian Islamic Hebrews shaking hands with members of the Nation of Islam.[64] Isa laments that with the passing of Elijah Muhammad a dismal change overtook the Nation of Islam, which had once been the salvation of the black man. He accuses Warith Deen of perpetuating a philosophy of "all whites aren't bad," which is weakening the community that had for so long served as a fortification to striving black Muslims. By seeing the pale man as brother, warned Isa, blacks will begin to forget who the devil really is and what their leader Elijah had taught them. The present misguided direction of the Nation is destroying the hopes of those who believed that they were following the true path of Islam.[65]

Later, however, Isa distanced himself and the Ansar from the Nation and some of Elijah Muhammad's doctrines. As he told a group of dignitaries in Egypt in 1981, the Ansar firmly believed in the ideas of Elijah relating to separation and economics.[66] But Isa clearly denounces the doctrines of the divinity of Fard Muhammad (Master Wallace Douglas [Dodd] Ford [Fard], whom he identifies as one of recent history's false mahdis)[67] and of Elijah's claim to prophethood.[68] He has absolutely no use for Malcolm X or for Elijah's son Wallace (Warith Deen),[69] both of whom he feels sold Islam out to Arab white supremacists, and very little appreciation for

Louis Farrakhan,[70] self-styled advocate of Nation of Islam ideology. "Wallace D. Muhammad is not bringing Islaam to its pristine purity in the West. He has recently resigned as the leader of the Nation of Islam. How could he call himself the MUJADDID [Reformer] and run away from his job and his duty! ! ! Minister Farrakhan has also come to the surface and claimed to be the final call, the Reformer. He is an eloquent preacher but not a teacher. . . . He holds a Qur'aan in his hands, but never uses it. . . . His sessions are always speeches not backed up by any scriptures or facts. This is definitely not the sign of a reformer!"[71]

Isa's assertion of his own connection with the mahdi of the Sudan and his legitimate assumption of that role himself was reinforced by his claim that he was born exactly one hundred years after the birth of the Sudanese mahdi and that his community was established exactly one hundred years after the mahdi established the Ansar in Aba Island in the Sudan.[72] His later writings make it clear that if he ever did claim the title *mahdi* as more than his given name, he will not admit to it. In the interviews he includes at the end of *The Ansaar Cult* the question is repeatedly asked, "Have you ever heard As Sayyid Isa Al Haadi Al Mahdi declare himself 'The Mahdi'?" to which the answer is a consistent no. Addressing himself specifically to Philips, he insists, "You say that I began to use the symbol of the Mahdi (AS) after I came back from the Sudan and again you are lying."[73]

Isa Muhammad has distinguished between three kinds of religious leaders: (1) The Prophet, who received a divine revelation from God and is granted certain powers to explain the message; (2) the apostle, whose duty was to convey the revelation received by the last prophet; and (3) the guide, *hadi*, and reformer (mujaddid). He categorically states that he is not a prophet but a reformer whose role is to restore the messages brought by others to their pristine state.[74]

Not only is Isa the reformer of the age, he is also depicted in Ansar literature as one whose coming was prophesied by the Prophet Muhammad: "Al Hajj Al Imam Isa Abd'Allah Muhammad al Mahdi is to us the raisin-headed slave of whom the Prophet Mustafa Muhammad Al Amin (PBUH) spoke; and the rising of the sun in the West. . . . As the Prophet Mustafa Muhammad Al Amin (PBUH) before him, he does not claim to be a Prophet. . . . The information found within the books that he writes is the only of it's [sic] kind that has been able to awaken and set free from the chains of ignorance the Black man and woman."[75]

Increasingly Isa began to understand his role in global dimensions. He affirms that his mission is essential not only for Muslims in the United States but for the salvation of Muslims everywhere, who have gone astray since the beginning of Islam by emphasizing politics and dividing over the issue of legitimate succession to the Prophet Muhammad. "The knowledge has risen out of the West in the countenance of al Hajj al Imam Isa Abd'allah Muhammad al Mahdi (WU), the Mujaddidun; reformer for this day and time. It is my job as the reformer to reform Islam and re-institute it in its pristine purity; not only here in the West but also in the East, where it is needed. Despite the fact that the people of the East were raised speaking Arabic, and were thus able to read the Qur'an, they still do not understand it, nor its relationship to the Old and New Testaments."[76] This in a sense is an affirmation that the fact that Arabs can read the Qur'an and read its meaning does not make them authoritative Muslims. "English, a language of the Devil, is confusing and corrupt. And because of this, finding the English equivalency to Arabic words is in some degrees difficult. This aspect makes the task of translating burdensome; yet, it is a divine duty and assignment that must be attended to. Many Arabic speaking foreigners, who profess to be 'Muslim,' have had their chance to help in your quest toward a clear understanding of the Holy Qur'an. They are status-seekers, and power-hungry, wanting to do no more than mislead by altering the words of Allah Subhana wa Ta'ala. These who speak Urdu, Yemen [sic], Egyptian dialects and other substandard languages, attend universities and religious philosophy."[77]

Thus the Arabs are criticized for their apparent arrogance because of their knowledge of Arabic. "They think that they have the authority to decide who can and cannot enter Makkah, argue over whose translation of the Qur'an is the *best* translation."[78] Despite their knowledge of Arabic, they, described as "pale man," have deliberately mistranslated some verses in order to conceal the definite consignment of all "blue eyed" criminals to Hell's Fire as he renders the translation of Sura 20:102 in his Qur'an.[79] Thus there is a need for special insights which only Isa, the scion of the mahdi, is able to provide because of his special lineage. It is a rejection not only of Warith Deen, but of Arab religious authorities.

The recognition of Warith Deen Muhammad as the leader of the convert Muslim community in North America, which was accorded to him by the Muslim immigrants and by the Muslim leadership of the Gulf States, inspired a scramble for international acknowledgement of other Muslim leaders and authentication of their message. Much of Isa Muhammad's writing is devoted to a justification of his own role as the one chosen to save the black man from the domination of the pale race. In that sense he considers himself to be in a direct line with other leaders of the African-American community. His visit to the Sudan, and Saadiq al-Mahdi's visit to the community in the United States in 1978, are cited as proof of authenticity and of international credibility. Saadiq al-Mahdi's speech to the Ansar is quoted as confirmation of the unique knowledge possessed by Isa and the special world leadership role that awaits him. Al-Mahdi is reported to have assured him that he is admired and welcomed in the Sudan and that there is great potential there for him to preach his message. The influence of Christian missionaries has spread ideas of racial superiority of the kind that blacks all over the world have suffered from whites, said the Nubian leader. Isa Muhammad could be of help because of his experience with what it means to be Christian and black. "This all means that your potential is not only here [in the United States], but it can also be seen in your homeland of the movement that's in the Sudan."[80]

Ansar literature portrays this recognition in a favorable light, as an affirmation of Isa's innate possession of the truth. Isa chastises others for not recognizing his leadership when even those from overseas are coming to him for the truth. To look for the meaning of Islam among foreigners, he says, is to maintain dependency on others. Muslims should be ashamed of themselves for looking outside this country for the truth since persons from overseas are taking "a giant step toward ALLAH" by coming here.[81] The visit of Sudanese dignitaries to his headquarters was also extremely important to the Ansar as support of Isa Muhammad's claim that he is of Sudanese lineage.

As late as 1984, after seeking and receiving this "international legitimacy" through his contacts in the Sudan and Egypt,[82] Isa Muhammad continued to see himself as the legitimate heir of Elijah Muhammad. "The Honorable Elijah Muhammad (HWON) was the only individual who attempted to get rid of that white-washed image of a pale god by putting the pale man's concept in reverse. He taught that THE CREATOR is Black. . . . Many have slandered him and labeled him a racist. But the Honorable Elijah Muhammad (HWON) was far from being a racist. UNDERSTAND THIS: *He did not teach racism, he taught balancement.*"[83] Isa Muhammad's loyalty to Elijah stemmed not only from Isa's desire to appeal to disaffected members of the Nation of Islam who were not happy with Warith Deen's reforms, but also from his wish to continue preaching that Islam was the religion of the black man. His references to himself as the *mukhlas,* or "purifier" and as "The Final Link" were meant to underscore this continuity, and also to appeal to the followers of Louis Farrakhan. The Ansaru Allah organization has peddled portraits of black leaders including Elijah Muhammad, Noble Drew Ali, and Malcolm X (although, as was noted above, Isa Muhammad in 1989 rejected Malcolm, calling him an agent of the Saudis).

Isa Muhammad has considered himself the interpreter of all scriptures mentioned in the Qurʾan, although it can be argued that he took this role more seriously at the beginning of his mission than later. Muslims from the East have erred because they have ignored the Torah and the Gospels in their attempt to understand God's revelation. He alone is able to discern the comprehensive (and consequently syncretistic) truth and to clarify the Torah, the Psalms, the New Testament and the Qurʾan. To this end he has coined a special reference to the Qurʾan as "The Last Testament," as he wrote in 1977: "We believe in all the Holy Scriptures which include the Taurat [Old Testament], the Injil [New Testament], and the Qurʾan [Last Testament]. All of the above serve as a guidance in all we do."[84] He is insistent that all scriptures must be read carefully and in their correct order of revelation.

Isa Muhammad's teaching is sprinkled with references to the Old and New Testaments. In a sermon on paradise, for example, he says that "when there are other people who call themselves believers they pursue their daily world, yet they have not 'dropped their nets and become fishers of men.' "[85] The back cover of *The Book of Lam* features a large picture under the heading "O You Who Are Faithful Be Aiders of Allah," in which the four scriptures are shown united: the Psalms, the Gospels, the Torah, and (as he spells it here) the Quraan.

Isa Muhammad understands the role of reformer as involving the implementation of the Islamic law or Shariʾa. He reports that the

Ansar follow the Maliki school of law[86] and declares that Muslims who adhere to other legal schools are confused. This he says is because Malik's *al-Muwatta'* is the only collection of traditions published in the Arabic language. The others, he (incorrectly) argues, were originally written in Persian and then were translated into Arabic.[87] Reiterating the connection of the Ansar with the mahdi of the Sudan, he states that the sayings of the Prophet used by the Sudanese Ansar were related directly to al-Mahdi by the Prophet himself. Thus there is a direct link from Muhammad to the Sudanese mahdi to the Ansaru Allah community in America. This, he claims, is the difference between the Ansaru Allah community and other sects. Those who follow confused leaders are themselves confused. Calling the Islam of such leaders "mainly the opinions of egotistical fanatics" who cannot answer the questions of their followers because they themselves do not know the answers, he reassures his listeners that the Ansaru Allah community does not have this problem.[88]

Isa Muhammad has grown increasingly vitriolic in his attack against what he calls "Arab Islam." The piece entitled "Goals and Purposes of the Ansaru Allah Community," found on the back cover of many of his publications, specifically states that the difficulties of being Muslim in the United States are compounded by the fact that the "so-called Arab" has been sent to the West for the express purpose of confusing and confounding the Nubian man. He claims that many Arab concepts of Islam are Christianized, and yet Arabs do not believe in the Old and New Testaments. Among these deceivers the statement identifies the Sunni, the Ahmadiyya, the Wahabi [sic], the Shiʿi, the Akhwani Muslimin, and "a host of others." These immigrant Muslim groups were seeking converts in the African-American community, claiming to be the sole possessors of true Islam. In a sense they were competing for leadership of the same African Americans who had been disenchanted with Christianity and the American sociopolitical and economic system. Isa devotes an entire pamphlet, entitled "Racism in Islam," to an elaboration of his belief that Islam as it is practiced by what he calls pale Arabs is riddled with racial prejudice. "You can't tell me there is no such thing as Racism in Islam because I've seen it! There is more Racism inflicted upon Black Arabs in Arab speaking countries than the Black man experiences in America. He is subjected to degrading incidents of social, economic and religious racism at any time! Pale Arabs look down their noses at Black Arabs."[89]

One good example of racism in Islam, according to Isa, is the failure of some Muslims to recognize the legitimacy of succession from the Prophet directly to his son-in-law, 'Ali. The insistence by Sunni Muslims on the rightful claim to the caliphate by Abu Bakr, Uthman, and Umar is part of the pale people's allegation that Muhammad and 'Ali were also pale, when in fact, says Isa, they were not. The true line of descent, he insists, is only through Fatima and 'Ali and their sons Hasan and Husayn, who must have been black.[90] (This teaching came after Khomeini's revolution in Iran and the free distribution of Shi'a literature in English by the Mustazafan foundation.) All of the prophets are pictured in Isa's literature as black, having very similar features and with prominent almond-shaped eyes. "We stress this point not as a prejudice statement, but only to uncover the fact that all the Prophets (PBUT) were Nubian (Black) as is al Hajj al Imam Issa Abd'Allah Muhammad al-Mahdi. To denounce him is to deny your descendency through the prophets."[91]

One proof that "so-called Arabs" have no intention of uniting the Muslim world, says Isa, is the fact that in America they have not established schools or universities for Islamic education for children or adults, nor are they building Islamic mosques even though they have been in this country since the early 1900s.[92] Black Americans of various affiliations had hoped that parochial Islamic schools could be established across this nation by oil-rich countries in order to raise the educational standards of Muslim children as well as to provide proper Islamic training for living an Islamic life in a non-Muslim milieu. Isa identifies the cause of the lack of such schools as a simple lack of concern. Clearly the money is available, but there is simply no evidence that "so-called Arabs" have any interest in providing the kinds of resources, educational or otherwise, that could serve to unite the many sects in Islam around the world through proper Islamic education, he argues.

Isa reviles Arabs for modernizing and Westernizing, which he equates with Christianizing. Even Egyptians, whom he is quick to praise when that supports his cause, are faulted for emulating Western fashions and ideas in their homeland. Yemenis, Malaysians, Jordanians, and others have also become victims of the devil's plan to eliminate the pure seed. These (pale) Arab Muslims are portrayed as unfit to be citizens of any place, since they neither live up to Isa's expectations of what it means to be Muslim nor recognize his leadership. Finally, then, they are to be seen as agents of Satan, working to perpetuate his realm in this world.[93] Most recently, in *The Ansaar Cult*, Isa accuses the Muslim World League of being a communist organization hiding in an Islamic country and says that the Wahhabis, the weakest group in the Muslim world, are trying to rule the world with their great wealth.[94]

As well as claiming that blacks are the true descendants of the original seed, Isa warns his followers not to be misled by those false Arabs who merely occupy this country and cannot even speak English well. They are aliens, he says, and blacks should not be awed by them. Even more, they are fraudulent, taking the liberty of acculturating Islamic customs to American life and portraying Islam falsely to the world. Certainly they are incapable of understanding the experience of the black man.

Despite heavy barrages of criticism, Isa points to growth in the number of members in his community as proof of its divine origin. Quoting a Hadith of the Prophet Muhammad that declares that Allah will raise up a nation who will enjoin good, prevent evil, and kill those who cause turmoil, he identifies the Ansar with that nation. "These small splinter groups are always saying how the Ansars are so wrong. But if we were in that much error, why are we steadily progressing, and they are regressing?"[95] Persecution is used as a badge of election. "Many people say that the Ansars are crazy, but remember, the day that people stop calling you crazy, then you know that you're not living in righteousness, meaning, the day that people stop persecuting you, and stop throwing rocks at you . . . then you know that something is wrong with you. And you are backsliding." Responding to the fact that different groups in New York and Philadelphia have harassed and persecuted the Ansar, he says that Allah will give them the strength to withstand.[96]

• • • • • *Life in the Ansaru Allah Community*

Other Muslims in both the immigrant and the indigenous communities of America have levied criticism against the Ansaru Allah sect for many reasons. Not the least of these is that Ansars traditionally have lived in isolation, separating themselves from the rest of society. Isa Muhammad stresses the importance of group unity in different ways. He sees strength as coming through community, and his emphasis on isolation is a means of ensuring that there will be no integration into white society, which would dissipate the power of the Ansar and make them susceptible to oppression. In a basic way the unity of the brotherhood is necessary for the survival of the group. This unity Isa sees as promoting both the material and the spiritual growth of its members.[97]

The methods Isa employs in perpetuating the community, he claims, are superior to all others. While other leaders concentrate on educating the adults, Isa prides himself on raising a generation of Muslim children through specialized teaching, particularly in training the children to recite the Qur'an. "As Ansars, we sacrifice our lives and the pleasures of this world, so that our children may grow to be the true believers in Allah Subhana wa ta'ala. We must provide them with the proper education and environment to be successful."[98] Community propaganda makes much of the fact that the very ability of the Ansar children to recite the Qur'an so beautifully means that the Ansar are in possession of the truth of Allah and obviously under his guidance.[99]

Much of what characterizes life in the Ansar community, however, is controversial. There is some question as to whether or not members are expected to give all of their possessions for the general maintenance of the community. Isa Muhammad himself denies it in a rather vague way, but interviews with disaffected members of the community cited by Philips give testimony to such hardships; some former members have recounted instances when Isa Muhammad's family has worn the good clothing donated by members of the community while the former owners of the clothing went about in rags.[100] Even those persons who profess full allegiance to Isa Muhammad and the Ansar community interviewed in *The Ansaar Cult*[101] suggest that such donations are required, although they insist that most members make them willingly and gladly.

Another point of contention between those who have left the community and those interviewed on its behalf relates to the ruling that male members are required to bring in money through begging. (Women are limited to their roles as wives and mothers and are not expected to work outside the community or to beg.) That this has been the practice since the early days of the Ansar is not disputed; the issue is whether or not it is helpful. Those who have left tend to view it as humiliating and degrading and to protest that it is often impossible to bring in the forty or fifty dollars a day that Isa requires. They charge that various forms of "punishment," including being forbidden to sleep with their wives, are levied on those who do not succeed. Isa defends the practice as fully Islamic. After his visit to Egypt in 1981, for example, he saluted the Muslim beggars in Cairo as proof of what the Ansars have been saying for years, that "to beg donations for the upliftment of Islaam" is in accord with Islamic law and the Qur'an and all the prophets.[102]

Members of the Ansar community traditionally have lived with the sexes segregated. Men have had one dormitory and women another, with the children living in a third section. This practice as well has been justified as Islamic, a manifestation of the importance of insuring propriety between the sexes. One of the most controversial aspects of this sexual segregation is the obvious difficulty it poses between husbands and wives. Isa has provided for occasional conjugal relations in what is commonly called "the green room"; to share this room with his wife a male has to sign up well ahead of time. Detractors charge that this is too humiliating, particularly since everyone in the community knows why a couple is going to spend the night in the room. They also say that those who are not in Isa Muhammad's favor are never allowed to have a turn. Some feel that sexual segregation encourages members of the community to obtain sex in illicit ways. Isa has provided a fairly detailed defense of the green room,[103] whose color he says represents fertilization. "The green room was the only alternative that we had to keep certain people who didn't have sexual control from going totally berserk and that was their doing, not mine." He says that as soon as the community developed to the point where people could rent their own apartments and live together, the green room was discarded.[104] Reports from some of the Ansar communities, however, indicate that segregation of the sexes is still practiced.

Despite Philips's charge, supported by some of those he interviewed, that Isa Muhammad seems to regard marriage lightly and refuses to let many in the community get married,[105] Ansar literature emphasizes the sanctity of the institution of marriage. A pamphlet entitled "Islamic Marriage Ceremony and Polygamy" goes to great lengths to describe the importance of the contract ("marriage is a sacred contract between men and women, they enter a mutual agreement with respect and love, and it is a mutual stronghold and foundation of human society")[106] and the various steps of the ceremony itself. Four roles are suggested that women can play in order to be good wives: domestic ("the domestic woman's every thought is of her family and home"), companion ("she is the wife that her husband can depend on for emotional stability"), educated ("her job is to be an encyclopedia for her husband"), and cultured ("she deals with all aspects of culture" [one of which seems to be the ability to please her husband sexually]).[107] The five types of women a man should avoid when looking for a wife are the yearner (a widow who has a child by a former husband), the favorer (who constantly reminds her husband of her favors to him), the deplorer (who compares her present husband with her former), the backbiter (or gossip), and the toadstool (a vain, unprincipled beauty). Polygamy is recognized as Islamic and legal, although it does not seem to be encouraged; Isa acknowledges that polygamy is one of the reasons why young black women may find it difficult to contemplate converting to Islam.[108]

One of the criticisms levied against Ansar doctrine by the Sunni community is the insistence that women, even black women, do not have spirits. Isa responds to the charge not by denying it—men and women are essentially equal, he says, but black women have no spirits[109]—but by citing verses from the Qur'an itself as proof. For example, Sura 2:228 talks about man being a degree above woman, 2:31 specifies that Adam (not Eve) knew the nature of things, 7:11–12 says that angels will prostrate themselves before man, and 2:30 says that Adam will rule the earth with his intellect. Eve had no knowledge of any of these things and had to be instructed by Adam, Isa argues. In short, man is both older and wiser, and it is man's responsibility to instruct and women's to listen and learn.

This does not mean that Isa is unconcerned about women, however; much of his writing deals with female dress and behavior. Since the late 1970s the official clothing for males of the Ansar community has been white pants, a white robe, and a white cap on which the mahdist symbol of spear and crescent between two pyramids is displayed. From puberty women are expected to wear full loose garments covering the entire body except the hands and feet and to wear a complete face veil with only a slit for the eyes. (Women as well as men are expected to wear nose rings.) Photographs in Ansar publications show women participating in many different kinds of activities, such as dancing, picnics, volleyball, and going to the laundromat wearing these full coverings. According to Ansar doctrine, wearing a headpiece that covers the hair but leaves the face exposed, to say nothing of not wearing a veil at all, is unlawful and sinful.[110] Regional and cultural variations in Islamic dress are denounced. The wearing of pants is anathema, because pants are seen as a foreign (Pakistani) and even a polytheistic invention. "In this day and time," Isa says, "it is very difficult to tell which are men and which are women, especially among pale people. Pale men have grown their hair past their shoulders, while their women trim their hair to the neck. The beauty that were [sic] once reserved for women are now shared by a majority of the men."[111] Ansar men are allowed to shave and cut their hair only on pilgrimage.

Immigrant and convert Muslims who reject the the full face veil for women as un-Islamic and say that those who insist on it are subject to foreign influences are accused of compromising Islam in the interests of modernity. "Some so-called Muslims even go so far as to say that Islam modernizes itself and being that we are in a Western society, the veil is no longer necessary. Our answer to that is the fact that we are in a western society means absolutely nothing to ALLAH SUBHANA WA TA'ALA. If you believe in ALLAH . . . you will live His laws no matter where you are on the face of the Earth."[112]

A small pamphlet called "Attention! If You See an Ansaar, This is What You Should See" warns that women should never be found in pants or in bright colors that are shocking to the eyes such as red, blue, orange, or bright yellow. The material of the garment should be thick so that one cannot see through it, and should not be tight-fitting. The idea, the pamphlet insists, is that a woman's beauty should be concealed and not revealed.

Isa Muhammad took advantage of his 1981 trip to Egypt to take a great many photos of Cairene women fully veiled, which he demonstrates as one more proof that this kind of dress is in accordance with Islamic law.[113] Although most Egyptian women who veil do not wear the niqab or full face covering, he was able to discover and photograph many who were dressed that way. "You women from the different Islaamic communities here in America who have submitted to the truth by wearing the *khimar:* veil," he says, "Don't short-change yourselves—put it on right! ! ! The wearing of short headpieces and veils made from prints and stripes along with pants is not the proper attire of a believing Muslim woman." Along with the photos of Muslim women in Cairo is one of a blond (unveiled) tourist, looking particularly unhappy, with a caption reminding the viewer that it was Satan who expelled Adam and Eve from the garden, pulling their clothing from them.

Ansar women are allowed to be seen in public places only if they are on some specific business, never for pleasure alone. When they do go out they are urged to keep their gaze lowered and to walk decently. Women are not to laugh or talk loudly while in the street and should not eat in public unless they turn their backs to others. "The Muslim woman should carry herself like the invisible man. She should be able to move about without being noticed."[114] At no time should a woman be caught gossiping, slandering, or using vulgar language, but should comport herself with dignity by keeping her mouth closed and her mind and heart open. Women should not display any ornamentation while in public, since this might attract the attention of men.

This is not to say, however, that the Ansar are not interested in having their women keep themselves as beautiful as possible so long as that beauty is not displayed publicly. It is a great mistake, says Isa Muhammad, for women to think that because they are covered from head to toe they should neglect personal grooming. Concerned that there has never been a standard of beauty for Muslim women, he wrote an extended piece on "Islamic Beauty Aids and Customs" for their benefit.[115] Nubian women should cast away the customs of the Amorites, he says, and come back to their own customs and traditions, those of Islam. He tells women that traditionally there are ten virtues characteristic of Muslim women, of which three are related directly to personal grooming and beauty: always be clean, always smell good, and always be beautiful in front of one's husband.[116] The use of cosmetics is acceptable, but they must be natural products taken directly from the plants of the earth and not harsh chemicals. (An advertisement in "Islamic Marriage" for Ansar incense, "A Garden of Aromatic Ambrosia," tempts the reader with such scents as jasmine, musk, mystic violet, and Blue Nile.) *Kuhl* is recommended for the eyes, *halawa* (candy) as a way to remove unwanted body hair, and *khamrat* as a homemade perfume and aphrodisiac. Drawings of the hands and feet illustrate how beautiful they can be when decorated with *henna*. The article concludes with a passage from Song of Solomon (4:7): "Thou art all fair, my love; there is no spot in thee."

Prayer is extremely important in the Ansar community, and various publications of Isa Muhammad contain injunctions to pray regularly as well as sample prayers. "Salaat brings relief and a release from depressions through the stimulation of faith," Isa affirms. "Salaat is like music. It becomes a natural impulse molded into beautiful and responsive talent by diligent practice."[117] Prayer and recognition of Allah are natural to man; one says "AAA" when breathing in and "LAAA" when breathing out. The diaphram is even shaped like two letter L's, as in Allah. The four prayer positions are shown in an illustration to physically demonstrate the four letters of the name Ahmad, with the Arabic letters resembling the form of the worshipper in these respective positions: "alif" is the standing, "hah" the bowing, "mim" the prostration, and "dal" the sitting.[118]

For years Isa Muhammad worked hard to fund the building of a new masjid in Brooklyn and urged his followers to be generous in their contributions. The mosque, called Masjidu'l Mukhlasina, was finally completed in the early 1980s and is pictured repeatedly in Ansar publications. It is said to be the largest mosque and only one of its kind in the Western hemisphere. The complex includes a school, called a university, offering classes in art, music, Qur'an and Qur'an recitation, history, science, religion, vocational science, and more, "a highly concentrated submergence of knowledge comparable to the curricula offered at the most highly acclaimed universities anywhere in the world." The facility also contains lecture halls, playground facilities, a library, and a museum of ancient Islamic relics.[119] Isa Muhammad is proud of the fact that the school teaches Islamic religion and Arabic language.

• • • • • *Conclusion*

Isa Muhammad's accusations of racism against the white community of the West and against Sunni Arab Muslims and others whom he perceives as "collaborating" with the pale people often have been viewed by those outside the Ansaru Allah community as his own form of racism. Muslims who hear Isa's teachings, particularly concerning his own role, or who are privy to prejudiced reports by others who for a variety of reasons resent the Ansar movement, are quick to denounce him as a fraud and his movement as existing outside the sphere of Islam. Immigrant Muslims in the United States as

well as in Saudi Arabia and elsewhere understandably have questioned the motives of all people who aspire to charismatic leadership roles in Islam, recognizing that unscrupulous opportunists use
the religion as a means of promoting their own causes, often solic-
iting funds from overseas in the process. The kind of scrutiny that
they give to convert communities is seen by their members, in this
case the Ansaru Allah, to be particularly demeaning.

While Isa Muhammad's teachings have undergone some fairly
subtle changes over the several decades of the life of the Ansar community, his hostility toward the pale man has remained constant.
To the extent to which Arabs in his opinion have been co-opted by
the white establishment, he includes Arabs in his indictment. He is
eager, however, to maintain his own direct relationship with the
true line of Islamic leadership, and thus emphasizes the blackness
of all of the prophets through Muhammad. In order to dissociate
himself from Wahhabi Islam, he has increasingly drawn links with
Shi'ite genealogy and its interpretation of Islam. His obvious appropriation of Shi'ite terminology, which appears to date from around
1982, seems to be the result of factors other than his antipathy to
"false Arabs." Among them are his own lack of an extensive Islamic
education as well as the exposure given to Shi'ite interpretations after the 1979 Islamic revolution in Iran. There was a great deal of
Shi'ite literature available in English translation at that time, and it
is not out of character for Isa to have synthesized it into his own interpretation of what constitutes true Islam. Affirmation of the role
of 'Ali, whom he understands to be black, thus becomes a rejection
of Sunni Islam. It is also important to note that by 1982 it is estimated that there were more than one thousand blacks in the Philadelphia area who had converted to Shi'ism.

Stressing the fact that Fatima was the only child of the Prophet
Muhammad to bear children, Isa Muhammad uses identification
with the Shi'ite interpretation of 'Ali's role to affirm his own geneo-
logical descent from the Prophet through Fatima and 'Ali. It also
seems to be another of his efforts to appropriate the titles that others
have claimed as part of his ongoing quest for legitimacy as a leader.
His self-identification as the mahdi fits with Shi'i expectations. Realizing that what he teaches deviates from the teachings of Muslim
scholars through the ages, Isa insists that this is because his original
uncorrupted knowledge comes from a divine source. Consequently,
his own teachings supersede those of traditional Islam. Any devia-

tion from orthodoxy is due not to shortcomings in his own education or knowledge, but because overseas (pale) Arabs have corrupted
the teachings of Islam to fit their own racist prejudices. Thus he
calls on his followers, the Ansaru Allah, to rise up to the nobility of
their descent not only from the original creation but as direct heirs
of the line of the Prophet.

Whatever one might think of Isa Muhammad, he clearly has been
a figure of enormous significance to the members of his movement.
Those who have defected from the community (according to Philips)
refer to him as an extreme egotist, a fraud, a swindler and a thief,
vicious, and licencious (encouraging adultery, homosexuality, lesbi-
anism and orgies). "He's like the Jinn that whispers into your heart
that plays upon your lower desires."[120] Interviews with those who
are in the community (as reported by Isa Muhammad in his *Ansar
Cult*), however, reveal him as teacher, father figure, friend, guide, pa-
tient and merciful, the redeemer of the Nubians. "What he has
given me, us, the world, is priceless. What he has done for us is end-
less. . . . The generosity, mercifulness and forgiveness that he exhib-
its is beyond human understanding."[121]

By Isa Muhammad's own most recent word, he is not a prophet,
not an incarnation of God, not the Second Coming of Jesus, and not
the Mahdi. He is, again by his profession, a teacher, a guide, a leader,
an Imam (though not the Imam of Shi'i expectation), a qutb (axis) of
the Ansar Sufi order[122] and the mujaddid of this age. He is also, by
attestation of many of his followers and by his own admission, a
worker of miracles.[123] All of the members of his sect interviewed in
his defense (as cited in his *Ansar Cult*) claim to have seen him perform miracles, which range from healing the sick to raising the dead
to astrological intervention to making himself appear larger than
life. That he indeed has seemed larger than life to at least some of
his followers is clear.

Isa Muhammad retired as Imam of the Ansaru Allah community
in 1988; the new leader is referred to as "Imaam Musa." Obviously
Isa remains actively involved in the defense of the community and
its doctrines, as is indicated by his quick and lengthy response to the
attack of Philips and others. "I've watched him answer questions,
year after year many have come to talk him down, the Jews, the Sunnis, the Black Muslims, the 5%, the Egyptians, etc., but none of
them can stand against the truth," says one of his followers.[124]

Whether or not the community will continue to have access to that truth and to grow under the leadership of another Imam is yet to be seen.

• • • • • *Postscript*

Since the writing of this chapter, Isa Muhammad has engaged with renewed vigor in the task of calling orthodox Sunni Muslims to account for the ways in which, in his opinion, they have distorted the true teachings of Islam by following the Hadith to the exclusion of the Qur'an and by venerating the Prophet Muhammad. In the introduction to a volume entitled *360 Questions To Ask the Orthodox Sunni Muslims*, published in 1989 under the facetiously adopted name of Rev. Dwight York, Isa writes, "I, as the founder of the Ansaru Allah Community in America, have to confess that it was upon my retirement that I began to see and realize how much of the teachings that I have passed on were altered by Orthodox Sunni Muslim's opinions and Hadiths, and I stand to correct the deception right now. . . . I felt it necessary to come out of retirement so that I can aswer the lies by these self-proclaimed Orthodox Sunni Muslim scholars" (p. M).

In the book, Isa lashes out at Sunnis for their cowardice in levying death threats against such supposed apostates as Salman Rushdie and accuses the Sunnis of actually carrying out executions of Muslims in the cases of Malcolm X and Rashad Khalifa (see chapter 6 concerning Khalifa). He argues that the Sunnis are trying to play God in determining who has the right to interpret Islam and notes wryly that God does not need the intervention of small-minded orthodox Sunnis. He saves his harshest attacks for the Saudis, who are depicted as supporting Ameenah Abu Bilal Philips, Isa's most severe critic. Isa calls the Saudi Darul Ifta "the biggest innovators and liars in Islam" and accuses Saudis in general of being so concerned for money, prestige, and world power that they will kill for it (pp. K, 299). Egyptians as well are identified as "devout, merciless killers," but it is clear that this is primarily because they came to the aid of Saudi Arabia during the Gulf War (p. 111).

Isa also declares strongly in *360 Questions* that the Ansaru Allah community is racist in its interpretations of Islam, and for good reason. Emphasizing repeatedly that the orthodox Sunni are "pale Arabs" (in contrast to those Isa calls "Black Orthodox Sunni Muslims"), Isa focuses on what he identifies as the Sunni objective of preventing blacks from knowing the truth. "We will no longer stand for your name calling, slandering or death threats made against the Ansaaru ALLAH. We promise that if you attack any of our members, there will be a blood bath of Sunni Arab blood and their flunkies on American soil anywhere we find you" (p. J). "If there is any attempt on our community," Isa goes on to say, "there will be a war" (p. 113).

In the book Isa continues the ongoing process of redefining the identity of his own community. A real Muslim, he now says, is actually a Christian or Messiahite. This is his indication that the Ansar are now followers of Jesus and are awaiting his return. The Saudis, in contrast, do not talk about the return of the Messiah but instead worship the Prophet Muhammad (pp. A, 299). Adopting for himself the name Rabboni Y'shua (literally Lord Jesus, although he makes it clear that he does not consider himself to be the returned Christ), he indicates that it would have been more appropriate for him to have been given the title of Rabbi rather than Imam. Members of the Ansar are still Muslims, but Isa identifies the community as Muslims for Christ. He states that he has never considered himself to be the Mahdi, although he is of the family of the Mahdi, but that he is the Mujaddid or reformer of this age, whose spiritual guide is the angel Michael (p. 588).

# CHAPTER 6

# United Submitters International

Early in the morning of January 31, 1990, fifty-four-year-old Rashad Khalifa was stabbed to death in the mosque in Tucson, Arizona, of which he was the Imam. When the mosque secretary arrived to meet him for morning prayers, she discovered his body in the kitchen, bloody and lying on top of the handgun he carried for his personal protection.[1] Khalifa's followers knew that he was aware of the danger to his life, having constantly received death threats on the phone at the mosque for years.

No persons or organizations claimed responsibility for the slaying, and the killer was never apprehended. Mohammad T. Mehdi, spokesman of the National Council of Islamic Affairs in New York, expressed his opinion that the murder was most likely the work of a single individual: "The stupid person who did this will give him [Khalifa] more credit. Over time he could become a martyr, even if he was not able to obtain any meaningful standing within the Islamic world during his lifetime."[2] It is not difficult to imagine why Khalifa knew that he had enemies or why the preaching of his understanding of the message of Islam would be so difficult for many in the Islamic community to understand. Khalifa's explanation of the miracle of the Qur'an as proven by his computer analysis of its structure, and his conclusion that the key to the book is in the number nineteen, first excited and challenged the Muslim world. Many who were initially persuaded, however, became disenchanted (and some became outraged) when he used this analysis to announce the year of the End of the World, denounced two verses of the Qur'an as "satanic" in origin, severely attacked Muslims in general and Arab Muslims in particular for the idolatry of following the Hadith and the Sunna, and revealed his own designation as God's messenger in the line of Abraham and Muhammad.

Khalifa's supporters were, and continue to be, persuaded not only of the validity of his mathematically based "confirmation" of the miraculousness of the Qur'an, but of his own role as the person selected by God to reveal these heretofore unknown secrets to this age by means of modern electronic equipment. His detractors have spared no effort in denouncing him as heretical. A former disciple, Ahmed Deedat of the Islamic Center International in Durban, South Africa, enthusiastically presented Khalifa's findings in a 1979 booklet entitled *Al-Qur'an the Ultimate Miracle*. Deedat lectured widely on the subject, including at forums organized by the international World Association of Muslim Youth, affirming that the discovery of the miracle of nineteen is scientific proof of the existence of God as the divine source of the Qur'an. One of these talks was videotaped and distributed around the world with the title "Al-Qur'an, A Visual Miracle."[3] Along with many other Khalifa enthusiasts, however, Deedat later denounced and dissociated himself from the self-proclaimed messenger. In 1988 he described Khalifa as *kadhdhab*, a liar or charlatan, the derogatory term cited in the Qur'an (Sura 38:4–5) as having been used in reference to the Prophet Muhammad by the unbelievers. (Khalifa interpreted this as further proof of his identification in the line of messengers and challenged Deedat to a debate as to his identity.)[4] The Mufti of Saudi Arabia, one of its leading Islamic scholars, denounced Rashad Khalifa in a fatwa as a heretic and an apostate.[5]

Despite its detractors, however, Khalifa's message continues to be discussed by persons interested in a modern, scientifically verifiable validation of the uniqueness and authenticy of the Qur'an. Many of those who knew Rashad Khalifa continue to express their great appreciation for his work, his message, and his person. Journalist Karima Omar, now known as Virginia Marston, remembers Khalifa with fondness and gratitude, even though she is not willing to affirm without qualification the claims that he made for himself. "A heretic?" she asks. "Many thought so. A reformer? In a sense. A herald? Well, some heard his call. An eccentric? Had to be in his line of work, with his kind of God." She praises Khalifa for his candor and honesty, his humor, his courage, his wisdom and deep care for friends and enemies alike. "Rashad Khalifa smoothed out the lumps, distributing divinity evenly across ethnic, linguistic and cultural boundaries," she says. "Thanks to Rashad, God indeed seems stark raving sane."[6]

Members of Masjid Tucson who knew Rashad Khalifa remember him as "a wonderful man with a tremendous sense of humor" and "a kind, caring and humble person deeply concerned about others." They say he had the ability to help people laugh, to ease their burdens, while rarely getting upset no matter what difficulties arose; that he was very generous and spent his own money on anyone who had need; that he would take care of members of the community in all kinds of ways, including cooking and providing meals for them. "He fed us all," they say, with food both physical and spiritual.[7]

• • • • •  *Rashad Khalifa and the Miraculous Nineteen*

Rashad Khalifa was born in 1935 in a small village in Egypt; his father was a master of the Shadhili Sufi order. Although Rashad was raised in that tradition, members of the Tucson Masjid report that he never described himself as a Sufi. His professional training was not in religion as such but in the physical sciences, one of the reasons why his scientific explanation of the Qur'an initially aroused the interest of so many in the Islamic world. He came to the United States in 1959 and received his doctorate in biochemistry from the University of California at Riverside in the early 1960s; he taught at Riverside for two years.[8] In 1963 he married Stephanie Hoefle, a native of Tucson,[9] and later he became a U.S. citizen.

Khalifa's credentials as a scientist seem solid. He worked as head of horticultural research in the Egyptian Ministry of Agriculture, was senior research chemist for Monsanto Corporation in St. Louis, and was on the roster of scientists referred to as "Technical Assistance Experts" with the Industrial Development Organization of the United Nations.[10] In the middle 1970s he was sent as a United Nations agricultural adviser to Libya where he worked in consultation with Colonel Mu'ammar Qaddhafi. From 1980 to 1986 he served as supervising chemist in the pesticides section of the Arizona Commission on Agriculture and Horticulture. He resigned from that position because he believed that he had been denied a promotion because of his Egyptian heritage and Islamic faith; a

Rashad Khalifa.
Courtesy of United
Submitters
International.

lawsuit was unsucccessful in proving this charge. Khalifa's initial findings in relation to the Qur'an were noted in the respected journal *Scientific American* as "an ingenious study of the Koran."[11]

For eleven years Khalifa was Imam of the Tucson Masjid. He established an integrated community of American converts and immigrants from several countries and distributed free of charge a small monthly journal initially entitled *Muslim Perspective*. Much of the appeal of Khalifa's message, along with the authenticity afforded to his mathematical interpretations by his own scientific credentials, seems to have been the result of his flexible understanding of what constitutes reasonable and appropriate Islamic thought and action. By denouncing the Hadith and Sunna he cleared the way for an elimination of dress codes, segregation of men and women, and other restrictions that seem so important to many Muslims today, especially those engaged in the fundamentalist movement, who find them an essential part of the faith.

Basic to Khalifa's message throughout his career was his absolute conviction of the miraculousness of the Qur'an. This, of course, has been Islamic doctrine since the beginning; what Khalifa contributed was "the irrefutable proof" of that miraculousness. In brief, through a computer analysis of all of the verses of the Qur'an, he determined that the number nineteen (and its multiples) was the organizing principle of the entire book. His conviction was that this mathematical system was so extremely complex that (1) no human being could ever have worked it out (thus the Qur'an is the product of the divine hand), and (2) it was only in the age of computer science, "the era of mathematical sophistication,"[12] that it was possible to begin to understand this complexity.

Khalifa worked on his interpretation of the Qur'an's mathematical code from 1968 to 1981. In 1973 he published his first book explaining this theory, *Miracle of the Quran: Significance of the Mysterious Alphabets*. As a result of that work and of the many talks and lectures he gave on the mathematical composition of the Qur'an, he became widely known in the Islamic world. The first published reports of his findings appeared in Egypt in the middle 1970s.[13] Even then, however, there were many who recognized that the logical conclusion to some of his findings ran counter to popularly held Muslim beliefs, and accusations of apostasy began to be leveled.

The work that first attracted the attention of a wider audience was Khalifa's 1981 volume *The Computer Speaks: God's Message to the World*. In this volume he presented his first thoroughgoing claim, cited on page 1, that he had "physical, touchable, verifiable, and utterly indisputable proof for: (1) the existence of God, (2) a message from God to you, and (3) the exact year when this world will end." The book itself was written on a Hewlett-Packard HP-1000, E-Series computer and was based on what he called a "coded message" to our world from its creator. Khalifa reflects that while many scientists, philosophers, and theologians have been convinced of the existence of God, they have been unable to make the transition from that reality to its relevance for daily life. This time, however, the practical data provided will engage that relevance, precisely because the proof is 100 percent physical with no opinions, conjecture, or interpretation involved.

It was also in 1981 that Khalifa published his first English version of the Qur'an, believed to be the first translation of the sacred scripture of Islam into English by a native speaker of Arabic, entitled *Quran: The Final Scripture.* (Two revised translations were published in 1989 and 1992.) In the commentary accompanying the translation of the text he provides the basis for the mathematical understanding of the Qur'an, his views on Hadith and Sunna, and a number of other explanations. These interpretations are given again in greater detail in nineteen appendices. In the commentary serving as a preface to the translation he displays an inclusiveness in relation to persons of other traditions that developed much more fully toward the end of his life. "You may be Jewish, Christian, Muslim, or anything else," he says. "But you can fulfill the purpose of your life, attain perfect happiness, and achieve salvation, ONLY if you submit to God; the omnipotent, omniscient, omnipresent, Lord, cherisher, and sustainer of the universe."

In the following year, 1982, the materials already presented in his previous writings were published in a work initially designed to be shown through a series of photographic slides—each page of the book, entitled *Quran: Visual Presentation of the Miracle,* represents a separate slide. The premise of this work, continuing the theme already developed, is that there was physical evidence that God had provided messages to the human world. Faith was therefore no longer needed; belief could give way to the knowledge that God exists through the "overwhelming physical evidence" that has been encoded in God's final scripture, the Qur'an. The book contains photocopied passages from the Arabic Qur'an prefacing Khalifa's translations, along with diagrams illustrating the "physical facts" that he cites as proof of the divine authenticity and miraculousness of the holy book.

A fourth publication, one about which there seems to have been as much consternation as anything Khalifa wrote earlier, is the 1982 volume entitled *Quran, Hadith, and Islam.* It continues much of the attack on Hadith and Sunna that Khalifa set forward in *Quran.* The points are presented in a style that scarcely allows for misinterpretation, bold type outlined in boxes asserting such things as "Hadith & Sunna = 100% Conjecture," "You Shall Not Idolize Muhammad," and "Muhammad Does Not Know the Future" and decrying what he calls the myth of Muhammad the intercessor and "The Deification of Muhammad."[14] He spells out in the most direct way his deep concern that Muslims are in danger of falling into gross idolatry, the worst of sins, by venerating the Prophet Muhammad to the point where they see him as more than human the way that Christians have seen Jesus as more than human. To look to Muhammad for intercession, he says, is nothing more than idol worship. He specifies that because of this idolatry, and because most Muslims continue to follow the Hadith and Sunna which encourage it, there are "Two Unfortunate Facts of Life." These facts are that the majority of people are disbelievers, and that the majority of those who believe in God are going to hell. Quoting from Sura 12:103, 106, he says, *"IF YOU ARE WITH THE MAJORITY, YOU ARE IN DEEP TROUBLE."*[15] The only legitimate Hadith is the Qur'an itself.

Since the last four of these works came out at more or less the same time, they can reasonably be said to represent Rashad Khalifa's thinking at what was perhaps the high point of his career. He was developing his ideas to their logical conclusion, and despite the rising tide of criticism, even outrage, in the Islamic world he was widely acknowledged as having propounded a theory for the proof of the divine origin of the Qur'an worthy at least of serious attention. The basic themes that Khalifa developed in these works of 1981 and 1982 were sufficient to attract the notice of the Islamic world and in many cases its condemnation, particularly his ideas about Hadith and Sunna and his calculation—based on the mathematical code— of the year of the end of the world. His rejection of the Sunna came at a time of heightened concern about compromising on any of its content. Muslim revivalists and fundamentalists saw and continue to see in the preservation of the traditions and the emulation of the Prophet a dam against erosion of the faith. For them the Sunna of the Prophet is the guarantee of authenticity, a grounding in a distinctive practice that gives the faithful a special and unique identity at a time when the Muslim World is threatened by Westernization and secularization.

It is clear in all of the writings that Khalifa intends to condemn others in the Islamic world, particularly Arab Muslims, for what he calls their abuses and misrepresentations of true Islam. Working on the presupposition of an underlying divine plan, he says that God allows these abuses to come about in order to purge them. "God Almighty has decided to substitute new recipients of His message," he writes, "and to forsake the original recipients who disregarded and desecrated His valuable teachings."[16] Those who claim to be the very guardians of the Islamic message he accuses of having perpetrated "erroneous impressions" under the guise of "Islamic revolution."

One of the obvious ways in which Arab Muslims have abused, misrepresented, and perpetuated an erroneous Islam is through their reliance on the Hadith and the Sunna. Khalifa declares over and over his contention that it is only the Qur'an that is valid as a guide to proper living, and that the Hadith and Sunna are the invention of Satan, what he repeatedly calls "Satan's trap" for humans. "Many Muslims have fallen into Satan's trap, and invented a long list of unauthorized prohibitions, based on the great blasphemy known as 'hadith' and/or 'sunna'," he claims in *Qur'an: The Final Scripture* in explanation of Sura 3:94 ("anyone who invents lies about God, after this, these are the wicked"). His exegesis is full of even more specific references, as in the commentary on Sura 6:44 ("consequently, because they discarded the message given to them, we opened for them the gates of everything. Then, just as they rejoiced with such givings, we seized them suddenly, and they became stunned"). His response to this is, "The Muslims of today have abandoned the Quran, and adopted the inventions of 'Hadith' and 'Sunna' in complete defiance of God and the prophet. . . . Therefore, it appears that the vast oil wealth given to Saudi Arabia, the Arabian Gulf states, Kuwait, Iraq, Iran, Indonesia, and North Africa is in fact a curse that leads to the inevitable retribution predicted in this verse."[17]

The only mission of the Prophet was "to deliver Quran, the whole Quran, and nothing but Quran," Khalifa claims. Every messenger has been supported by miracles given by God. Moses' staff became a live serpent, and Jesus was able to create birds out of clay. The miracle of Muhammad is the Qur'an itself.[18] The Prophet is said to have admonished his followers not to write down anything he said except Qur'an, and anything else would be erased.[19] It is interesting to note that Khalifa uses this report from the great collector of traditions Ahmad Ibn Hanbal to show that traditions are full of contradictions, while the word of God (the Qur'an) is always consistent. In his appendix he repeats arguments about the comparison of the Mishnah and Gemarah with the Hadith and Sunna, adding that among these "false sources of jurisprudence" is the doctrine of the trinity in Christianity. God allowed these fabrications in order to

Convention meeting of the United Submitters International. Courtesy of United Submitters International.

distinguish true believers from false. For true believers in Islam the only source of divine instruction is the Qurʾan.

It is in *The Computer Speaks* and *Quran: Visual Presentation* that Khalifa gives the full details of his discoveries about the number 19. *The Computer Speaks* outlines thirty-one "physical facts" to prove beyond any doubt the significance of the number 19 and its multiples. Of these thirty-one, he says that nineteen are so straightforward as to be easy for anyone to understand.[20] The rest he calls "the more intricate facts," dealing with the mysterious letters or Qurʾanic initials which serve to prefix twenty-nine chapters of the Qurʾan. His rather complex calculations concerning these mysterious letters, based on the transposition of letters into numerical equivalents, are detailed in his writings of this period.[21] He feels he can show mathematically that they have been divinely designed and placed in their locations, proving that the Qurʾan is God's word and that it has been perfectly preserved.[22]

Much of the literature that is distributed by Masjid Tucson contains some version of the nineteen facts that serve to introduce the uninitiated to the miracle of the mathematical code of the Qurʾan.

These facts are not always given in exactly the same order or form in his various publications, but however presented they serve as the basis of his message. Generally the first several points he makes are that there are nineteen Arabic letters in the first verse of the Qur'an,[23] that there are 114 Suras in the Qur'an (19 × 6), and that the first Sura to be revealed to the Prophet Muhammad is to be found by counting back nineteen Suras from the end of the Qur'an. The reader is invited to see appendix 2 for a reproduction of one of the pieces of literature of the Masjid Tucson that lists all nineteen facts, entitled "Let the World Know."

The literature of the masjid assures those who see the nineteen facts in their abbreviated form that "the [full] details are absolutely stunning." It is in the four works written at this period of Khalifa's life that these fuller details are provided for the reader, all replete with charts and numbers. Here it may be helpful to look in more detail at some of the themes that Khalifa developed in his *Quran: The Final Scripture* as corollaries to the numerically based interpretation. These themes are suggested in his commentary on specific verses and amplified in the series of appendices to the volume.[24]

Khalifa states that one of the miraculous aspects of the Qur'an is that it is easy to memorize. That is because every letter is positioned so as to remind the reader of the verse or the expression that comes next. In memorizing the Qur'an, then, one is aided by what he calls "an intricate audio system."[25] This, of course, is directly related to the fact that the Qur'an was revealed in Arabic. He says that during his work as a technical expert for the United Nations he had the opportunity to compare the efficiency of most of the world's languages and discovered that Arabic is in fact the most efficient and uses the least number of words to express an idea or concept. He also applauds the fact that the words "he" and "she" do not necessarily imply gender in Arabic, making it therefore the right medium for conveying the genderless quality of God.[26] "God Almighty is neither male nor female," he notes in commenting on Sura 2:20, where he is forced in translating the Arabic into English to use "He" for "God."

Khalifa spends a good deal of time developing themes that are part of the process of death and resurrection. First, he says that death is just like sleeping, complete with dreams.[27] Most of us will not even know that we have died, and will be quite surprised when the day of resurrection comes. In *The Computer Speaks* he provides the specific year of the end of the world, calculated according to his mathematical system to be the year 2280 A.D. He does not identify this as the day of resurrection, however, and does not include this dating information in any of his discussions about death and the afterlife.

Among the traditional signs of the coming of that day is the appearance of what has been called "the beast of the earth," sometimes identified as al-Dajjal.[28] In commenting on Sura 27:82 ("we will produce for them a creature from the earth who will speak to them, saying that the people did not firmly believe in our scripture"), Khalifa says that there is strong evidence pointing to the fact that the creature is in fact the computer, and that through decoding the numerical miracle of the Qur'an it is actually speaking to the world. Sura 36:65 says that on the day of resurrection our hands and feet will speak to us and testify to our deeds. "God invented the video recorder," says Khalifa, "in order to give us an idea how our hands and feet will testify on the day of judgment." And he adds in commentary on Sura 41:20–22 that "we will view our lives from birth to death. While the disbelievers cannot edit their audio-video record, the believers enjoy this advantage through repentance. Repentance edits out all sins, and thus, they will not exist on the record." The videotape image is evoked again when he talks about "predestination," which he explains in a classical way as the combination of human freedom to believe or disbelieve and God's absolute knowledge of what that choice is going to be. Our ongoing decisions throughout life are recorded on "something like a videotape from birth to death."[29]

Part of Khalifa's emphasis on the Qur'an as the only miracle of Muhammad, and his efforts to cleanse Islam of what he sees as the idolatry of attributing special powers to Muhammad,[30] is the Qur'anic insistence that on the day of resurrection there will be no intercession with God. Sura 2:48 says, "Beware of the day when no one can avail another, no intercession will be accepted, and no one can be helped." As he claims in *Quran, Hadith, and Islam,* Khalifa believes that intercession is a myth applied to Jesus in Christianity and to Muhammad in Islam, but that the truth is that nobody has the power of intercession, adding the slight caveat in commenting on Sura 2:254–55 that the only way in which there might be intercession is if God so decides. The truth is that the myth of intercession is another of the tricks of Satan to dupe the people into idol worship.[31] Like Wahhabi Muslims, modernist Muslims, and the fundamentalists who also do not believe in intercession, Khalifa is challenging the "popular" beliefs and practices of most Muslims, who think that Muhammad will have some influence, despite the fact that they deny belief in intercession.

Finally in relation to death and resurrection, Khalifa is absolutely clear that while heaven and hell are realities, what is said about them in the Qur'an is meant only as allegory. The real nature of these abodes is beyond our wildest imagination.[32] This emphasis on the allegorical, which implies a rejection of a literal understanding of the abodes of recompense, is paralleled by an emphasis on the importance of the soul. Every time one does a religious duty such as prayer the soul grows by leaps and bounds, he says. While our bodies are growing to their normal physical size, our souls may be either gaining greatly in size and weight or diminishing. "Those who fail to develop their souls will end up weak, shrunken, and 'weightless' on the day of resurrection."[33]

We will find later in Khalifa's thought that he identifies himself as one of three primary messengers of Islam, the other two being Abraham and Muhammad. There is no hint of that in these writings, although he does emphasize the fact that while Muhammad is the last prophet (nabi) the Qur'an does not refer to him as the last messenger (rasul). "Note the distinction between a 'prophet' and a 'messenger,' " he says in commenting on Sura 3:81. "God has made a covenant with the prophets that He will give them the scripture and wisdom: then, when a messenger comes to you (O people), confirming the scripture, you shall believe in him and support him." "The prophet is one who was given a scripture, while the messenger merely confirms and preaches existing scriptures. Since Qur'an is the last scripture, Muhammad is the last prophet."[34]

Khalifa is also very clear about his understanding of the role that Abraham played as the source of religious practices in Islam, usually done in the context of insisting that Muhammad was not the source of these practices (as those who venerate the Hadith and Sunna would claim). Abraham was the first to use the word *islam*, submission, and was the first recipient of the religious duties that are practiced by Muslims today.[35] (See also his commentary on Suras 2:182, 3:65–68, and 4:103, in which he specifies that the commandment to establish the five daily prayers, or salat, was revealed to Abraham.) Islam in its final form, he says, is based on two things: Qur'an and religious practices through Abraham.[36] All religious practices in Islam existed before Muhammad. The Hadith and Sunna to which the "so-called Muslims" adhere serve in effect to make Islam particular, bound in time and space to the practice of the Prophet Muhammad in the seventh century and to the political, social, economic, and cultural dimension of the religion as it developed in Medina between 622 and 632 A.D. With the emphasis on Abraham, Islam is freed to be timeless and connected not only with the faith of the first believer, but also with the faith of any and all sincere believers.

Khalifa carries forward this discussion of prophets and messengers in what is appendix 19 of his *Qu'ran: The Final Scripture,* entitled "The Bible's Preview of Muhammad."[37] Here he says that one of the amazing features of the Bible, even in its present and distorted form,[38] is that it makes clear that divine revelation would proceed through a series of prophets and would finally culminate in one prophet (whom he identifies as Muhammad) with a message of such universality that no further prophets would ever be needed. The biblical name for this final prophet is the paraclete, who would not be a follower of Jesus because Jesus himself said that the paraclete would be able to reveal things of which he, Jesus, was not aware. Commenting on Sura 2:146, he says that both the Old and the New Testaments are clear in their prediction of the coming of a final paraclete who will reveal all truth.[39] Khalifa rejected traditions that reported that Muhammad went on a night journey from Mecca to Jerusalem, from where he ascended to heaven, where he received the prescription of the five daily prayers after repeated bargaining with God to reduce the number from the initial fifty. Khalifa taught that Muhammad's night journey as reported in the Qur'an talks about travel from Mecca to the farthest place of prostration (which was interpreted as being out of this world) "to receive the Qur'an."[40]

For the remainder of his career Khalifa seems to have confined the dissemination of his ideas mainly to the medium of the monthly publication of the Masjid Tucson, the *Muslim Perspective,* with the exception of the lengthy appendices to his second translation of the Qur'an. Attacks on Khalifa's credibility were only to increase as he attempted to persuade the rest of the community of Muslims that his explanations were valid and his understanding of the message of the Qur'an correct. Let us turn, then, to the course of his thinking from the early 1980s to his death at the end of the decade.

Rashad Khalifa at work analyzing the Qur'an. Courtesy of United Submitters International.

##### • • • • • *Rashad Khalifa: Messenger of God?*

One of Khalifa's consistent themes was his assertion that the mathematical base of nineteen protects the Qur'an from distortion, addition, or loss. Either supporting that or in effect proving that it is not true, depending on one's perspective, he announced in 1985 that nine violations of the mathematical code of the Qur'an had been discovered, and that all of these violations are in the last two verses of Sura 9. He therefore announced that these two verses were fabricated and inserted by scribes into the text, and are not a legitimate part of the Qur'an.[41] This, as can be imagined, was very unfavorably received by most Muslims and has constituted one of the major bases for their continuing attack on Khalifa and his interpretation.[42]

Khalifa's next announcement of note was of what he said would be referred to by future generations as "The Tucson Declaration of

September 15, 1985." In this declaration he proclaimed the establishment of "the richest and most powerful nation on earth," specifically the United Islamic Nation (UIN). The UIN was declared to be not Sunni and not Shiʿa, but only Muslim. (Khalifa at several places in his earlier writings had stressed, following the Qurʾanic warnings in Suras 6:15a and 23:53, that the Islamic community should not be divided into sects.) Characterized by the ideals of peace, love, freedom, prosperity and justice, the UIN was described as stretching (when finally realized) from Morocco to Indonesia and from Nigeria to Turkey, with Mecca as its capital.[43] The date for the announcement of the UIN was based on the fact that the number nineteen is found in Sura 74, and $19 \times 74 = 1406$, the year of the Islamic calendar corresponding to 1985.

The constitution of the UIN is to be the Qurʾan, where the basis for the legal and economic system is found. Emphasizing again that the Islam practiced in the area of the Middle East is severely distorted by traditions, innovations, and superstitions, Khalifa called for the abolition of all shrines and tombs of saints, including the tomb of the Prophet in Medina. Khalifa stressed that he was not advocating the overthrow of any government; such matters were in God's hands. He predicted that sooner or later all Muslim countries in the region would join; if not, their governments could expect to fall. Well aware that he was likely to be scoffed at and rejected by present governments, he quoted verses from the Qurʾan to show that those who mocked his prediction would suffer humiliation and retribution. He identified the two "stubborn corners" of the world that would refuse to join the UIN as the USA and the USSR, calling them "Gog" and "Magog."[44] His Qurʾanic support came from Sura 110:1–3, whose nineteen words describe victory and triumph as coming from God.[45]

The next month, October 1985, Khalifa offered the startling news that the identity of Imam Zaman (Imam of the age), "the promised one, the expected Savior, the long-awaited Benefactor," would soon be revealed. Readers did not have long to wait to find out that identity. Huge headlines in the November issue of *Muslim Perspective* asked, "WHO IS IMAM ZAMAN?" Millions of Muslims, said Khalifa, have been waiting for the hidden one "to come out and deliver them from humiliation, defeats, misery and wars." This hidden one has been known by many names, including Imam Zaman, Saheb Zaman, Al Mahdi, and the Twelfth Imam. The Devil has led people over the ages to have false expectations about this Imam Zaman, particularly in the Shiʿi understanding that it will be Muhammad Ibn al-Hasan al-ʿAskari, the twelfth Imam of Ithna Ashʿari Shiʿism, reappeared. The discovery of the miraculous mathematical code of the Qurʾan has now made it possible to identify this hidden one, he reported, the proof for which he offered by using extended mathematical calculation.

Those who might have expected that the Imam Zaman would be identified as a person, possibly even Rashad Khalifa himself, were to be surprised. Some of the older Muslims who hung on to the traditions, said Khalifa, would probably be greatly disappointed to discover that *"IMAM ZAMAN, THE HIDDEN ONE, THE GREAT SAVIOR AND BENEFACTOR* turned out to be none other than *AL-QURAN AL-KAREEM*, the word of Almighty God."* The Qurʾan itself is called rasul, messenger, in Suras 3:101 and 65:11. Once again Khalifa affirmed the ultimacy of the Qurʾan as the guiding principle for human lives, denouncing the traditions, the superstitions, and by implication the foolishness of expecting a human savior.

Khalifa soon began to see what he interpreted as the realization of his prediction that nations that did not accept the United Islamic Nation would fall. "First Government Falls In Bloody Coup," said the headlines of the January 1986 issue of *Muslim Perspective*. Only four months after his announcement of the establishment of the UIN the government of South Yemen collapsed. Who will be next? he asked, renewing his invitation for all Islamic states to declare their membership. "Those who ridicule the UIN declaration will not laugh for long."

In the same issue Khalifa also attacked the traditionist al-Bukhari, saying that in his *Sahih* (compendium of Hadith traditions) he blasphemed against the Prophet Muhammad. Khalifa juxtaposed two versions of a Hadith telling the story of people who, having gone to the Prophet wanting to embrace Islam, were ordered by him to go to his flock of camels and sheep and drink their urine and milk. When they reportedly changed their minds, the Prophet sent his men to bring them back, after which he gouged their eyes with heated nails, cut their hands and feet, and threw them into the desert until they died of thirst. Sunni Muslims have been angry at what they assert was a misrepresentation of this passage from Bukhari's *Sahih*; photocopies of the passages are reproduced in the magazine, however, and the meaning of the Arabic is correctly given.

For the most part the articles in *Muslim Perspective* from that point on reiterate what Khalifa already said in the journal as well as in his works of the early 1980s. In July 1986 he devoted the issue to a diatribe against those who would undermine the true unity of the faith, leading to the unhappy reality of sectarian divisions, by following the false doctrines of Hadith and Sunna. This was followed in August by the reproduction of a lengthy article written by a Malaysian scholar, Dr. Kassim Ahmad, on why Muslims should immediately abandon Hadith. "There is no doubt that God and His invisible and invincible soldiers are supporting Kassim in his current historical stand against Satan's feeble troops who call themselves 'Ulama' (Muslim scholars! ! !)," says the introduction to the article.

Throughout his career Khalifa tried to purge Islam from the accretions of traditions and to present it as a reasonable and workable Qur'anically based faith viable for the twentieth century. Convinced that those who rely on Hadith and Sunna as the basis for a repressive Islamic law are misled (by Satan) and misrepresent the faith, he consistently worked to get back to the basics of the Qur'an. His discussion of polygamy is a good example. In his commentary on Sura 4:3, the only Qur'an verse mentioning the possibility of marrying more than one wife, he insists that it is only by the invention of the Hadith that people are under the false impression that Islam limits men to four wives. The fact is that there is no specific limit on the number of wives one may have. Then in the September 1987 issue of *Muslim Perspective* he clarified what he really felt about polygamy. Making it clear that he was not saying that polygamy was against God's law, he nonetheless urged Muslims to resort to more than one wife only under very particular circumstances, especially in America. "If the circumstances do not clearly dictate polygamy, we [had] better give our full attention to one wife and one set of children; it is our duty to raise one happy and healthy family. The children's psychological and social well-being, especially in a country where polygamy is illegal, dictate monogamy on us."

It was around this time that Khalifa's flexibility in including Christians and Jews in the community of those who believe in God's laws began to get expanded into a call for what he termed "universal unity." Observing that Hindus and Sikhs fight in India, Protestants and Catholics in Ireland, Sunnis and Shi'is in Iran and

Iraq, Jews and Muslims in Jerusalem, and so on, he noted the irony of such enmity among persons all of whom have in common the belief in one God. What we must do, he said, is concentrate on that common link. "If our true love and our true objective is our Creator *ALONE*, we will be surely united. . . . War will be eliminated."[46]

By late 1987 Khalifa's tone had turned from one of excitement about his new discoveries to a kind of tense defensiveness against a continuing series of attacks by Sunni Muslims.[47] Members of the community recall that at the same time he viewed the attacks against him as an honor, reflecting the Qur'anic assertion that all messengers of God had been ridiculed and rejected. They also recall that during periods of respite from attack, Khalifa would smile and say, "I must have been complacent; I have to work harder in spreading the Truth." He accused the Muslim World League[48] of urging the Egyptian government to arrest Dr. Ahmad Sobhy Mansour for sedition, for example, inciting a "blessed revolution against idolatry." (Mansour was for some time associated with Rashad Khalifa's Masjid Tucson, but left in the late 1980s.)[49] He persisted in his attacks against Saudi Arabia as Satan's official agent, against the Azhar religious establishment in Cairo for preaching false Islam, and against the veneration of the Prophet, and he noted with great pleasure in December 1987 that (in line with his prediction) three leaders of Muslim countries had then fallen—President Numeiry of Sudan, President Mahmoud Ali of South Yemen, and President Bourguiba of Tunisia. (In March 1988 he predicted that Egypt, the rest of the Arab world, and Pakistan would "die" by 1990.)[50] Meanwhile some of the brothers and sisters from among his supporters were reported to have made new discoveries relating to the mathematical base of the Qur'an,[51] proof of the validity of the message.

Since the beginning of his announcement of his mathematical theory Khalifa had been severely criticized by some in the Muslim community.[52] He was accused of buying into an ancient and superstitious belief in the numerical value of letters and the importance of digits.[53] "Some people have tried to attribute many miraculous qualities to these digits," said one critic, "but such superstitions have no basis in Islam."[54] The system of nineteen, it was said, is integral to the belief of the Bahai and the central core of their understanding of the cosmos.[55] Since the Bahai are considered heretical, such a comparison was hardly calculated to enhance Khalifa's standing in the Muslim community. He was accused of trying to

confuse and divide Muslims by propagating his "misleading" interpretations, and of "duping" the uneducated and underprivileged
who have no understanding of real Islam.[56]

One of the most thorough critics of Khalifa's claims was Abu
Ameenah Bilal Philips, who in 1987 published a point-by-point
rebuttal of his claims for the mathematical calculations around
the number 19, entitled *The Qur'an's Numerical Miracle: Hoax
and Heresy.* Philips put Khalifa in the company of Mirza Ghulam
Ahmad, founder of "Qadianism," and Elijah Muhammad of the Nation of Islam as deviants and apostates.[57] He wrote the book, he
says, to challenge and disprove most of the fundamental "facts" on
which Khalifa's theory is based, and to "expose his deliberate falsification of data and alteration of the Qur'an to show conclusively
that Khalifa's numerical theory is a shoddily concocted hoax unable
to withstand scientific scrutiny."[58] Philips proceeds through his arguments with an almost ruthless rigor, accusing Khalifa of number
juggling and arbitrary letter identification. To set the scene for his
critique he announces in his foreword that even his class of high
school students was able to work with a computer and discover the
inconsistencies in Khalifa's arguments.

Rashad Khalifa was quick to come to his own defense through a
counterattack on Philips. In the January 1988 issue of *Muslim Perspective* he sarcastically tried to turn the tables by taking Philips's
recognition that there is at least some truth in the number code
(Philips admitted that there are four chapters in which the total
occurrence of the prefixed letters does add up to a multiple of nineteen) as an indication that he is in fact coming around to an acceptance of the whole theory. "Well, congratulations, Abu Ameenah:
You are just beginning to see the light," he said, calling Philips's attempts to discredit God's miracle heroic. "Abu Ameenah's hatred of
God's miracle drove him to this kind of misleading criticism, only
to prove beyond doubt that those who agree with him are mindless
sheep." The fact remains that Philips's work is generally accepted
among Sunni Muslims as the most exhaustive rebuttal of Khalifa.

Attempting to counter the criticism leveled by Muzammil Siddiqi,
then an official of the Muslim World League Office in New York and
presently Imam of the Islamic Center of Orange County, California,
that he was outside of the fold of Islam Khalifa again tried to turn
the tables and say that it was Siddiqi who was not a true Muslim.[59]
Rashad Khalifa may be outside of the fold of Muhammadanism, he

said, but he is certainly not outside of the fold of Islam.[60] The January 1990 issue of what was by then called *Submitters Perspective* contains another attack on Siddiqi in which he is accused of upholding a "trinity" by citing the three basic sources of Islam as the Qur'an, the authentic Sunna, and the *ijma'* (consensus).

Khalifa's greatest follies in the eyes of the rest of the Muslim world were his insistence on what they saw as the hoax of his system, his claim to know the year of the end of the world, his attack on the Sunna and Hadith, and his rejection of the last two verses of Sura 9 as illegitimate. In May 1988 he made the announcement that was the final straw even for some of those who had heretofore been loyal followers. In a special bulletin of *Muslim Perspective* entitled "GOD INSISTS" he confirmed that "God has provided powerful, physical, proof in support of my mission as His commissioned messenger to the New World." America as the new world, he said, has never had a messenger commissioned by God. The time has now come. The support for his mission is the physical evidence that he has brought of the miracle of the Qur'an. He provided nineteen more facts based on that system which were intended to confirm beyond any doubt the veracity of his claim. Among them were that the root word for Rashad occurs nineteen times in the Qur'an; that the addition of the Sura numbers plus the verse numbers where roots of Rashad and Khalifa are found comes to 1463 ($19 \times 11$); that the total of Sura and verse numbers where the root word of Rashad occurs is $19 \times 72 + 1$, while the total for the root word Khalifa is $19 \times 5 - 1$. The numbers of Suras and verses where the words Rashad and Khalifa are mentioned equal 171 ($19 \times 9$); Rashad Khalifa was born on November 19 which happens to be the 323d day of the solar year ($19 \times 17 = 323$). And so on. In his *Quran: The Final Scripture* he reaffirmed the importance of Abraham and put himself squarely in the line of messengers. "Abraham was the religion's original messenger, while Muhammad delivered its scripture, and Rashad was blessed with delivering the religion's proof of authenticity." He cited Sura 15:87 ("we have given thee seven of the oft-repeated [verses] and the great Qur'an [Pickthall]") as proof that the period between Muhammad and the next messenger is "seven pairs" of centuries, then observed that he was born in 1935[61] and was thus forty-five years old in 1980, exactly 1,400 years after Muhammad.

Subsequent issues of *Muslim Perspective* devoted considerable attention to the reaffirmation of his claim to be a messenger. Khalifa made much of the fact that Muhammad was the last nabi, but that there is no Qur'anic affirmation that he was the last rasul. Many in the Muslim community have neglected to credit him with that distinction (with which in any case they do not agree), and have accused Rashad Khalifa of claiming for himself the status of prophet. In August 1988 he sent a message to presidents and kings in the Islamic world announcing "great news and an urgent alert for the Muslims," the irrefutable evidence that he has been sent as a messenger to "1. save the Muslims, 2. remove all innovations, traditions, and superstitions, and 3. restore Islam to its original pristine purity." Khalifa never claimed for himself the role of mujaddid, believed by Muslims to appear once in every century. It could be argued, however, that by his third claim in this list he did indeed understand that to be one of his functions. He accompanied his announcement with further warnings to those who refused to believe that retribution would be imminent. He pointed to Sura 54:43 as proof that the severity of retribution is in proportion to the miracle, indicating that God's miracle to this generation is greater than the miracles of all previous messengers.[62]

During all of this time Rashad was working on his second translation of the Qur'an. This 1989 work, entitled *Quran: The Final Testament*, appeared just a year before his death. Unlike his earlier translation, it does not have an extensive page-by-page commentary. Most of his exegesis is contained in thirty-eight appendices to the text. What it does provide, like the new Pickthall and the Yusuf Ali translations, is the Arabic text of the Qur'an juxtaposed to the translation. Allah in the text is always translated GOD; at the bottom of each page are two numbers—on the left signifying the number of times the word *God* appears on that page and on the right showing the number of times it has appeared in the text to that point.[63] The text of the Qur'an is rendered into very clear and readable English, a translation that is generally faithful to the Arabic.

In the appendices, however, we find again and carried to even greater lengths the particular interpretations common to Khalifa's writing. A few examples will serve as illustrative. The numerical tables showing all of the ways in which the number nineteen has been discovered to be operating in the Qur'an are again reproduced in appendix 1, and the relationship of the number 19 to the five pillars of Islam carefully spelled out. These pillars or responsibilities do not differ from those accepted by the body of Islam except in relation to the first, the shahada or bearing witness. While this is normally rendered as "There is no God but God and Muhammad is the Prophet of God," Khalifa and his followers insist that one should affirm only that there is no other god besides God. This rejection of one of the twin pillars of the shahada constitutes one of Khalifa's most controversial positions. It was necessary for him, however, as part of his firm sense that bearing witness to anyone other than God, even Muhammad in his designated role as God's prophet, is to violate the Qurʾanic injunction forbidding the association of anyone with the one God.

Appendix 2, entitled "God's Messenger of the Covenant," explains what we already have seen in terms of his understanding of his own role. "God's Messenger of the Covenant is a consolidating messenger," Khalifa says. "His mission is to purify and unify all existing religions into one: Islam."[64] He bases his understanding of his role as "Messenger of the Covenent" on Malachi 3:1–2 in the Hebrew Bible,[65] saying that he is to confirm and purify existing scriptures in the process of consolidating them into one divine message. It is also based on Suras 3:81, 33:7, and 33:40, which he sees as prophesying the coming of the consolidating messenger. "It is only befitting that a message with such a crucial mission must be supported by the most powerful miracle," he says, identifying Sura 74:31 ("Over it is nineteen") as describing that miracle, with 74:31–34 elaborating it. "While the miracles of previous messengers were limited in time and place, God's miracle supporting His Messenger of the Covenant is perpetual; it can be witnessed by anyone, at anytime, in any place."[66]

All righteous believers, including Jews, Buddhists, Sikhs, Hindus and others as well as Muslims, will be led by the messenger (Khalifa himself) from darkness to the light. By righteous believers is meant those who worship God alone. "The existing religions including Judaism, Christianity and Islam are severely corrupted and will simply die out," he says, referring to Suras 9:33, 48:228, and 69:9. The only religion approved by God is Islam, affirmed in Suras 3:19 and 3:85.[67]

It is in this context that Khalifa talks about his own encounter with the prophets of history who confirmed his identity as the Messenger of the Covenant. He first announced this in *Muslim Perspective* in September 1988. "On Tuesday, the third day of Zul-Hijja, 1391 (December 21, 1971)," he said, "I, Rashad Khalifa, the soul, the real person, not the body, was taken somewhere in the universe, where I was introduced to all the prophets. . . . All of them, one by one, declared that they believe in me as the 'Apostle of the Covenant.' " He elaborates on this in appendix 2 to *Quran: The Final Testament*, specifying the experience occurred when he was on Hajj pilgrimage at Mecca in December 1971. "What I witnessed, in sharp consciousness," he says, "was that I was sitting still, while the prophets, one by one, came towards me, looked at my face, then nodded their heads. God showed them to me as they had looked in this world, attired in their respective modes of dress." He then comments, interestingly, that he was quite taken aback to realize that Abraham (whose specific identity was revealed in a special thought communication to him) actually looked very much like his own relatives and even like himself. It was not until Ramadan of 1408, seventeen years after this experience, that he became aware of the real significance of this event as informing him of his role as the Messenger of the Covenant.[68]

Members of the community of Masjid Tucson point to the Qur'anic indication of the three ways to distinguish God's true messenger from a fake messenger, contained in appendix 2, as proof of the validity of his claim. God's messenger (1) advocates the worship of God alone and the abolition of idol worship, (2) never asks for any personal wages or remuneration, and (3) brings divine and incontrovertible proof of his messengership. They feel that Khalifa fulfilled each of these responsibilities, always preaching God's oneness, never asking for any money for himself, and bringing the proof of the original message of the mathematical pattern. In *Quran: The Final Testament*, Khalifa identifies several more specific ways in which he sees his responsibilities as a messenger, or more exactly, the particular messages that he is to convey. He says, for example, that the age of responsibilitity is forty, and that anyone who dies before that age automatically goes to heaven (based on Sura 46:15).[69] Another of the ways in which he chastises the "so-called Muslims" is by affirming that Muhammad wrote the revelations of the Qur'an with his own hand, undercutting the classical Islamic assertion that the Prophet was unlettered (*ummi*).[70] Identifying the death of Jesus as the most controversial subject in the world, he says that the mathematical code reveals that Jesus' soul was raised to God before he was arrested and crucified (explained "scientifically" by analogy with a death after heart surgery while the body technically functions).[71]

He lists fourteen principal duties of God's Messenger of the Covenant in the appendix to *Quran: The Final Testament*, of which the above are but a few.[72]

Khalifa's followers report that he used to talk about how his announcement that he was a messenger would be a tremendous test for people, and that many of them would not pass that test (for example, those convinced of his legitimacy would be few). They are comfortable with this in two ways. First, they recognize that there never will be a large company of believers and are content to be a kind of "remnant." Second, they interpret the "messengership" of Rashad in a fairly loose way. As they put it, it was not really such a "big deal." Just because he was chosen to be a messenger of God does not mean that others might not be better or more pious people. While they firmly believe that Khalifa was chosen to be the vehicle of a particular message, they also say that on another level all people who have something to say about God to others are messengers, because on the Day of Judgment the believers will serve as witnesses among the people. Khalifa did announce at one particular moment his own acknowledgment of his role, and that was taken very seriously. However his followers say that they pretty much knew it anyway, and wondered why he had not said earlier what they felt that they already knew. Or as they put it, "What took you so long?" Khalifa related that when he was struggling with whether he should publicly announce that he was a messenger (his agonies over whether or not to accept the responsibilities of such a role are reminiscent of narratives about the lives of such figures as Buddha, Jesus, and Muhammad) his daughter said to him, "What are you trying to say, Dad? I knew all along that you are God's messenger."[73]

The trend toward a kind of universalism that was nascent in Khalifa's earlier writings became much more evident at this time, no doubt part of his attempt to dissociate himself from and to counter the attacks of Islamic orthodoxy. In confirming the Qur'anic message that Islam is the only religion approved by God, insisting that *islam* is not a name but a description of the act of submitting to God, he stated that "a Muslim is anyone who submits to God, be they Jews, Christians, Muslims, Hindus, or Buddhists. . . . One can be a Muslim Jew, a Muslim Christian, a Muslim Hindu, or a Muslim Muslim."[74] All believers in God were urged to heed the divine call to "Purify, Unify, Consolidate Your Religions Into One,"[75] a theme that runs all through the materials of his appendices to *Quran: The Final Testament.* What all religious people have in common is their belief in God, and what separates them, he said, is their identification with what he called "the human factors" of putting too much emphasis on Muhammad, Jesus, Mary, Imams and saints, and the like. If we concentrate on our creator and submission to him we can forget about these divisive and potentially idolatrous distractions. It is not surprising in the light of this theme that in the middle of 1989 the name of the bulletin of Masjid Tucson was changed from *Muslim Perspective* to *Submission Perspective* and then to *Submitters Perspective.*

Given Khalifa's contention that two verses of Sura 9 were falsely inserted, it is also not a surprise to discover that he is said to have been intrigued by Salman Rushdie's extremely controversial book *The Satanic Verses* (1989). One of Khalifa's followers, Edip Yuksel, spoke of what he saw as a divine plan and a symbolic connection between Khalifa and Rushdie, both of whom have the same number of letters in their first and last names (in both English and Arabic), and who share in one of their names the Arabic root R–Sh–D (which appears nineteen times in the Qur'an).[76] There was no connection, really, said Yuksel in a May 5, 1991, conversation with the authors, yet in another way there was a very mysterious connection. It was a kind of Satanic trick or game to take attention away from Rashad and focus it on Rushdie. In any case, after Khalifa's death his followers made clear what they thought about Rushdie. Calling him "the infamous writer," the author of the lead article "Tales vs. Truth" in *Submitters Perspective,* November 1990, insisted that it was by the hand of Satan that Rushdie chose the name Rashid Khalifa for the storyteller in his new children's book *Haroun and the Sea of Stories.* He did reflect the hope that perhaps through this demonic attempt to confuse the storyteller with the messenger people may get inquisitive about the real Rashad Khalifa and the message for which he was killed.

And so in January 1990, Khalifa was murdered. "The Messenger of the Covenant is in Heaven with his Lord," said the *Submitters Perspective* headline.[77] His followers continue to interpret world affairs in the light of the consequences of rejecting Khalifa's message. Events in the Middle East are not a coincidence, they say; God in his plan has raised up a tyrant (Saddam Hussein) for the express purpose of making life miserable for those who reject.[78] The community at Masjid Tucson continues to carry on its activities as much as possible as it did while Rashad Khalifa was Imam. They disseminate Khalifa's interpretations by selling his books and tapes of his lectures and sermons. According to those responsible for this distribution, the number of publications sold has remained fairly constant. Members also continue to write, publish, and distribute *Submitters Perspective* through the auspices of the mosque. Since Khalifa's death the harassment that he was experiencing toward the end of his life has not continued to plague the community, although they acknowledge that at first a variety of individuals and groups of the "so-called Muslims" would stop them on the way to the masjid and call them to return to acceptance of the Hadith and Sunna. These efforts were short lived, probably in part because of the expectation that without the leadership of Rashad Khalifa the movement would soon disintegrate. His followers continue today to be both criticized and rejected by Sunni Muslims.

Members of the community profess a strong allegiance both to Khalifa's teachings and to the style of life that he proclaimed right and appropriate for Submitters. They have no association with the other two mosques (one Sunni, one Ahmadi) in Tucson because they believe that the other groups do not abide strictly by the Qur'an and because they believe that overtures of communication would be rejected. The group continues to be sharply heterogeneous, with a number of immigrants as well as converts, both African-American and Anglo. The central core of the followers appears to be Iranians and Turks, highly educated, who are attracted to a new interpretation of Islam where they can maintain their belief in the essential divine message, now scientifically proved, and live in the modern world. Among the converts are people who have been searching for some kind of meaning in life and cannot find it in Christianity. Some of them have gone through Muslim and Christian fundamentalist groups and not found them satisfactory. What appeals to them in Khalifa's message is that it makes sense, bringing together all humanity in submission to the one God.

They perform the five duties (pillars) required of all Muslims with their own modifications. The call to prayer, *adhan*, omits the name of the Prophet Muhammad: "Ash-Hadu Allaa Elaaha Ellaa Allah (I bear witness that there is no other god beside God) Wahdahu Laa Shareeka Lah (He ALONE is God; He has no partner)."[79] It consists

of saying four times "Allahu Akbar (God is Great)" and saying once
"Laa Elaaha Ella Allah (There is no other god beside God),"[80] reflecting Khalifa's absolute conviction that according to the Qur'an no
name should be associated with that of God. During Ramadan,
members fast but do not celebrate the 'Id feast at the end of the
month of fasting.[81] The pilgrimage to Mecca is considered a religious duty although they know that because of the fatwa against
Rashad applications would not be accepted by the Saudi government. Zakat or paying the alms tax is very important. They give individually 2.5 percent of their income to charity every time they
receive any money. If contributions are made to the masjid they are
above and beyond that percentage.

The community of Masjid Tucson is very articulate in its agreement with Khalifa that what other Muslims (whom they regularly
refer to as "so-called Muslims") are doing is wrong. "Not one single
commandment they follow coincides with the commandments of
God, *not one,*" members affirmed. Among the specifics cited in
terms of wrongdoing are: (1) Adding the second part of the shahada
testifying to the Prophethood of Muhammad. The issue is not that
the "so-called Muslims" are testifying to the prophethood of Muhammad as such, but rather that they associate the name of Muhammad with that of God. There are many injunctions in the
Qur'an to obey God and the Prophet, but not to bear witness to both
in the same testimony. What is really objectionable, therefore, is
that the Hadith calling for that double witness is given equal status
with the Qur'an, and Muhammad seemingly equal veneration with
God. (2) Adding to the commandments about *wudu'* or ritual washing before the prayer. The Qur'anic instruction on wudu' is found in
Sura 5:6.[82] By adding the washing of other parts of the body besides
those mentioned in the Qur'an, Muslims, according to Khalifa, "fell
into Satan's trap, disobeyed their Creator, and incurred misery and
defeat."[83] (3) Mentioning Muhammad and others during the salat or
prayer in direct contradiction to the Qur'anic injunction in Suras
20:14 and 72:18. In commenting on the verse, Khalifa affirms that
"The 'Muslims' have been duped by Satan into uttering the innovation known as '*Tashahhud*' where they shower praises and glorifi-
cations on Muhammad and Abraham."[84] They also disobey the
clear instruction of the Qur'an regarding the vocalization of prayer
noted in Sura 17:110.[85] The Muslim masses, he reports, maintain silence during the noon prayer, the afternoon prayer, and the third

unit of the sunset prayer, and the second half of the night prayer.[86] (4) Paying 2.5 percent of total worth rather than individual income "on the day of harvest" (Sura 7:146) in the zakat. (5) Interpreting the time for the hajj or pilgrimage to be a few days in the month of Zul-hijja only, while the Qur'an says it can come in any of the four sacred months (Sura 9:36–37). (6) Prescribing the wearing of the hijab or conservative dress for women. (7) Stoning for adultery or cutting off the hand for stealing when the Qur'an really recommends much more lenient punishment for crimes. (8) Taking Sura 4:34 to mean that women literally can be beaten if disobedient to men. Khalifa's followers see his interpretation of the Qur'an as pointing to its function as a guide to the wise and proper living of life: "God prohibits wife beating by using the best psychological approach."

As is the case with all of the groups considered in this study, members of Masjid Tucson put great emphasis on raising children within the context of the community. There are groups of young people of all ages, and the women in particular are active in creating opportunities for keeping them involved and for teaching proper moral behavior. There is no Arabic instruction as such, although some Arabic is learned through Qur'an study and in doing readings and songs. A booklet entitled "God's Teachings thru Songs" reproduces the words of some children's music (available for sale on tape) adapted with a few changes in wording from well known songs, with a few written especially for the children of the community.[87]

Khalifa strongly encouraged the participation of women in the worship activities of the masjid and they continue in that tradition. While members will not agree to having a woman lead the prayer or deliver the *khutba* at the Friday prayer, principally because it would constitute *bidʿa* or innovation in which they do not see themselves as engaging, they stress the importance of women's contribution to theological discourse by leading study of the Qur'an for both men and women. Members are in general agreement that if there is no man available or prepared to lead the prayer, then it is acceptable for a woman to do it. This reflects the general atmosphere of the Masjid Tucson, which is one not of laissez-faire, but of trying to determine reasonably and rationally how best to follow the commands of God as outlined in the Qur'an (and, it is important to add, as explicated by Rashad Khalifa in light of the miracle of the number 19). Women do not wear headcovers or other forms of conservative dress even in the masjid, but they wear modest dress that covers the chest, following Suras 24:31 and 33:59. A booklet printed by the masjid describing step by step how one performs the prayer has illustrations of the worshipper in various prayer positions. It is interesting that the sketches are of a girl with short sleeves, a skirt just below the knees, and her ponytailed hair uncovered. Although Khalifa does not have a specific appendix in either of his Qur'an translations dealing with the role of women, it is clear throughout his writings that he interprets the verses of the Qur'an as providing for full participation of women in the life of the community.[88]

Without the leadership of the "Messenger of Covenant," the future of United Submitters International at first looked uncertain at best; however, the community remains stable and has recently experienced some growth. Members of the Masjid Tucson are reluctant to call themselves a group. In conversation with the authors they engaged in a lively discussion of how they would like to be identified, concluding that perhaps the name "Submission: The Only Religion Acceptable to God" would be most appropriate.[89] There are, in fact, other followers of Rashad Khalifa located in such places as Phoenix, Arizona; Riverside and the Bay area in California; Vancouver, British Columbia; and other parts of the world. There does not seem to be available, however, any kind of register of these groups. The only da'wa or propagation that seems to go on, at least now that Khalifa is gone, is through the dissemination of the monthly *Perspective* and other published materials, old and new.

While the question of leadership of Masjid Tucson remains an issue, there is little indication that Khalifa's followers will cease to function as a mosque community. There have been defections over the past decade as Khalifa made claims that were difficult to accept. Some left when he identified the two verses of Sura 9 as spurious,[90] some when he predicted the year of the end of the world, and some (such as his close associate Ahmad Mansour) when he took the final step of proclaiming himself a messenger of God. It might actually be the case that with the death of their leader, and the solidification of the members over an acceptance of his role and message, there is a kind of renewed strength in the community. Edip Yuksel, a well-educated former participant in the Islamic fundamentalist movement in Turkey, is providing religious leadership. He is grounded in the faith of Islam and has a good knowledge of current ideological teachings. (His father is a Muslim scholar who has condemned his son's recent writings.) He sees himself as continuing much of

Khalifa's work, particularly in identifying groups who reject as did Rashad the dependence of the "so-called Muslims" on Hadith and Sunna and reaffirm the message of the Qur'an alone.[91]

• • • • • *Conclusion*

It is clear that Rashad Khalifa's interpretation of Islam takes seriously the challenge that the last quarter of the twentieth century has posited for religions in general and Islam in particular. His attempt to reform Islam by grounding its teachings in the Qur'an alone is not new, having echoes in the Ahli Qur'an reform movement of the Indian subcontinent in the last century.[92] What is new is the affirmation of "the scientific proof" that the Qur'an is the revelation of God, utilizing the latest, most modern technological development in the form of the computer as its validation.

Like his detractors among the contemporary Islamists, Khalifa was pained by the condition of Muslims in the contemporary world. He was of the generation that saw the Ayatollah Khomeini return to Iran and establish an Islamic Republic. For many in the Muslim world Khomeini's victory was interpreted as an empowering of the Islamic community by God because the Iranians heeded God's commandment to obedience. As a result they believe firmly that salvation can only come through a similar process, one in which the Muslims take charge of their lives by eschewing Western values and adhering to the teachings and example of the Prophet. Khalifa, as we have seen, drew the opposite conclusion.

Khalifa was also writing at a time in which the Arab world was experiencing, as it continues to experience, a profound feeling of humiliation as a consequence of defeat by Israeli forces. Together with all the Muslims of the world he witnessed the Israeli invasion of Lebanon in 1982, the year in which he published his controversial book *Quran, Hadith, and Islam*. In that volume he specified what he saw as the link between following the Hadith and Sunna and the present woeful political and military circumstances of Muslim countries: "For as long as the Muslim ummah upheld Qur'an, and nothing but Qur'an, the Muslims led the world scientifically, technologically, culturally, socially, militarily and economically. They never lost a single battle. The borders of Islam extended from West Africa to China; into Southern France and Eastern Germany. With the appearance of Hadith & Sunna at the beginning of the third century AH, a progressive deterioration of the Muslim Ummah began. Since the appearance of these innovations as sources of guidance beside the Quran, the 'Muslims' never won a single battle. Why do 3 million Israelis consistently defeat 150 million Arabs??? Does it make any sense that 3 million Israelis should force 1,000 million 'Muslims' out of their mosque in Jerusalem?"[93]

Muslims today continue to ask the same questions the reformers have asked for several centuries. What is wrong with the Muslims? Why does it appear that God has abandoned them to their enemies? They all agree that the reason they lag behind other nations and that their condition is not what God promised in Sura 3:110 of the Qur'an, "the best community brought forth to mankind," is that somehow Muslims are not interpreting Islam correctly and are not living according to the way God intended. Where they differ is in their understanding of the role of the Qur'an and the Sunna in the lives of the community. The Islamists, including the Muslim Brotherhood of Egypt and other Arab countries and the Jamaati Islami of the Indian subcontinent, believe that what is wrong is the penetration of modern reformist ideas borrowed from alien cultures that have weakened Muslim adherence to the practice of the Prophet. The remedy, as they see it, lies in the rigorous enforcement and implementation of traditions, the details of worship and ways of life that operated as an impetus for the empowerment of the Muslim community in its formative period. Khalifa felt that it was precisely this insistence on the "emulation" of the Prophet that rendered the Muslims weak and powerless. He had a deep respect for the Prophet as the one who brought the Qur'an, but was persuaded that Muslims in their effort to venerate him have raised him to the level of God. He always took his direction from the Qur'an, justifying his criticism of the "so-called Muslims" with verses such as Sura 6:116, "If you obey the majority of people on earth, they will divert you from the path of God," his refusal to venerate the Prophet Muhammad with Sura 18:110, "Say, 'I am no more than a human like you,' " and his reliance on the Qur'an alone with such passages as Sura 6:114, "Shall I seek other than GOD as a source of law, when He has revealed to you this book fully detailed?"[94]

Rashad Khalifa's ideas, like those of the Sudanese reformer Mahmoud Mohamed Taha, seem both liberal and progressive, and for that reason have been attractive to the young and the educated. It is absolutely the case, of course, that Khalifa is at the same time fully grounded in the Qur'an as the indisputable foundation for faith and for living. Because he died suddenly and at a relatively young age, and because he spent so much of his time trying to prove the validity of his interpretation of the system of nineteen as verification of the divine origin of the Qur'an, he did not go far in spelling out what a true Islamic community might look like. In appendix 36 of *Quran: The Final Testament,* however, he did reveal some of his image of a truly Qur'anically based state, entitled "What Price A Great Nation." Such a nation is one which, upholding God's laws, is guaranteed victory, prosperity, happiness and prominence among nations. Among the characteristics of this nation—all based on the injunctions and the promises of the Qur'an—are maximum freedom for its people; guaranteed human rights regardless of race, creed, social status, financial circumstances or political affiliation; economic prosperity and social justice for all; a political system based on unanimous agreement rather than a majority rule; the highest standards of moral behavior with strong families; no alcohol or illicit drugs or illegitimate pregnancies or abortion and (practically) no divorce; no crime against the lives or properties of others; environmental protection; prevalence of love, courtesy, peace, and mutual respect among all citizens and between the Islamic nation and the other communities of the world.

Here are the beginnings of a description of an Islamic system which is both "postmodern" and fully based on the Qur'an. It can only be guessed what more time to develop such a vision might have done to enhance the level of tolerance and understanding between Khalifa and his fellow religionists.

# The Druze Covenant (Al Mithaq)

I lay my trust in Our Lord [al-Hakim] who is unique in His Oneness, who is above numbers and partners.

I solemnly declare, in my free will, sound of mind and body, my soul be my witness:

I absolve myself of all creeds, doctrines and beliefs.

I shall be totally obedient to Our Lord [al-Hakim], hallowed be His name, for obedience is worship;

I shall not include in my worship anyone else past, present, or expected;

I dedicate my body and soul, my wealth, possessions and loved ones to our Lord [al-Hakim], exalted be His Name;

I accept without protest all His judgments, denying none of His acts, whether favorable or unfavorable to me.

If I renounce this Covenant with Our Lord [al-Hakim] to which I have committed, or if I disobey any of its tenets I shall cause my fall from His favor and be deprived of the knowledge of His spiritual luminaries and be deserving of His punishment.

If I so confess that there is no God on earth or heaven save our Lord [al-Hakim], Hallowed be His Name, I would be among the victorious in the ranks of the true believers—Ahl-al—Tawhid.

Written in the month of ———in the year of ———according to the calendar of the servant of our Lord [al-Hakim], Hamza Ibn Ali Ibn Ahmed, Guide of the respondents, Avenger of the atheists and renegades with the power and might of our Lord [al-Hakim], glory to Him in the highest.

(Translated by Abdallah E. Najjar, June 17, 1985)

# United Submitters International Creed

1. The first verse of Quran consists of **19** Arabic letters.

2. The Quran consists of 114 suras (**19** × 6).

3. The first sura ever revealed (Iqra') is number **19** from the end of Quran.

4. The first sura ever revealed (Iqra') consists of **19** verses.

5. When Gabriel came down with the first Quranic revelation, he gave Muhammad **19** words, namely, the first five verses of sura Iqra'.

6. The **19** words of the first revelation consist of 76 letters (**19** × 4).

7. The whole sura (Iqra') consists of 285 letters (**19** × 15).

8. The last sura ever revealed (Al-Nasr = No. 110) consists of **19** words.

9. There are 114 (**19** × 6) suras in the Quran, and each sura, except one, opens with the Quran's opening statement, which is the foundation of this code. Since the code must be perfect, we find that the statement missing from sura 9 is made up in sura 27. Thus, while sura 9 does not have the opening statement, sura 27 has two of them, namely, one at the beginning, and one in verse 30. This makes the total frequency of the opening statement 114 (**19** × 6).

10. When we start counting at the missing statement, i.e., count sura 9 as number 1, we find that the sura containing two statements is number **19**. In other words, to find the missing statement of sura 9, you have to count **19** suras starting at sura 9. This is God's sign to us that the sequence of suras in Quran is divinely designed.

11. The number of words between the two "Basmalas" of sura 27 is 342 (**19** × 18). [The Basmala is the designation for the phrase that opens all of the Suras of the Qu'ran except one, namely, "In the name of God, the Merciful, the Compassionate."]

12. Taking only one "Basmala" to represent the 114 Basmalas of Quran (only the first one, in the first sura, is given a number), we find that every word in the Basmalah is repeated in the whole Quran a number of times that is always a multiple of **19.**

i. the word "Ism" is found in Quran **19** times.

ii. the second word "Allah" is mentioned 2698 times (**19** × 142).

iii. the third word "Alrahman" is mentioned 57 times (**19** × 3).

iv. the last word "Alraheem" is mentioned 114 times (**19** × 6).

13. There is a whole sura about this secret numerical code, entitled "The Hidden Secret," namely sura 74. In this sura, God informs us that if anyone claims that the Quran is manmade (verse 25), God will prove to him otherwise by the number **19** (verse 30). [In exegeting this verse in *Quran: The Final Scripture,* Khalifa says that in retrospect we now know that the whole sura is about this miraculous code which has been hidden for 1,400 years.]

14. The Quran states that the number **19** will serve five functions: 1. to disturb the disbelivers; 2. to assure the good Jews and the good Christians that Quran is indeed a divine scripture; 3. to strengthen the faith of the believers; 4. to remove any lingering doubts in the hearts of the Muslims, Christians, and Jews that the Quran is God's message to the world; and, 5. to expose the hypocrites, who are indifferent to this overwhelming Quranic miracle.

15. God informs us that this numerical code is "one of the greatest miracles." (See verse 35 of sura 74.)

16. In the sequence of revelation of Quran, which is different from the written sequence, the **19** letters of "Basmala" (verse 1 of sura 1) were revealed immediately after the number **19** mentioned in Quran (verse 30 of sura 74).

17. A unique feature of Quran is the existence of "Quranic Initials" at the beginning of 29 suras. These 29 suras, in terms of size, make up half the Quran. Exactly half the Arabic alphabet (14 letters) participate in forming 14 different sets of Quranic Initials. Thus, 14 letters make up 14 sets of initials, to prefix 29 suras. When we add 14 + 14 + 29, the total is 57 (**19** × 3).

18. It was discovered that the letters of ALL the Quranic initials, without any exceptions, exist in their suras in multiples of 19. Any

reader can easily verify this physical fact by counting the letter "Q" (Qaf) in the sura entitled "Q" (Qaf) (sura 50). He will find that the letter "Q" (Qaf) occurs in this sura exactly 57 times ($19 \times 3$). The only other sura intitled with "Q" (Qaf), namely sura 42, also contains the same number of "Q" (Qaf), 57, even though sura 42 is more than twice as long as sura 50.

19. The sura initialed with the letter "N" (Noon), namely sura 68, contains 133 "N's" ($19 \times 7$).

# Notes

• • • • • *Chapter 1*

1. There are several studies on medieval groups that were deemed heretical or sectarian by the Sunni majority. Most have been prepared by enemies, raising questions concerning the accuracy of the accounts. See Helmut Ritter, "Philologia III: Mohammedanische Haresiographen." There are variations on the firqa tradition. Abu Da'ud, *Sunan*, claims that the Jews will have seventy-one or seventy-two firqas, the Christians seventy-one or seventy-two, and the Muslims seventy-three.

2. Muhammad ibn 'Abd al-Karim al-Shahrastani, "Muslim Sects and Divisions," 9–10.

3. Ibid., 10.

4. Other variations report that the Prophet said, "Those who will not be in the fire are those who follow what I and my companions do." Ibn Hanbal, *Musnad*, 3:145, claims that the *jama'a*, the group, will not perish.

5. For more information on Islamic sects see Abu'l-Hasan 'Ali ibn Isma'il Ash'ari, *Maqalat al-Islamiyin*; 'Abd al-Qahir Baghdadi, *Al-Farq bain al-Firaq*; 'Ali ibn Zaid Zahir al-Din al-Baihaqi, *Tarikh Hukama' al-Islam*; Shahfur ibn Tahir Isfara'ini, *Al-Tabsir fi'l-Din wa Tamyiz al-Firqa al-Najiya 'an al-Firaq al-Halikin*; 'Abd al-Rahim Muhammad al-Khayyat, *Kitab al-Intisar wa'l-Radd 'ala Ibn al-Rawandi al-Mulhid*; Ahmad ibn Yahya al-Murtada, *Kitab Tabaqat al-Mu'tazila*; Salah al-Din Khalil ibn Aibak al-Safadi, *Kitab al-Wafi bi'l-Wafayat*; Muhammad ibn 'Abd al-Karim al-Shahrastani, *Kitab Nihayat al-Iqdam fi 'Ilm al-Kalam*; and 'Abd al-Wahhab ibn al-Subki, *Tabaqat al-Shafi'iya al-Kubra*.

6. Marshall S. G. Hodgson, *The Venture of Islam*, 1:66–67.

7. Recent literature on religious groups in America illustrates the variety of distinctions made between the designations *sect* and *cult*. See, for example, Robert S. Ellwood and Harry B. Partin, *Religious and Spiritual Groups in Modern America*, which defines *cult* as a group that is "small, has authoritative and charismatic leadership, offers powerful subjective experiences which meet personal needs, is separatist, and claims a relation to a legitimating tradition" (p. 27), a definition that fits most of the groups considered in this study. Joseph R. Washington, Jr., *Black Sects and Cults*, blurs the distinctions between sects and cults in pointing to characteristics that clearly apply to the Moorish Americans and the Ansar: "The cult-type is an extreme sectarian movement which in Africa and among Blackamericans often takes the form of nationalistic racial and ethnic group cohesion" (p. 6); "The single element black church-, sect-, and cult-types hold in common and which is without parallel in white counterparts is the **cult** of power for black realization in the here and now" (p. 8). For other definitions of sect and cult see Marc Galanter, ed., *Cults and New Religious Movements*; Roy Wallis, ed., *Sectarianism: Analysis of Religious and Non-Religious Sects*; Thomas Robbins and Dick Anthony, eds., *In Gods We Trust: New Patterns of Religious Pluralism in America*; and David Bromley and Phillip Hammond, *The Future of New Religious Movements*.

8. The Shiʿa believe that the Prophet designated his son-in-law ʿAli as his successor, a fact the Shiʿa defend through a corpus of traditions they ascribe to the Prophet.

9. Hodgson, *The Venture of Islam*, 1:197.

10. Shahrastani, "Muslim Sects and Divisions," 19.

11. The Abbasid caliphs assumed the title *Imam* in order to co-opt the opposition Shiʿite groups that helped them to power.

12. The Mustaʿilians are also known as the Bohras.

13. See Seyyed Hossein Nasr, Dabashi, and Nasr, *Expectation of the Millennium: Shiʿism in History*, 8ff. Compare Saiyid Athar Abbas Rizvi, *A Socio-Intellectual History of the Isna ʿAshari Shiʿis in India*; Muhammad Husayn al-Tabatabai, *Shiite Islam*; and Husain M. Jafri, *Origins and Early Development of Shiʿa Islam*.

14. The ʿAlawi's affirmation of faith is the following: "I testify that there is no God but Ali ibn Abi Talib *al-Maʿbud* (the worshipped one), no veil but Muhammad *al-Mahmud* (the praised one), and no gate but Salman al-Farisi *al-Maqsud* (the intended one)." Matti Moosa, *Extremist Shiites: The Ghulat Sects*. See also Umar F. Abd-Allah, *The Islamic Struggle in Syria*; ʿAbd Allah al-Husayni, *Al-Judhur al-Tarikhiyya li al-Nusayriyya al-ʿAlawiyya*; and Samuel Lyde, *The Asian Mystery: Ansaireeh or Nusairis of Syria*.

15. John Kingsley Birge, *The Bektashi Order of Dervishes*.

16. The Druze, for example, were Arab nationalists who fought valiantly against the French occupation of Syria.

17. Among leaders of jihads against foreign intrusion were Ahmed Brewli in India, Usman Dan Fodio in Nigeria, Abd al-Qadir in Algeria, Al-Hajj Omar Tal in Guinea, Senegal, and Mali, the Sanusiyya in Libya, and Sayyid Mohammad Hassan of Somalia. See B. G. Martin, *Muslim Brotherhood in Nineteenth-Century Africa;* E. E. Evans Pritchard, *The Sanusi of Cyrenaica;* and Mervyn Hiskett, "Material Relating to the State of Learning among the Fulani before Their *Jihad*."

18. P. M. Holt, *The Mahdist State in the Sudan.*

19. William S. Hatcher and J. Douglas Martin, *The Baha'i Faith: The Emerging Global Religion;* William McElwee Miller, *The Baha'i Faith: Its History and Teachings;* H. M. Balyuzi, *Baha'u'llah: The King of Glory;* Balyuzi, *The Bab: The Herald of the Day of Days;* Ruhi Muhsin Afnan, *The Revelation of Baha'u'llah and the Bab;* and Moojan Momen, *Studies in Babi and Baha'i History.*

20. Allan D. Austin, *African Muslims in Antebellum America: A Sourcebook.*

21. Yusuf Nuruddin, "The Five Percenters," unpublished manuscript.

22. See, for example, the writings of 'Ali 'Abd al-Raziq and Sa'id al-Ashmawi as well as the controversial book by Farag Fuda, *Qabl al-Suqut.*

23. Sura 4:135.

24. "The Arabs said, 'We have believed.' But you say, 'You have not believed'; what you should say is, 'We have submitted,' until belief enters your hearts."

25. Isma'il Raji al-Faruqi, *Tawhid: Its Implications for Thought and Life.*

26. Abu al-Hassan 'Ali al-Nadawi, *Al-Qadyani wa-al-Qadyaniyya,* 19.

27. Rashad Khalifa claimed a distinction between *nabi* and *rasul* on the basis that prophets have been given scriptures, while the role of the messenger is only to confirm and preach scriptures already in existence.

28. Willem A. Bijlefeld, "A Prophet and More Than a Prophet?" 1–28. Bijlefeld concludes (p. 25) that "the combination *rasul*-Book . . . occurs so often that this functioning in the history of the Book-revelation can hardly be seen as the primary distinction between the prophet and the apostle."

29. A. J. Wensinck, "Rasul," in *Shorter Encyclopaedia of Islam,* 469.

30. 'Uthman 'Abd al-Mun'im 'Aysh, *'Aqidat Khatm al-Nubuwwa bi al-Nubuwwa al-Muhammadiyya,* 9.

31. Nadawi, *Al-Qadyani wa-al-Qadyaniyya,* 21–30; here Nadawi affirms the doctrine of *khatm al-nubuwwa* as a direct refutation of the possibility of revelation coming to Ghulam Ahmad, founder of the Ahmadiyya, as he claimed. Later (p. 96) he claims that Ahmad used the teachings of extremist Sufis and others about receiving intimations from God to justify his claim to prophethood.

32. D. S. Margoliouth, "On Mahdis and Mahdism," 2.

33. Ibid., 1. Compare Abdulaziz Abdulhussein Sachedina, *Islamic Messianism*, 1–2, where the author apparently bases his understanding of messianism on Margoliouth. Sachedina does add that the Islamic doctrine differs from the Christian in that Muslims do not regard man as a sinner who must be saved through spiritual regeneration.

34. That is, by a Hanafite woman and not by the Prophet's daughter, Fatima.

35. Margoliouth, "On Mahdis and Mahdism," 7.

36. Sachedina, *Islamic Messianism*, 2.

37. The Shi'ites cite the Hadith attesting to the name, identity and function of the Mahdi as descriptive of the reappearance of the twelfth Imam: "In a *hadith* upon whose authenticity everyone agrees, the Holy Prophet has said, 'If there were to remain in the life of the world but one day, God would prolong that day until He sends in it a man from my community and my household. His name will be the same as my name. He will fill the earth with equity and justice as it was filled with oppression and tyranny.' " Nasr, Dabashi, and Nasr, *Expectation of the Millennium*, 8.

38. Rashad Khalifa gives this concept a very novel interpretation, as is explained in chap. 6 herein.

39. This lack of clarity is mirrored in the confusion over whether Isa Muhammad, who assumes the title Mahdi, also in any sense considers himself to be the returned Jesus. See chap. 5 herein.

40. D. B. Macdonald, "'Isa," in *Shorter Encyclopedia of Islam*, 174. Macdonald notes that Ghulam Ahmad, founder of the Ahmadiyya, claimed to be both the returned Jesus and the Mahdi.

41. See Geoffrey Parrinder, *Jesus in the Qur'an*, 32. Parrinder notes that "[Fakhr al-Din] Razi [theologian and commentator on the Qur'an] and others suggested a derivation of Masih from a verb meaning 'to travel,' for Jesus was said to have travelled much or gone in pilgrimage. For later Muslims Jesus became the model of pilgrims and the example of mystics. 'Take Jesus as your patron,' said the theologian-mystic al-Ghazali. Ahmadis have applied this idea of the wandering Jesus to their belief that he travelled eastward as far as Kashmir."

42. See Jane Idleman Smith and Yvonne Yazbeck Haddad, *The Islamic Understanding of Death and Resurrection*, 69–70, quoting historian Ibn Khaldun's *Al-Muqaddimah*: "It has been well known (and generally accepted) by all Muslims in every epoch, that at the end of time a man from the family (of the Prophet) will without fail make his appearance, one who will strengthen the religion and make justice triumph. . . . He will be called the Mahdi. Following him, the Antichrist will appear, together with all the subsequent signs of the Hour (the Day of Judgment), as established in (the sound tradition of) the *Sahih*. After (the Mahdi), 'Isa (Jesus) will descend and

kill the Antichrist; or, Jesus will descend together with the Mahdi, and help him kill (the Antichrist), and have him as the leader in his prayers."

43. Throughout the history of Islam many of those who have claimed the title *Mahdi* have been in turn labeled "Antichrist" by other Muslims. Aziz Ahmad, *Islamic Modernism in India and Pakistan, 1857–1964*, includes in that list some of the key players of the sects considered in this study: "To this category belong the Shi'i extremists (ghulat), the Fatimids, the Hululis, who believe in divine incarnation, the Alfi heretic Mahdi of Jaunpur in sixteenth-century India, and modern false messiahs like the Mahdi of the Sudan or Mirza Ghulam Ahmad of Qadian" (p. 118).

44. al-Nadawi, *Al-Qadyani wa-al-Qadyaniyya*, 30.

45. 'Abd al-Qadir 'Ata, *Al-Mahdi al-Muntazar: Bayn al-Haqiqa wa'l-Khurafa*, 66.

46. Abu Da'ud, *Mishkat Kitabul Ulum*, 2:24.

47. Gustave E. Von Grunebaum, *Medieval Islam*, 246.

48. Von Grunebaum, ibid., notes that four hundred years later the sciences of Islam had sunk so low that it was hard to find someone believed capable of reviving them; one likely candidate, at least in his own understanding, was al-Suyuti, whose erudition could well have fulfilled the prerequisites of this position.

49. Seyyed Hossein Nasr, *Traditional Islam in the Modern World*, 107–8, observes that it is important to understand the distinction between modern utopianism and Islamic teachings in regard to the mujaddid. The modern reformer, he claims, "can hardly be said to have brought about the renewal of Islam." Nasr argues that the kind of revivalism that is based on utopianism but uses Islamic images is not truly Islamic, although it is characteristic of certain kinds of Islamic "fundamentalism."

50. For studies on the Muslim community in the United States see Yvonne Yazbeck Haddad, ed., *The Muslims of America;* Haddad and Adair Lummis, *Islamic Values in the United States;* Earle H. Waugh, Baha Abu-Laban, and Regula B. Qureshi, eds., *The Muslim Community in North America;* Waugh, Sharon McIrvin Abu-Laban, and Regula Burckhardt Qureshi, *Muslim Families in North America;* and Raymond Brady Williams, *Religions of Immigrants from India and Pakistan.*

51. Michael M. J. Fisher and Mehdi Abedi, *Debating Muslims: Cultural Dialogues in Postmodernity and Tradition.*

52. John Norman Hollister, *The Shi'a of India.*

53. Ahmed ibn Hamed al-Khalily, *Who Are the Ibadhis?*

54. Frances Trix, "Bektashi Tekke and Sunni Mosque of Albanian Muslims in America," unpublished manuscript.

55. *National Spiritual Assembly of the Baha'is of the United States and Canada.*

• • • • • *Chapter 2*

1. Several theories have been proposed for the origin of the term *Druze*, the most common being that it comes from the name of the heretical missionary Muhammad al-Darazi, a disciple of al-Hakim who was killed after disputing with Hamza (see below). In the April 1985 issue of *Our Heritage*, Fouad Sleem discusses myths that have circulated about the origin of the Druze, for example that they were descendents of the Crusaders or were of Persian origin. The truth, he says, is that they are descendants of the Tanouh and other Arab tribes (p. 36).

2. Abdallah E. Najjar, interview with the authors, February 1991. The authors express their gratitude to Dr. Najjar, who read a draft of this chapter and offered comments.

3. Writing about the Druze in America, Alixa Naff, in *Becoming American: The Early Arab Immigrant Experience*, claims that "the sect's distinctive esoteric beliefs and practices so diverged from its Islamic origins as to be considered semi-Islamic by some Muslims and non-Islamic by others. Present-day Arab-American Druze have adopted the latter opinion" (p. 25).

4. Wahbah Sayegh, "Know Your Druze Faith," *Our Heritage* 9, no. 3 (May 1989): 19. Azhar has issued a fatwa defining the Druze as Muslims.

5. Abdallah E. Najjar, interview with the authors, June 23, 1990. Najjar makes the distinction that Druzism is a *madhhab* (sect or school) rather than a religion. The definition of a Druze that is reported to have satisfied at least some in the community in the 1970s was "a Muslim in a hurry to be close to God."

6. "Sunni Moslem historians . . . remembering him as the heretic who abolished the five pillars of Islam and ordered the names of the early caliphs associated with a curse in the public prayer, have portrayed him in terms of a medieval Nero, tyrannical and unbalanced to the point of mental derangement. The Christian historians . . . were equally merciless in his condemnation." Philip K. Hitti, *The Origins of the Druze People and Religion*, 26–27.

7. Nejla M. Abu-Izzeddin, *The Druzes: A New Study of Their History, Faith and Society*, 77.

8. The Shi'i branch of Islam split several times, the major time in the middle of the eighth century over a matter of succession. Those who accept the imamate or leadership of Isma'il, son of Ja'far al-Sadiq (d. 765) are known as the "Seveners" (Isma'ilis), while those who believe that the imamate carried through Abdallah al-Aftah to a twelfth Imam (now in occultation) are called the "Twelvers" or Ithna Ashari.

9. See, for example, Robert Brenton Betts, *The Druze*, 8ff.

10. Abu-Izzeddin, *The Druzes*, 85, 105.

11. E. Toftbek, "A Shorter Druze Catechism," 38.

12. Abu-Izzeddin, *The Druzes*, 101.

13. "The Creator will not hold the creature accountable on the Day of Judgment except if he had changed his condition from misery into well-being, from weakness into health and from a physical or intellectual handicap into perfection." Tawfiq Salman, *Adwa' 'Ala Madhhab al-Tawhid*, 26. The June 1983 issue of *Our Heritage* features an article on reincarnation by Dr. Ian Stevenson of the University of Virginia. Stevenson visited Lebanon in 1964 and was warmly welcomed by the Druze community, which is eager for more scientific study of a concept that has been so long debated among the world's religions.

14. The five luminaries are believed to have been personified in human form in order to provide instruction for the faithful. They are: (1) Al-Aql or the Universal Mind (Hamza ibn 'Ali); (2) An-Nafs or the Universal Soul (Isma'il al-Tamimi); (3) Al-Kalima or the Highest Word (Muhammad al-Qurashi); (4) Al-Sadiq or the Precedent or Cause (Salman al-Samiri); and (5) Al-Tali or the Follower or Effect (Al-Muqtana Baha'uddin).

15. Sami Nasib Makarem, *The Druze Faith*, 39.

16. This discussion is based on Makarem, *The Druze Faith*, 89–113. Compare Sayegh, "Know Your Faith," 19–20.

17. In the Islamic tradition, *islam* is understood as the external submission to God, while *iman* means faith or the submission of the heart. There was much discussion in the early Islamic community as to whether or not *islam* had to include *iman* to be valid for one's admission into the Islamic community.

18. "To the Muwahidun," says Abdallah E. Najjar, "[*zakat*] means edification and purification of one's soul that lead to helping and safeguarding the brethren. It is to be given freely without the feeling of imposed duty. It is to be motivated by love and could be (a) a testimonial of an exemplary way of life for others, (b) a constructive guidance and counsel or (c) a material assistance to one in need." Interview with the the authors, 1991.

19. Makarem, *The Druze Faith*, 109.

20. That *tawhid* continues as the central plank in the Druze platform is evident from the title of the keynote address at the ADS Convention in 1987: "Is America Ready for Tawhid?" *Our Heritage* 7, no. 3 (Summer 1987): 8–11, and from the subject of a seminar held at the 1989 convention: "Druze Women in America: Between Tawhid and Reality," *Our Heritage* 9, no. 3 (May 1989): 14.

21. See Makarem, *The Druze Faith*, 43.

22. Al-'Aql is also the term for Universal Mind. "God made al-Aql the cause of all causes—the center of the circle, the axis of all thoughts and

beliefs, the pride of the worlds in all matters, temporal and religious." Abdallah Najjar, *The Druze: Millennium Scrolls Revealed*, 68.

23. Amin Muhammad Tali', *Asl al-Muwahhidin al-Druze wa-Usuluhum*, 106.

24. Betts, *The Druze*, 43. Toftbeck, "A Shorter Druze Catechism," asks, "Q. Is it fitting that Unitarianism should be granted to women? A. Yes; because the covenant was written for them; and they obey the summons of al-Hakim, as is mentioned in the document of the covenant of women, and so too in the document with regard to girls" (p. 40).

25. There are also three persons in southern Syria who have the title Shaykh al-'Aql. Betts, *The Druze*, 22.

26. Riad S. Yakzan, "The Sheykh El Akl Speaks," *Our Heritage* 2, no. 2 (June 1982): 16.

27. The May 1989 issue of *Our Heritage* (p. 21) lists the now twelve Mashaykhat al-'Aql in the United States and Canada as follows: Mouazza Aridi, Escondido, Cal.; Riyad Abi Faker, Reseda, Cal.; Ramiz Mohib Mounzer, Edmonton, Sask.; Adeeb Shami, Missusauga, Ont.; Walid Farhat, Bethal, Conn.; Fawzi Rawdah, Middletown, Conn.; Afef Hatoum, Titusville, Fla.; Dr. Galeb Maher, North Adams, Mass.; Dawood Jawhari, Fenton, Mich.; Sami Merhi, Paramus, N.J.; Moustafa Moukarim, Houston, Tex.; Ramiz Saab, Mclean, Va.

28. At burial the head of the deceased Druze is turned to face Mecca, but unlike the case of the burial of a Muslim no words of preparation are spoken in the ear to prepare the dead one for the coming of the questioning angels Munkar and Nakir. The Druze believe that the soul of the dead will be immediately reincarnated into another living Druze.

29. Tali', *Asl al-Muwahhidin*, 7.

30. Naff, *Becoming American*, 46–47.

31. Nada F. Najjar, "The Role of Women in Tawhid," unpublished manuscript, July 1988. "Historical records show that in the early stages of the 'Da'wa,' " writes Najjar, "women not only participated in learning, understanding and adopting the faith but were equally active and responsible in spreading its virtues" (p. 4).

32. Nada F. Najjar, "The Role of Women in Tawhid," 5–6.

33. Tali', *Asl al-Muwahhidin*, 130. Tali' notes that the restriction on multiple wives is based on the Qur'anic insistence that all wives must be treated justly; Druze belief is that justice to more than one wife is not possible and that polygamy does social, natural, and economic harm to the persons involved. If a man leaves his wife for three years without support or for five years even if he is supporting her, then they are divorced.

34. For a full treatment of the traditional role of women in Middle Eastern Druze society see Nissim Dana, *The Druze: A Religious Community in Transition*, chap. 9.

35. Nada F. Najjar, "The Role of Women in Tawhid," 11.

36. Dana, *The Druze*, 2–3, suggests that of the more than 400,000 Druze in the world, some 180,000 live in Syria, 140,000 in Lebanon, and 40,000 in Israel. Louis Perillier, *Les Druze*, 65, puts the figures quite a bit higher. A publication of the American Druze Women's Committee cited in Betts, *The Druze*, 64, indicates that there were an estimated 27,000 Druze in the United States in April 1984.

37. Makarem, *The Druze Faith*, 1.

38. See, for example, Naff, *Becoming American*, in which the author refers to the belief of both Druze and Muslims in their "religiously sanctioned superiority" and to their feelings of bitterness that Christian Arabs and Christian Europeans exhibit an obvious sense of superiority, indicating in her citing of the 1860 massacre some of her own sectarian bitterness.

39. Abu-Izzeddin, *The Druzes*, 107–8.

40. The memorabilia library and icons were taken by Druze militia to the Shouf for safekeeping and were recently returned to the monastery.

41. Muhammad Said Massoud, *I Fought as I Believed*, xiii-xiv.

42. See Naff, *Becoming American*, 34–37.

43. Ibid., 84–85.

44. Ibid., 241–43.

45. *Our Heritage* 5, no. 3 (September 1985): 27.

46. Fred Massey, "Albakourat al-Durzeyat Memorabilia," *Our Heritage* 2, no. 4 (December 1982): 18.

47. These branches, in order of establishment, were in Cleveland; Detroit; Waterbury, Conn.; Princeton, W.Va.; Kingsport, Tenn.; Charleston, W.Va.; Houston, Tex.; Hopewell, Va.; Washington, D.C.; and Oklahoma City, Ok. To qualify to form a branch a local group needed to have at least ten members. Henry Flehan, "History of A.D.S.," *Our Heritage* 2, no. 2 (June 1982): 10–13, 48.

48. See E. D. Beynon, "The Near East in Flint, Michigan: Assyrians and Druses and Their Antecedents." Beynon discusses the determination of the first Druze who came to Michigan to get along in their new home, working as sugar beet weeders, cement mixers for construction companies, and grocery store clerks. At the time of that writing they had developed a significant retail trade with several subsidiary stores owned by Druze.

49. "On Looking Back Seventy Years," *Our Heritage* 10, no. 2 (Fall 1990): 26.

50. The conventions were rotated among various cities to allow for the attendance of members who could not travel every year to different places. Flehan, "History of A.D.S.," *Our Heritage* 2, no. 1 (March 1982): 16.

51. Flehan, "History of A.D.S.," *Our Heritage* 2, no. 1 (March 1982): 16.

52. Ajaj N. Andary, "History of the A.D.S.," *Our Heritage* 2, no. 4 (December 1982): 30.

53. Andary, "History of A.D.S.," *Our Heritage* 2, no. 4 (December 1982): 30.

54. Today *Our Heritage* is published biannually and contains articles on Druze history, identity, and faith as well as on other matters of concern to the community. The *Druze Newsletter*, with specific news about Druze in various parts of the country, is published five times a year.

55. Makarem is also the author of *The Doctrine of the Ismailis* (Beirut, 1972).

56. Abdallah E. Najjar, "The Druze's Role and Dilemma in America," *Our Heritage* 2, no. 4 (December 1982): 23.

57. Ibid., 30.

58. This concern for the youth, and responsibility for their education, continues to be strong in the community. Writing in the fall 1990 issue of *Our Heritage*, ADS national president Ajaj N. Andary comments on the 1990 convention in Costa Mesa, California: "The main theme of this year's convention was centered on the 'Druze Youth.' Although we did have more youth participating in these panels than in other years, the interest shown in learning more about our faith and heritage seems to still be lacking in enthusiasm, seriousness, and dedication" (p. 3).

59. The election issue of the 1990 *ADS Bulletin* (no. 1) contains the platforms for the campaigns of candidates for positions such as president-elect and member of the Board of Directors. One of the candidates for the latter, acknowledging that he is articulating a "different" agenda for the Druze, expresses his hope for opening up the community: "We dream of the day when our children's children can invite their playmates to come to the Assembly of Wisdom, our Khalwa. We dream of the day when we can publicly declare the tenets of the Tawhid faith and embrace any who can qualify as brother and sister" (p. 10).

60. "Like all Gnostic beliefs, At-tawheed is surrounded with secrecy. Such practice is to protect the Gnostic knowledge from those who are not prepared to comprehend it. At-tawheed is not achieved by common logical approaches ... but rather [by] deep desire to achieve unity with the universe by denying the lower self and its earthly desires, and striving to rise to the higher self, so that the unity with God can be achieved." Naji Jurdi, "At-Tawheed, A New Approach," *Our Heritage* 10, no. 2 (Fall 1990): 22.

61. On the agenda of the Feb. 7–8, 1987, meeting of the ADS Committee on Religious Affairs, for example, were the questions "What is a Druze Descendent?" and "What is a Druze Follower?" *Our Heritage* 7, no. 2 (Spring 1987): 3.

62. Richard Childs, *Flint Journal*, November 5, 1981; reprinted in *Our Heritage* 2, no. 1 (March 1982): 24–25.

63. *Our Heritage* 5, no. 3 (September 1985): 40.

64. "Profile," *Our Heritage* 2, no. 4 (December 1982): 20.

65. Yakzan, "The Sheykh El Akl Speaks."

66. "Report of the Michigan Branch of the American Druze Society," *Our Heritage* 5, no. 1 (April 1985): 15.

67. *Our World* 1, no. 1 (Fall 1984): 53. In *The Druze*, Betts writes, "Popular misconceptions of the Druze as a secretive band of savage warriors who showed no mercy" have given way to "a fairer, more balanced view reflecting some well-intentioned research [that] had begun to appear in the media" (p. 108). Betts credits ADPAC with much of this improvement and reports that ADPAC is now in abeyance pending the establishment of an official Druze lobby in Washington.

68. ADPAC, letter to ADS members, December 20, 1984.

69. See Jay Goldsworthy, "How Hollywood Came Together for Jesse Jackson," *News Circle on Arab American Community Affairs* 16, no. 176 (August 1988): 33–36.

70. *Our Heritage* 5, no. 3 (September 1985): 27.

71. Many Druze, especially in earlier decades, became at least nominally Christian in the American environment, usually either Presbyterian or Methodist. Betts, *The Druze*, 64.

72. Ajaj Andary, "American Druze Youth Issues & Concerns," *Our Heritage* 10, no. 2 (Fall 1990): 34.

73. Flehan, "The History of the A.D.S.," *Our Heritage* 1, no. 2 (June 1981): 10.

74. Mohamed Khodr Halabi, "Tawhid Faith, A Personal View," *Our Heritage* 11, no. 1 (Spring 1991): 11.

75. Sahar Muakasa, "Marhaba, Ikhwani fi al-Tawhid," *Our Heritage* 11, no. 1 (Spring 1991): 5.

76. Samah HeLal, "Is America Ready for Tawhid?," *Our Heritage* 7, no. 3 (Summer 1987): 8–11.

77. In traditional Druze services in the villages of Lebanon congregants meet on Thursday night. The first part of the service is instructional in character, open to juhhal and children. It consists of explication of the texts by the elders and includes advice to the juhhal. Then the juhhal and children are dismissed, and the 'uqqal continue their service and chanting.

78. Letter from a reader, *Our Heritage* 10, no. 2 (Fall 1990): "The greatest damage to this movement of enlightenment is the apologetics by, of, and for a glorious past. Tradition is the antithesis of Tawhid" (p. 6).

79. Abdallah E. Najjar, unpublished devotional talk to members of the ADS Committee on Religious Affairs at the thirty-eighth annual Druze convention, June 19, 1985.

• • • • • *Chapter 3*

1. Some Ahmadi officials put the figure considerably higher. M. A. Rashid Yahya, missionary to the midwest region in Glen Ellyn, Illinois, said several years ago that there were more than 10,000 Ahmadis in the United States alone.

2. "Introduction to Ahmadiyyat," pamphlet of the Ahmadiyya Movement in Islam (Canadian National Headquarters, 10610 Jane Street, Maple, Ont. L6A 1S1), March 1989.

3. An Ahmadi translation of the Qur'an with commentary provides excellent information on the Ahmadiyya understanding of the Qur'anic message.

4. Muhammad Zafrulla Khan, *Ahmadiyyat: The Renaissance of Islam.*

5. Alhaj Ata Ullah Kaleem, unpublished manuscript, 1982.

6. Hazrat Mirza Ghulam Ahmad, *The Essence of Islam*, 1:ix-x.

7. "In my early youth I saw in a dream that I was in a magnificent building which was very clear and neat where people were talking about the Holy Prophet (on whom be peace). I enquired from the people where the Holy Prophet was and they pointed to a room which I entered along with other persons. When I presented myself to him he was much pleased, and returned my greeting with a better greeting. I can still recall and can never forget his charm and beauty and the kind and affectionate look that he directed toward me. He won my heart with his love and the beauty and glory of his countenance." Ghulam Ahmad, *Tadhkirah*, 1.

8. Muhammad Zafrulla Khan, *Ahmadiyyat: The Renaissance of Islam*, xiii.

9. Ahmadis understand this possibility differently, and cite a Hadith attributed to Aisha and reported by Jalal al-Din al- Suyuti, "Say he was Khataman Nabiyyeen, but do not say that there will be no prophet after him." B. A. Rafiq, *Truth about Ahmadiyyat*, 41.

10. Alhaj Ataullah Khallem, "Holy Prophet Muhammad as Khataman Nabiyyeen," *Muslim Sunrise* 56, no. 4 (1990): 36.

11. According to Humphrey J. Fisher, *Ahmadiyya*, 62–76, in 1891 Ahmad claimed that he was the promised Messiah of Islam. Muhammad Zafrulla Khan, *Ahmadiyyat*, xii, observes that Muslims have generally agreed that the Mahdi-Messiah would come in the last decade of the Christian nineteenth century, or the fourteenth century Hegira. There are reports that in 1904 Ghulam Ahmad proclaimed himself to be the second advent of the Avatar Krishna. Mohammed Elias Burney, *Qadiani Movement*, 9; compare Muhammad al-Khadr Husayn, *Al-Qadyaniyya*, 10.

12. Ghulam Ahmad, *The Philosophy of the Teachings of Islam*, vii.

13. From the inside of the front cover of Ghulam Ahmad, *Objectives Explained.*

14. The present khalifa of the Ahmadiyya has addressed the matter of the name of the community, defending its continuity with Islam: "The names Ahmadi, Ahmadiyyat, etc., do not point to a new religion. Ahmadis are Muslims and their religion is Islam. . . . Ahmadis have adopted the names Ahmadiyyat, Ahmadiyya Movement, Ahmadiyya Jama'at and so on. But the adoption of a name is not the adoption of a new religion. . . . The names Ahmadi, Ahmadiyyat, etc., are meant only to distinguish Ahmadi Muslims from other Muslims, Ahmadi interpretation from other interpretations of Islam." Hazrat Mirza Bashir-ud-Din Mahmud Ahmad, *Invitation to Ahmadiyyat*, 3.

15. Muhammad 'Ali, *The Ahmadiyyah Movement*, 20.

16. The headquarters of the Lahore Jamaat is 36911 Walnut Street, Newark, Cal., 94567, and the organization's official publication is the periodical *Islamic Review.*

17. N. A. Faruqui, *Ahmadiyyat: In the Service of Islam.*

18. Bashir-ud-Din Mahmud Ahmad, *Introduction to the Study of the Holy Quran*, 438.

19. *Ahmadiyya Gazette* (May 1982): 2.

20. Bashir-ud-Din Mahmud Ahmad, *The Ahmadiyya Movement in Islam*, 12.

21. Quote from Burney, *Qadiani Movement*, xii. Burney also quotes Ghulam Ahmad himself has having said, "It is our duty not to recognize non-Ahmadis as Muslims, and not to offer prayers behind them, because they are disbelievers in one of the Prophets of God (Mirza Qadiani himself). This is an affair of religion. None has discretion to do anything in the matter" (p. xii).

22. Spencer Lavan, *The Ahmadiyah Movement*, 110–14; compare 'Ali, *Ahmadiyyah Movement*, 17.

23. See Faruqui, *Ahmadiyyat*, 1, in which the author describes Islam in India in the nineteenth century as being "under severe attack from Christian missionaries and orientalists, and like-minded opponents of Islam (such as the Hindu Arya Samaj)."

24. Ghulam Ahmad, *Message of Peace*, 8–9.

25. "Instead of rebutting the monotheism or other actual teachings of Islam, [Christian missionaries] tried to destroy the faith of the Muslims in their religion by attacking what was, in fact, the misrepresented form of certain of its teachings, and to weaken their devotion to the Holy Prophet Muhammad by carrying out a character assassination based on a completely distorted picture of some aspects of his life." Faruqui, *Ahmadiyyat*, 5.

26. Rafiq, *Truth about Ahmadiyyat*, 33. See also p. 29, quoting Ghulam Ahmad's *Nurul Quran:* "The Jesus who is presented by the Christians, who claimed to be God and condemned everyone else except himself, both those who had gone before and who were to come after, as accursed, as having

been guilty of vices the recompense of which is a curse, is regarded by us as deprived of Divine mercy. The Holy Qur'an makes no reference to this impertinent and foul-mouthed Jesus. We are surprised at the conduct of one who considered that God was subject to death and himself claimed to be God and who reviled such righteous ones as were thousand times better than him."

27. Ibid., 33.

28. Ibid., 20.

29. Faruqui, *Ahmadiyyat*, 6, remarks that in the nineteenth century there were beliefs prevalent among the Muslims that made Ghulam Ahmad's task of counteracting Christian attacks on Islam even more difficult. Most prominent among those beliefs were that Jesus did not die but was taken straight to heaven, where he is still alive, and that Jesus will come again toward the end of time to save the Muslim community. These ideas, he says, were taken from the Christian creed of the ascension and the Second Coming. Christians, therefore, were able to exploit the situation by citing the Qur'an itself to prove that no human being or prophet could physically ascend to heaven and that prophets needed food for their physical bodies (which Jesus did not after the ascension). Thus, they could argue, Muslims must agree with Christians that Jesus was more than human, i.e., the Son of God. See chapter 2 of this work for a summary of the arguments and teachings regarding the death of Jesus.

30. Rashid Ahmad Chaudhri, *A Book of Religious Knowledge*, 69–70; J. Gordon Melton, ed., *The Encyclopedia of American Religions*, 340.

31. Bashir-ud-Din Mahmud Ahmad, *Invitation to Ahmadiyyat*, 12.

32. *Mubahala* is a synonym for *mula'ana* (curse contest). The event to which this Qur'an verse refers is the meeting of the Prophet Muhammad in 632 with a deputation from the Christians of Najran over a dispute on Christology and prophetology. See L. Massignon, "La mubahala de Medine et l'hyperdulie de Fatima," 550.

33. Lavan, "Polemics and Conflicts in Ahmadiyya History," notes that in 1891 a mubahala was issued to Ghulam Ahmad by 'Abd al-Haqq Ghaznavi over the issue of the death of Jesus, the first recorded time of such a challenge issued by one Muslim to another rather than by a Muslim to a non-Muslim.

34. *Review of Religions* 84, no. 1 (January 1989): 46. The mubahala is also the object of ridicule on the part of Ahmadi detractors. A 1966 publication from South Africa, strongly opposed to the Ahmadi movement, reported that cases are known in which the last "Mirza Qadiani" cursed someone in the context of such a contest and prophesied his death. The death occurred, in which "Mirza Qadiani" was suspected but not actually implicated. Burney, *Qadiani Movement*, 18. In 1989 a certain Hafiz Bashir Ahmad Masri made what were deemed to be "deragotory and baseless" al-

legations against the second and third Ahmadi khalifas and against the family of the fourth khalifa. In response the Imam of Jamaat Ahmadiyya issued another mubahala.

35. Faruqui, *Ahmadiyyat*, 108.

36. *Al-Hakim*, May 31, 1901, quoted in Faruqui, *Ahmadiyyat*, 115–16.

37. Bashir-ud-Din Mahmud Ahmad, *The Ahmadiyya Movement in Islam*, 13.

38. Bashir-ud-Din Mahmud Ahmad, *Ahmadiyyat or the True Islam*, 361–62.

39. Bashir-ud-Din Mahmud Ahmad, *Invitation to Ahmadiyyat*, 52. Ahmadi critics have long charged that the reason the early Ahmadi khalifas were so outspoken against the violent form of jihad was because they were strongly under the influence of Christian missionaries and that they hoped to win Western favor and Western support for their movement. Ghulam Ahmad has even been accused of announcing his readiness to shed his own blood as well as that of other Ahmadis in support of the cause of the colonial British government in India. Burney, *Qadiani Movement*, 34.

40. For a detailed summary of the controversy between Ghulam Ahmad and Muslims and Christians over such issues as his teachings about Jesus and jihad and his claim to be the Mahdi, see Lavan, "Polemics and Conflict in Ahmadiyya History," 283–303.

41. Bashir-ud-Din Mahmud Ahmad, *The Ahmadiyya Movement in Islam*, 440.

42. For Sunni views of the end of time see Smith and Haddad, *The Islamic Understanding of Death and Resurrection.*

43. Muhammad Zafrulla Khan, *Ahmadiyyat*, 175.

44. Webb, who later served as U.S. consul to the Philippines, sought financial support from Indian Muslims to spread Islam in North America. For several years he published a journal called *Moslem World*. He also published several books, including *A Few Facts About Turkey Under the Reign of Abdul Hamid II* (New York: Published by the author, 1895); *Islam in America* (New York: Oriental Publishing Co., 1893); and *The Three Lectures of Mohammed Alexander Russell Webb, Esq.* (Madras: Moulvi Hassan Ali, n.d.). Webb also represented Islam at the World Parliament of Religions in Chicago, founded the Oriental Publishing Company, established a mosque in New York City, and assisted the Ahmadiyya in some of their first translation projects. See Richard B. Turner, "The Ahmadiyya Mission to Blacks in the United States in the 1920's," 51.

45. Muhammad Zafrulla Khan, *Ahmadiyyat*, 175. Khan also cites a letter written by Webb to Dr. Mufti Muhammad Sadiq upon the death of Ghulam Ahmad: "Hazrat Mirza Ghulam Ahmad accomplished a great undertaking and conveyed the light of truth to hundreds of hearts. . . . I have been deeply affected by the fearless earnestness with which he continued to

spread the truth in the pursuance of his purpose. Without a doubt God Almighty had chosen him for this great enterprise which he fulfilled completely" (p. 176).

46. Ibid., 177.

47. 'Ali, *The Ahmadiyyah Movement*, 21–22.

48. Qazi Muhammad Barakatullah, "John A. Dowie—A False Prophet," *Muslim Sunrise* (Special Convention Issue, 1975): 4.

49. Barakatullah, "John A. Dowie," 4.

50. Turner, "The Ahmadiyya Mission," 50–51.

51. Turner, "Islam in the United States in the 1920's," 142–43. In "The Ahmadiyya Mission" (p. 52), Turner contends that Sadiq accomplished this by distinguishing between commandments and permissions. Muslims must follow the commandments, but have flexibility on the permissions. Therefore in countries in which polygamy is illegal, for example, they are expected to refrain from the "permission" of polygamy.

52. Ibid., 147, citing early *Moslem Sunrise* reports.

53. Turner, "The Ahmadiyya Mission," 56.

54. Mary Caroline Holmes, "Islam in America," *Moslem World* 16 (1926): 264. Holmes's final remark, clearly her own defense of Christianity, was that "He [Jesus] does not lie buried in Srinagar, but is alive forevermore, as Islam will yet find true" (p. 266).

55. M. Yusaf Khan, "Some of Our Missionaries," *Muslim Sunrise* 42, no. 4 (December 1975): 14.

56. For example, a Sunni Imam being interviewed for a recent survey of Muslims in America recalled information about the prohibition against the eating of pork taken from an Ahmadi manual. "Islam prohibits the use of the pig for the following reasons: male pig cohabits with male pig, and sodomy is in consequence expected naturally to prevail among pork eaters. Pig is too fond of cohabitations; excessive lust in men and women using pork is the result." Haddad and Lummis, *Islamic Values in the United States*, 114.

57. See Williams, *Religion of Immigrants from India and Pakistan*, 101–2.

58. Turner, "The Ahmadiyya Mission," 57.

59. *Moslem Sunrise* 22, no. 4 (October 1923): 263–64.

60. *Moslem Sunrise* 3, no. 1 (January 1924): 45.

61. A. T. Hoffert, "Moslem Propaganda: The Hand of Islam Stretches Out to Aframerica," *Messenger* 9, no. 5 (May 1927): 141.

62. Charles S. Braden, "Islam in America," 313. The Imam of the American Fazl Mosque in Washington, D.C., reported in 1982 that he estimated some three to four thousand black families were members of the Ahmadiyya movement and that they well outnumbered the white members.

63. Turner, "Islam in the United States in the 1920's," 154–58. "The Ahmadiyas were Indians—one of the 'darker races of the world,' and the

Garvey movement stressed the internationalist perspective which led Afro-Americans to think of themselves in concert with Africans and the 'darker races of the world' over against white Europeans and Americans" (p. 158).

64. As Mubasher Ahmad put it in a 1991 communication with the authors, "It was mainly the African Americans who responded firmly and strongly to Ahmadiyya missionary work. Later on the religious aspect was exploited by some of the new converts . . . and they left the Ahmadiyya fold to start new religio-political movements. Elijah Muhammad, though never taught the correct teachings of the Qur'an, always possessed a copy of the Ahmadiyya translation of the Qur'an and was much influenced by the Ahmadiyya literature and missionaries."

65. Turner, "Islam in the United States in the 1920's," 184, 187.

66. *Moslem Sunrise* 3, no. 3 (July 1930): 11. Other notices in this issue of the journal discuss the visit of a missionary from India who converted 200, 650, or 700 of Chicago's citizens, indicating (p. 34) that they were "Turks, negroes and a few whites."

67. *Muslim Sunrise* (Special Convention Issue, 1975): 5.

68. Turner, "The Ahmadiyya Mission," 62.

69. Braden reflected on his experience with this Ahmadi missionary: "Sufi Bengalee and I became warm friends, and often discussed the problems of a missionary in a foreign land, I having had a decade of missionary experience abroad. Sufi Bengalee was a deeply devoted Muslim, whose abiding faith in God and childlike trust in the goodness and guidance of Allah often left one with a feeling of deep admiration for him and of humility in his presence." "Islam in America," 312.

70. Life was not easy for missionaries such as Bengalee; an article by his wife entitled "Some Nostalgic Memories of the Early Years of the American Mission" has recalled the difficulties and hardships of those early years. *Muslim Sunrise* 42, no. 4 (December 1975): 13–15.

71. M. R. Bengalee, "Religious Prejudice—Can It Be Overcome?," *Muslim Sunrise* 56, no. 3 (1990): 18, 21.

72. Turner, "Islam in the United States in the 1920's," 188–89.

73. From information provided by Ata Ullah Kaleem, Imam of the American Fazl Mosque in Washington, D.C., in a communication with the authors, May 27, 1982.

74. Khalil A. Nasir, "The History of the Ahmadiyyat in America," *Muslim Sunrise* (Special Convention Issue, 1975): 10–11. Ahmadis have been diligent in their efforts to keep in touch with American government officials; early issues of *Moslem Sunrise* contain excerpts of letters sent by community officials to U.S. presidents and other political leaders.

75. "The Ahmadiyya Movement in Islam, Canada," in-house publication, lists offices in British Columbia, Alberta, Manitoba, Ontario, and Saskatchewan.

76. Mubasher Ahmad, communication with the authors, 1991.

77. Turner, "Islam in the United States in the 1920's," 197–200.

78. Chaudhri, *Religious Knowledge,* 60–61.

79. Muhammad Iqbal, *Islam and Ahmadism,* 2–7.

80. S. Abul A'la Maududi, *The Qadiani Problem,* 40.

81. S. N. Ahmad, *The Anti-Ahmadiyya Stance,* quotes a 1984 sermon by the Imam of the Shaki Mosque in Lahore in which the Imam supported the martial law ordinance: "1. The domes of all the Ahmadi places of worship should be demolished forthwith. 2. The direction of their places of worship should be so changed that they no longer face Mecca. 3. Ahmadis should be prevented from offering their prayers in congregation. 4. They should be stoned to death one and all" (p. 19). Ahmad wonders what logic there is in the remaining demands if the demand of stoning to death is implemented.

82. Hazrat Mirza Taher Ahmad, *An Open Invitation to the Mubahala.*

83. "Rabitat al-'Alam al-Islami Tuhadhdhir min Khitat Fi'at al-Qadianiyya," *Muslim Star* 20, no. 176 (December 1983): 28.

84. For specific accusations against the Qadianis in Saudi Arabia, in which they are put in a category with Masons, communists, existentialists, and Baha'is, see Abd al-Rahman 'Amira, *Al-Madhahib al-Mu'asira wa-Mawqif al-Islam Minha;* for a similar critique from Egypt see Muhammad Isma'il al-Nadawi, *Al-Qadyaniyya, 'Ard wa-Tahlil;* compare Abu al-Hassan 'Ali al-Nadawi, *Al-Qadyani wa-al-Qadyaniyya;* Hassan 'Issa 'Abd al-Zahir, *Al-Qadyaniyya: Nash'atuha wa-Tatawwuruha;* and Ahmad Muhammad 'Awf, *Al-Qadyaniyya: al-Khatar Alladhi Yuhaddid al-Islam.*

85. Mubasher Ahmad, communication with the authors, March 1991.

86. Presently there are seven mosques in America: the American Fazl Mosque in Washington, D.C.; Annour Mosque in Pittsburgh; Sadiq Mosque in St. Louis; Fazli Umar Mosque in Dayton, Ohio; Renaissance Mosque in Detroit; Qureshi Yusuf Mosque in Tucson, Ariz.; and Sadiq Mosque in Chicago. Ahmadi centers are located in thirty-five cities in the United States.

87. Mubasher Ahmad, communication with the authors, 1991.

88. G. H. Bousquet, "Moslem Religious Influences in the United States," 41–42; compare Turner, "The Ahmadiyya Mission," 56–57.

89. Braden, "Islam in America," 309.

90. Braden, "Moslem Missionaries in America,"335.

91. Mubasher Ahmad, communication with the authors, March 18, 1991.

92. Williams, *Religion of Immigrants from India and Pakistan,* 102–3.

93. *Muslim Sunrise* 51, no. 1 (March 1984): 5–6.

94. Mubasher Ahmad, communication with the authors, 1991.

95. Muzaffar Ahmad Zafr, "Islam in the U.S.A.: History and Prospects," unpublished manuscript.

96. One of the points repeated in sections of the instructional material for children (and, presumably, for new converts) is that the reason for accepting the claim of Mirza Ghulam Ahmad to be the Mahdi is that he is the only one in his time to have laid claim to that office. "To deny his claim is to deny the prophecies made by God and those of the Scriptures of other religions." *Lessons on Islam, Book IV,* 64–65.

97. Members of the Chicago Jamaat, for example, participated in a surplus cheese program sponsored by the U.S. government by which cheese products were distributed to needy individuals. *Ahmadiyya Gazette* (May 1982): 5.

98. *Lajna News* (April 1981), photocopy, 3.

99. The last two of these are not published but distributed in photocopy form to members of the community. Both contain teachings of the community, special news about members and groups, and occasional activities such as Muslim games and crossword puzzles related to Ahmadiyya teachings.

100. "Lajna Imaillah U.S.A. 1981–1982, National Program," unpublished manuscript, 16.

101. Nycemeah Ameen, "The Maidservants of Allah," *Muslim Sunrise* (Special Convention Issue, 1975): 8.

102. Ibid., 12.

103. "The Appeal of Islam," *Ayesha* (Winter 1987): 15–16.

104. Amatul Hakim, "Islamic Solution to Teenage Problems," *Ayesha* (Winter 1987): 22.

105. In a letter to the editor of *Ayesha* (Winter 1986) a high school student named Angie in Columbia, Penn., wrote: "Is it really possible for someone who is very involved in the American dating and social system to give all that up?" A reader replied at length in the next issue (Spring-Summer 1987) urging Angie to be steadfast. "Pious Muslim women observe the veil (purdah)," he insisted, "to shield them from male attention when they are outside their homes. Men and women restrain their eyes and do not look at each other. This may seem odd to you, but it has saved Muslim society" (p. 30).

106. Shaikh Mubarak Ahmad, communication with the authors, June 22, 1987.

107. Maryam Ahmad, "Personal Experience Attending American Schools in Purdah," *Ayesha* (Spring-Summer 1983): 49–51.

108. Khadija Israfil Ahmad, "The Mantle of Freedom . . . The Spoils of War," *Ayesha* (Spring-Summer 1983): 54–58.

109. Zainab B. Collidge, "Purdah in These United States," *Ayesha* (Spring-Summer 1983): 61–63. Another dimension of purdah is the practice of arranged marriages, defended by the faithful of the community as both Islamic and as the guarantee of a happier marriage than usually is the case

when young men and women choose each other. See, for example, Saira Zubair, "Muslim Life in the U.S.A.: What's Love Got to Do With It?," *Ayesha* (Spring-Summer 1986): 18.

110. Humma Ahmad, "Purdah in a Public Junior High," *Ayesha* (Winter 1984): 50–51.

111. See Farzana Tehmeen Quader, "College Life in the U.S.—Experience of a Muslim Girl," *Ayesha* (Winter 1984): 51–53, in which the author rhapsodizes over the opportunities that being a student at Sweet Briar College provided for her to practice and propagate her faith.

112. Shakura J. Nooriah, "The Suggested Relationship of American Muslim Parents to Non-Muslim Schools," *Ayesha* (Spring-Summer 1983): 51–54.

113. Ayesha Hakeen, "An American Muslim in Ghana," *Ayesha* (Spring-Summer 1984): 60–64.

114. "What's in a Name?," *Ayesha* (Summer 1988): 31; names suggested for women are Amtul Basir (Hand Maiden of the All-Seeing), Amtul Wadud (Hand Maiden of the Loving), Ayilah (Sublime, High), Ayesha (Living, Prosperous), Farida (Precious Gem), Atiya (Gift, Present), Safiya (Pure), Zahrah (Blossom, Shining), Nafeesa (Precious, Valuable), Sakina (Tranquility, Calmness), and Amtul Haiyy (Hand Maiden of the Ever-Living).

115. Zainab B. Asad, "Arabic in the Land of the Beautiful," *Ayesha* (Winter 1987): 17–18.

116. "Among the families with mixed cultural and religious values," writes missionary Mubasher Ahmad, "the maintenance of a family system with puritanical orientation is next to impossible" (letter to the authors, March 18, 1991).

117. For further information about the Ahmadiyya movement see Taher Ahmad, *Murder in the Name of Allah;* Naeem Osman Memon, *Ahmadiyyat or Qadianism! Islam or Apostasy;* Iain Adamson, *Mirza Ghulam Ahmad of Qadian;* and Chaudhri and Shamim Ahmad, *Persecution of Ahmadi Muslims and Their Response.*

● ● ● ● ●   *Chapter 4*

1. Oliver Jones, Jr., "The Black Muslim Movement and the American Constitutional System," 421.

2. Archie Epps, ed., *The Speeches of Malcolm X at Harvard*, 81.

3. "Noble Drew Ali—A Centennial Remembrance (1886–1986)" mimeograph.

4. Clifton E. Marsh, *From Black Muslims to Muslims*, 41.

5. Moorish Press, Edition 26 (October 1976), p. 3.

6. E. U. Essien-Udom, *Black Nationalism*, 46.

7. Marsh, *From Black Muslims to Muslims*, 43. Noble Drew Ali, *The Holy Koran*, ascribes a similar experience to Jesus in the course of his life and works in Egypt among the gentiles: "I pray you brothers, let me go into your dismal crypts; and I would pass the hardest of your tests" (XXX:14).

8. "Noble Drew Ali—A Centennial Remembrance (1886–1986)."

9. Arthur H. Fauset, *Black Gods of the Metropolis*, 41. Gayraud Wilmore, *Black Religion and Black Radicalism*, comments that Moorish American (and other) efforts to find identity outside the United States "introduced into the traditional stream of black Christian theology an entirely new, non-Western perspective that was to become a tenacious element in the further development of black religion in the United States, offering a powerful attraction to black youth" (p. 159).

10. Noble Drew Ali, *The Holy Koran*, XLVII:1–6; compare "Acts of Moorish Science Temple of America," cited in Frank T. Simpson, "The Moorish Science Temple and Its 'Koran,' " 56–57.

11. Fauset, *Black Gods of the Metropolis*, generally considered a classic study of the Moorish Americans, contains an interesting interview of a member of the community challenging Fauset to consider his own identity as an African American. Asserting that he himself is Moorish American, responsible only to God, Allah, the interviewee says that the term *negro* is a name of scorn and contempt designed to perpetuate the slave condition. Negroes have no nation, no flag, no claim to identity, and neither do "blacks" or "Ethiopians." "The time is coming soon when all free people will have to know their nationality. So what," he asks his interviewer, "are you?" (pp. 115–16).

12. Noble Drew Ali, *The Holy Koran*, XLVIII:10.

13. A newspaper account of a 1934 court case involving the Moorish Science Temple, recounted in "A New Islam in America," *Moslem World* 25 (January 1935): 79, suggests that Noble Drew Ali was a prophet "descended from Mohammad." There is nothing in *The Holy Koran* that substantiates such a claim.

14. Noble Drew Ali, *The Holy Koran* XLVII:12.

15. Wilmore, *Black Religion and Black Radicalism*, 159–60.

16. "Noble Drew Ali—A Centennial Remembrance (1886–1986)."

17. "Garvey moved onto the center of the Harlem stage with all the ease and self-confidence of the man with a mission," one commentator has written. "He took to the streets, joining the soapbox and stepladder orators, and formed political alliances with some of Harlem's prominent radicals." Tony Martin, *Race First*, 9. Arna Bontemps described Garvey as "short, squat, beaming with visions, regally attired," a person who "in a spellbinding West Indian cadence, gave voice to dreams that literally blew the minds of a large segment of his impoverished generation of black humanity in the New World." Bontemps, *The Harlem Renaissance Remembered*, 6.

18. Essien-Udom, *Black Nationalism*, 50.

19. See, for example, Winthrop S. Hudson, *Religion in America*, 355, in which Hudson argues that like the "Black Jews" of the early part of the twentieth century, Garvey's Black Nationalists and Noble Drew Ali's Moorish Americans stressed black separateness. Compare Wilmore, *Black Religion and Black Radicalism*, 158–59, in which Wilmore argues that like some of the Church of God movements, the Moorish Science Temple illustrated the "flowering of the blackenization and alienation themes" originally developed in the late nineteenth and early twentieth centuries.

20. Sandra Weaver Bey, interview with the authors, 1987.

21. Noble Drew Ali, *The Holy Koran*, XLVIII:2–3. See *The Marcus Garvey and Universal Negro Improvement Association Papers*, 5:681.

22. George Eaton Simpson, *Black Religions in the New World*, 128. Simpson quotes a report in which Nation of Islam leader Elijah Muhammad declared, "I have always had a very high opinion of both the late Noble Drew Ali and Marcus Garvey and admired their courage in helping our people (the so-called Negroes) and appreciated their work. Both of these men were fine Muslims. The followers of Noble Drew Ali and Marcus Garvey should now follow me and cooperate with us in our work because we are only trying to finish up what those before us started." See also Theodore G. Vincent, *Black Power and the Garvey Movement*, 222–23.

23. Eric C. Lincoln, *The Black Muslims in America*, 57.

24. Photocopy courtesy of the U.S. embassy of the Kingdom of Morocco, Washington, D.C.

25. "The restoration of the Moorish flag to the descendants of Africa in America by Noble Drew Ali was of especial historic significance to the Moorish community and the world, for it took place in the United States during a time when the government of Morocco was in a state of subjugation to French rule (1912–1955), and could not raise the red flag with the five-pointed green star in the center, on African soil" (mimeograph statement for the centennial celebration of the Moorish American Science Temple in 1986).

26. Bontemps and Jack Conroy, *Anyplace but Here*, 205–206.

27. Fauset, *Black Gods of the Metropolis*, 42; Lincoln, *The Black Muslims in America*, 53.

28. Weaver Bey, interview with the authors, March 1991.

29. "History of the Moorish Science Temple," photocopy, 1986.

30. "Noble Drew Ali—A Centennial Remembrance (1886–1986)."

31. Ibid.

32. Ibid.

33. Ibid.

34. Fauset, *Black Gods of the Metropolis*, 43, reports that Moors in Detroit were considered by the police to be gangs of thieves and cutthroats.

35. "I hereby order all Moors that they must cease from all radical or agitating speeches while on their jobs, or in their homes, or on the streets. Stop flashing your cards before Europeans as this only causes confusion. We did not come to cause confusion; our work is to uplift the nation." Bontemps and Conroy, *Anyplace but Here*, 207.

36. Ibid., 106. Bontemps and Conroy identify some of these as "Old Moorish Healing Oil, Moorish Purifier Bath Compound, and Moorish Herb Tea for Human Ailments."

37. Fauset, *Black Gods of the Metropolis*, 43; compare Essien-Udom, *Black Nationalism*, 47. Turner has observed that among the factors contributing to the decline of the Moorish movement was what he called "economic exploitation and self-aggrandizing competition among leaders." "Islam in the Unitd States in the 1920's," 56.

38. Ibid., 57.

39. Bontemps and Conroy, *Anyplace but Here*, 207.

40. Ibid., 207–8.

41. Fauset, *Black Gods of the Metropolis*, 43–44.

42. Marsh, *From Black Muslims to Muslims*, 48.

43. George Eaton Simpson, *Black Religions in the New World*, 270.

44. "Today Noble Drew Ali's corpse lies in a stately mausoleum in Lincoln Cemetery. It can be viewed from windows from all sides and he looks exactly as though he will keep his promise to 'rise up and walk with my people again' sometime in the very near future. Fez-wearing Moors (and there are many of them still to be seen around the city) keep a vigil at the cemetery to be on hand when Noble Drew gets up from his death couch." Dan Burley, "Elijah Muhammad: Part II—Pomp, Mysticism Key to Power," *Chicago Defender*, August 22, 1959, p. 2. See also Essien-Udom, *Black Nationalism*, 387 n.54.

45. The report of Marsh, *From Black Muslims to Muslims*, 49, that "he had the sign of the star and crescent in his eyes and they knew right then he was the prophet reincarnated into his chauffeur" has little credence within the Moorish American community.

46. As of the early 1990s his wife was a spiritual leader of the Chicago community.

47. Other splinter groups in the 1930s seem to have identified W. D. Fard, who according to one view was the mysterious figure who selected Elijah Muhammad to be Messenger to the Black Man, as Ali's legitimate successor.

48. "Moorish Science Temple Faithful Granted Contribution Moratorium," *Newark Evening News*, September 7, 1934, p. 17.

49. Wilmore, *Black Religion and Black Radicalism*, 160, 232.

50. Frank T. Simpson, "The Moorish Science Temple and Its 'Koran,'" 56–57.

51. Melton, ed., *The Encyclopedia of American Religions*, 340.

52. Noble Drew Ali, *The Holy Koran*, 3. On the same page Noble Drew Ali declares that "the lessons of this pamphlet are not for sale, but for the sake of humanity, as I am a prophet and the servant is worthy of his hire, you can receive this pamphlet at expenses."

53. A Moorish-American woman in New Jersey has compiled a "Holy Koran Definer" in which she has defined all of the terms used in the scripture.

54. One of the first analysts to reveal the teachings of the Moorish Science Temple Koran was Bousquet, "Moslem Religious Influences in the United States," 40–44. His work was followed by the first edition of Fauset's *Black Gods of the Metropolis* in 1944; Fauset admitted to having seen *The Holy Koran* but would not discuss its contents. Frank T. Simpson, "The Moorish Science Temple and Its 'Koran,'" 56–61, provided a much fuller description of its contents than did Bousquet. Simpson also reported the "discovery" by Duncan Black Macdonald that the first nineteen chapters of *The Holy Koran* were taken from a volume by Levy H. Dowling entitled *The Aquarian Gospel of Jesus the Christ* (reprinted in a paperback edition by DeVorss of Marina Del Rey, Cal., in 1988). In 1965 E. E. Calverly, "Negro Muslims in Hartford," identified the source of chapters 20–25 of *The Holy Koran* as a 1923 volume entitled *Infinite Wisdom*, a copy of which was at that time in the possession of Professor Elmer Douglas of the Hartford Seminary. The title page of the book suggests that it was translated into Chinese from ancient manuscripts found in the Grand Temple of Tibet six hundred years before the birth of Christ.

55. "Koran Questions for Moorish Children," with a brief introduction by Samuel M. Zwemer. Zwemer refers to the document as a catechism, a term which is not used by Moorish Americans because of its Christian connotations.

56. Weaver Bey, interview with the authors, 1987.

57. The address is 1000 North Hoyne, Chicago, Illinois.

58. Cynthia Hale, "A Study of the Moorish Science Temple of America," unpublished manuscript, 1979, reports that the headquarters of one branch of the movement moved on January 15, 1975, to Baltimore, Maryland, under the leadership of Dr. R. German Bey.

59. Information on the organizational structure of the community has been provided by members of the Hartford Moorish American Temple in interviews with the authors conducted in 1987 and 1991.

60. See, for example, Marsh, *From Black Muslims to Muslims*, 44.

61. Fauset, *Black Gods of the Metropolis*, 52, declares that the Moors are enjoined to pray three times a day, but that is not the understanding of many in the community.

62. Hale, "A Study of the Moorish Science Temple of America," reports that she has talked with members who say that the hand greeting

is equivalent to a kind of "high-five" given in the name of love, truth, peace, freedom, and justice.

63. Hale, "A Study of the Moorish Science Temple of America," 79.

64. "A field of grass will grow on its own, but a garden of flowers requires cultivation. And if our children are to bloom and grow, deliberate educational stimulations must be introduced early into each child's home." From a pamphlet advertising a parent/child development seminar in Newark, November 17, 1984, conducted by the Moorish Institute.

65. "Noble Drew Ali—A Centennial Celebration (1886–1986)," cites Haani Mary M. Bey of Williamstown, N.J., for the "Moorish Mother of the Year Award," and Joseph Jeffries El for the "Noble Drew Ali Award" in recognition of his work to "brighten the hopes of our youth in order that their courage is increased to dare and do wondrous things" (p. 22).

66. The turban is reminiscent of Indian garb and may possibly have been the product of Ahmadiyya influence.

67. "Tho we are not travelling in covered wagons, camel caravans, nor space shuttles, we pioneer a fiscal frontier whose joint exploration shall reveal revitalized Moorish-American and Moorish-African economies. The key to our successes lies in the phrase 'economic security.' " "Noble Drew Ali—A Centennial Celebration (1886–1986)."

68. This discussion of the reincarnation doctrine of the Moorish Americans is based on information provided by Sandra Weaver Bey of the Hartford community, March 1991.

69. See Abbie White, "Christian Elements in Negro American Muslim Religious Beliefs," for a detailed if highly interpretive comparison of some of the beliefs of the Moorish Science Temple and the Nation of Islam.

70. Marsh, *From Black Muslims to Muslims*, 45, presents in chart form the parallels (and differences) as he sees them between the Moorish Science Temple and the Nation of Islam.

71. *When I Grow Up*, 10–11.

72. "Noble Drew Ali—A Centennial Celebration (1886–1986)," 8.


• • • • • *Chapter 5*


1. The term *Ansar* is used by some in the African-American convert community to refer to themselves in relation to immigrant Muslims. In such instances Ansar is in reference to supporters of Muhammad in Medina at the time of the Hijra.

2. See Lincoln, *The Black Muslims in America*; Lincoln, "The American Muslim Mission in the Context of American Social History"; and Essien-Udom, *Black Nationalism*.

3. See Turner, "Islam in the United States in the 1920's."

4. Malcolm X, "God's Judgment of White America," 121–48.

5. Isa Muhammad, *The Book of Lam*, 29.

6. Isa Muhammad, "Christ Is the Answer," 33.

7. Ibid., 32.

8. Isa Muhammad, "Are the Ansars (in the West) a Self Made Sect?," 4.

9. Sayyid Isa al Haadi al-Mahdi [Isa Muhammad], *The Ansaar Cult. The Truth about the Ansaarullah Community in America. Truth Is Truth. Rebuttal to the Slanderers*, 30 (cited hereinafter as *Rebuttal*).

10. "Are you going to compliment me with the ability to have written all these books myself? . . . Obviously ALLAH is guiding my pen." Mahdi, *Rebuttal*, 62.

11. See Isa Muhammad, "Why Allah Should Not Be Called God." Muslims in the United States are not in agreement as to whether to use Allah or God in reference to the divinity. The early immigrants preferred God. Pakistanis and recent immigrants from the Arab world committed to a revivalist perception insist on Allah.

12. Isa Muhammad, *The Book of Lam*, 120.

13. The Sudanese Mahdi was the charismatic Sufi leader who led his followers, known as the Ansar, in an uprising against the British in the Sudan. He became famous when he defeated British commander Charles Gordon at Khartoum in the late nineteenth century.

14. Mahdi, *Rebuttal*, 55–62. See Isa Muhammad, *The Book of Lam*, 93–94, for a brief commentary on the Five Percenters, whose claims to a large organization he mildly dismisses as untrue.

15. An immigrant Muslim leader who was the head of a mosque in Brooklyn and who appears to have had a profound influence on African-American Islam in the city.

16. Isa Muhammad has a personalized license plate on his car which reads "Dr York." The "Dr." comes from his claim to have acquired a doctorate in Islamic law while he was in the Sudan for four months in 1973.

17. Abu Ameenah Bilal Philips, *The Ansar Cult in America*.

18. Although Isa Muhammad professes at the end of *Rebuttal* that he finds Philips "a confused young man being used by the Saudian government" and will not level any accusations against him, in numerous other places in the volume he condemns him in no uncertain terms, including prophesying that Philips will burn in hell for his blasphemies against the Ansaru Allah.

19. This continues to be a very popular Ansar symbol. Ansar publications frequently carry advertisements for signet rings that feature the crescent and six-pointed star, which Ansars say symbolizes the 144,000 who are destined to enter paradise.

20. Mahdi, *Rebuttal*, 70ff.

21. Isa Muhammad has continued to insist on the identification of the Ansars with the Hebrews. "We are Hebrews!" he asserted in the late 1970s. "Yes, Muslims are Hebrews!!!" *The Book of Lam*, 126.

22. Mahdi, *Rebuttal*, 607.

23. The Khidr is referred to in the Qur'an in Sura 18:60–82.

24. Isa Muhammad, "Four Horsemen of the Apocalypse: Can the Holy Qur'an Solve It?," 16. In 1985 Isa Muhammad began a mystical order within the Ansaru Allah that he called "Sons of the Green Light." "It is a green light, the light of Shaikh Khidr (Melchesidek, SRA) illuminated by Allahu Subhaanahu Wa Ta'ala. The true Sufi knows this, because when he enters the mystical orders, he enters as a baby, soon thereafter, he becomes a tilmidh; and eventually a taalib. To become ultimately a master of wisdom, a perfect being, master of self, learning many secrets. This is the goal of the Sufi order of the Sons of the Green Light." "The Night of the 100 Raka'aat," 35.

25. "The Mahdiyya are the rightful rulers of the Islamic world," Isa Muhammad writes. "If the Ansaars would have followed the Mahdi Muhammad Ahmad son of Abdullah [1845–85] of the Sudan, into Mecca, the Ka'ba would have been in the hands of the Ansaars. The Sudanese are true Arabs of the pure seed of the Prophet Muhammad." Mahdi, *Rebuttal*, 25.

26. Isa Muhammad, "Hadrat Faatimah," 3.

27. See Bernard Cushmere, *This is the One*; Elijah Muhammad, *Messenger to the Blackman*; Elijah Muhammad, *The Fall of America*; Elijah Muhammad, *Our Savior Has Arrived*; and Tynetta Muhammad, *The Comer by Night*.

28. Isa Muhammad, "The Dog," 17.

29. Ibid., 25.

30. Mahdi, *Rebuttal*, 213–14.

31. Isa Muhammad, "Disco Music: The Universal Language of Good or Evil?," 9. On p. 7 of this publication Isa Muhammad contends that the high shrilling sound of white music is like the language of the jinn (fire spirits), that the Amorite in fact is the jinn.

32. Ibid., 7–9.

33. Mahdi, *Rebuttal*, 293.

34. Isa Muhammad, "Islamic Marriage Ceremony and Polygamy," 1.

35. Isa Muhammad, "Racism in Islam," 95.

36. Isa Muhammad, "Disco Music: The Universal Language of Good or Evil?" 12. It is interesting to contrast this with a segment of a letter from the Ku Klux Klan to the black community: "Your desire for white women is an admission of your own racial inferiority. One reason why we whites will never accept you into our white society is because a nigger's chief ambition in life is to sleep with a white woman, thereby polluting her." *Al-Jihad Akbar* (February 1974): 9.

37. Isa Muhammad, "The Dog," 26. Compare Isa Muhammad, "Racism in Islam," 11: "The Devil's main objective is to get you (the original man) to corrupt your pure seed. He'll use every lie and gimmick he can to intermingle with you so as to perpetuate his cursed seed. The paleman and palewoman WANT to lay with you not only for sexual pleasure as you may be so naive to believe, but for the purpose of thriving off of your seed. Yet, had you researched the Scriptures . . . you would clearly see that it is an abomination in the eyes of the Lord to lay with the cursed Amorite."

38. Isa Muhammad, "The Night of the 100 Raka'aat," 46.

39. Isa Muhammad, "Christ Is the Answer," 47.

40. Isa Muhammad, "The Dog," 1. The name of this publication is a clear play on words, as Isa Muhammad associates whites with Canaanites (canines).

41. Isa Muhammad, "Al Imam Isa Visits Egypt 1981," 3.

42. Ibid., 3, 10, 22. Isa Muhammad cites the Steppe Pyramid as an example of the knowledge and power that blacks possessed as ancient people, the sons and daughters of Allah.

43. "The fourth kingdom is in reality GREAT BRITAIN; America is an offshoot and a part of this empire."

44. Isa Muhammad, "Four Horsemen of the Apocalypse," 7.

45. Ibid., 10.

46. Always enjoying word play, Isa Muhammad in the Goals and Purposes statement says that Sudanese all over the world are under the spell of the Great Seal of the United States, the dollar bill.

47. See William A. Maesen, "Watchtower Influences on Black Muslim Eschatology: An Exploratory Story," 322.

48. Isa Muhammad, "Christ Is the Answer," 55.

49. Ibid., 43.

50. Isa Muhammad, "Are the Ansars (in the West) a Self Made Sect?" 17.

51. Philips, *The Ansar Cult*, 80.

52. Mahdi, *Rebuttal*, 415–16.

53. Isa Muhammad, "Four Horsemen of the Apocalypse," 14.

54. Isa Muhammad, "Christ Is the Answer," 47.

55. The inside cover of *The Book of Lam*.

56. Isa Muhammad, *The Book of Lam*, 13.

57. Mahdi, *Rebuttal*, 161. See, however, an earlier version, in Isa Muhammad, "Christ Is the Answer," in which Isa Muhammad refers to himself as "the annointed one" (p. 27) as well as one who has had previous existence. "Before I came to this flesh in 1945, I was here in the spirit from one end of the earth to the other" (p. 28). According to a May 1993 communication from the community, "He is not the Messiah Isa the Son of Mary, Isa al Masiyh, Ruwhu Allah, any name you want to use. He was the first be-

gotten of these anointed ones but he is not the Messiah Jesus. He is here to herald in Jesus' coming. This is his job to prepare people for his return."

58. Isa Muhammad, *The Book of Lam,* 17.

59. Philips, *The Ansar Cult,* 58.

60. Isa Muhammad, *The Book of Lam,* 3.

61. As is illustrated in other places in this volume, Isa Muhammad was only one of many to claim for himself the status of reformer or renewer of the faith understood by Muslims to come once in every century.

62. Isa Muhammad, "Are the Ansars (in the West) a Self Made Sect?" 2; compare Isa Muhammad, "Christ Is the Answer," 25.

63. Philips, *The Ansar Cult,* 8.

64. Isa Muhammad, *The Book of Lam,* 134.

65. Isa Muhammad, "Racism in Islam," 101.

66. Isa Muhammad, "Al Imam Isa Visits Egypt 1981," 3.

67. Others Isa Muhammad places in this category are Muhammad ibn Tumart of Morocco; Muhammad ibn 'Abdullah Hasan of Somalia; Mohammed Al Mahdi of North Africa; Guru Nanak, founder of the Sikh religion; Shaikh Hasan al-Banna, founder of the Muslim Brotherhood; Mirza Ghulam Ahmad, founder of the Ahmadiyya; Abdul Baha, founder of the Bahai faith; and Rashad Khalifa, founder of United Submitters International. Mahdi, *Rebuttal,* 178.

68. Isa Muhammad excuses Elijah Muhammad for this claim, saying that since he did not know Arabic and was forced to rely on a translation of the Qur'an, and that done by the Ahmadiyya, it is no wonder that he did not quite understand what he was saying. *The Book of Lam,* 67.

69. See Warith D. Muhammad, *Challenges That Face Man Today* and Warith D. Muhammad, *Focus on Al-Islam.*

70. See Lawrence H. Mamiya, "From Black Muslim to Bilalian: The Evolution of a Movement"; and Mamiya, "Minister Louis Farrakhan and the Final Call: Schism in the Muslim Movement."

71. Isa Muhammad, *The Book of Lam,* 10.

72. Isa Muhammad, "Christ Is the Answer," 33.

73. Mahdi, *Rebuttal,* 118.

74. Isa Muhammad, "Christ Is the Answer," 54.

75. Ibid., 3.

76. Isa Muhammad, "Are the Ansars (in the West) a Self Made Sect?" 3.

77. Isa Muhammad, *The Holy Qur'an: The Last Testament,* 1.

78. Ibid., 2.

79. Ibid., 19.

80. Isa Muhammad, "Are the Ansars (in the West) a Self Made Sect?" 8.

81. Isa Muhammad, "Christ Is the Answer," 27.

82. In Isa Muhammad, "Al Imam Isa Visits Egypt 1981," Isa Muhammad

is shown in numerous photographs with leaders (usually but not always dark featured) of the Egyptian Muslim community.

83. Isa Muhammad, "Racism in Islam," 96.

84. Isa Muhammad, "Islamic Marriage Ceremony and Polygamy," 1.

85. Isa Muhammad, "The Night of the 100 Raka'aat," 42.

86. Isa Muhammad, "Are the Ansars (in the West) a Self Made Sect?" 4.

87. Ibid., 5.

88. Ibid.

89. Isa Muhammad, "Racism in Islam," 1.

90. Ibid., 15.

91. Isa Muhammad, "Are the Ansars (in the West) a Self Made Sect?" 4.

92. Isa Muhammad, "The Night of the 100 Raka'aat," 20.

93. Isa Muhammad, "Racism in Islam," 44–48.

94. Mahdi, *Rebuttal*, 9–15.

95. Isa Muhammad, "Al Imam Isa Visits the City of Brotherly Love," 13.

96. In Brooklyn the Ansar formed a "mujahaddin" group to defend themselves against the attacks of their enemies.

97. Isa Muhammad "Racism in Islam," 146.

98. Isa Muhammad "Al Imam Isa Visits the City of Brotherly Love," 14.

99. Ibid., 14.

100. Philips, *The Ansar Cult*, 133–82.

101. Mahdi, *Rebuttal*, 547–70.

102. Isa Muhammad, "Al Imam Isa Visits Egypt 1981," 18.

103. Mahdi, *Rebuttal*, 493–94.

104. Some disaffected Ansars charge Isa Muhammad with sexual misconduct, accusing him of sleeping with the wives of community members whenever he desired. He has denied such accusations.

105. "Marriage within the cult becomes no more than infrequent sexual relationships of 'mates' assigned by Isa without the marital contract. Consequently, marriage ceremonies became redundant and were discontinued from the early eighties." Philips, *The Ansar Cult*, 118.

106. Isa Muhammad, "Islamic Marriage Ceremony and Polygamy," 2. For additional information on the role of women, see Isa Muhammad, "Menstruation," "Thoughts of Muslim Women in Poetry," "Islamic Cookery," "Your Body," and "Childhood and Reproduction."

107. "After a hard day's work, and the husband comes home, he's mentally fatigued. This is the time when he needs most of all relaxation, someone to put his mind at rest. He finds this in the wife who has been gifted with the natural talent for sex, it can be any one of the four wives. She is superior in this field." Isa Muhammad, "Islamic Marriage Ceremony and Polygamy," 24–25.

108. Ibid., 26.

109. Mahdi, *Rebuttal*, 293. A May 1993 communication from members

of the Ansar Allah community says that "although man was created on the spiritual plane and woman was taken from man, woman was created on the earth and given a spirit by way of the X chromosome. From the Y chromosome of Adam Eve received her soul for he was her father and mother. This is most times interpreted as bone of my bone, flesh of my flesh. What you don't see is that he has different meanings for the word spirit and the word soul, and so does the Bible."

110. Isa Muhammad, "The Muslim Woman," 5.

111. Isa Muhammad, "Why the Beard?" 25. See also, Isa Muhammad, "Men Who Dress in Women's Clothes."

112. Isa Muhammad, "The Muslim Woman," 4.

113. Isa Muhammad, "Al Imam Isa Visits Egypt 1981," 16–17.

114. Isa Muhammad, "The Muslim Woman," 3.

115. Isa Muhammad, "Four Horsemen of the Apocalypse," 6, 11–12. Several of Isa Muhammad's pamphlets are devoted to specific issues concerning women's dress; see, for example, "Why the Nosering?" and "Why the Veil?"

116. Isa Muhammad is not solely concerned with the pleasure of the husband, however; a pamphlet entitled "The Sex Life of a Muslim" purports to be an aid to educating mature adults, male and female, in ways to make their relationships more rewarding. See also, Isa Muhammad, "Disco Music: The Universal Language of Good or Evil?" 18. In "Hadrat Faatimah," 7, Isa Muhammad cites the Prophet Muhammad's wife as a role model for Muslim women of today "in that she mastered her duties as a wife, as a mother and as a daughter."

117. Isa Muhammad, "The Night of the 100 Raka'aat," 31.

118. Ibid., 20.

119. "Al Imam Isa Visits the City of Brotherly Love," centerfold.

120. Philips, *The Ansar Cult*, 143.

121. Mahdi, *Rebuttal*, 550.

122. Isa Muhammad, "Sons of the Green Light." Since Isa says "I was the Qutb . . . of the Sufi Order" it appears that either he has relinquished this role or that the order is no longer in existence.

123. See "THE NUBIAN CREED: The Miracle Worker," in Mahdi, *Rebuttal*, 207–10, where Isa Muhammad insists that his miracles are very different from the tricks of a magician.

124. Mahdi, *Rebuttal*, 548.

• • • • •   Chapter 6

1. "Death of a 'Messenger,' " *Arizona Daily Star*, March 4, 1990, p. 2A.

2. "Lone Assassin," *Arizona Daily Star*, March 4, 1990, p. 4A. Mehdi was countering the speculation that the murder might have been commit-

ted by members of the Moslem Brotherhood. He stressed that Muslims should ignore people like Khalifa and Salman Rushdie rather than give them so much attention.

3. Philips, *The Qur'an's Numerical Miracle,* 3.

4. "They Will Find Out Tomorrow Who the 'Kazzab' Is! [54:25]," *Muslim Perspective* (October 1988): 1, 3.

5. Philips, *The Qur'an's Numerical Miracle,* 3.

6. Virginia Marston, "In Memoriam: Dr. Rashad Khalifa (1935–1990)," unpublished manuscript, 1990.

7. Interview with members of the Masjid Tucson, May 4–5, 1991.

8. Assad Nimer Busool, "A Refutation of Rashad Khalifah's Claim to be 'God's Messenger,' " unpublished manuscript, 1989. Busool claims that Khalifah's Ph.D. in chemistry gave him "no particular standing in the field of Islamic Studies" (p. 1).

9. Philips, *The Qur'an's Numerical Miracle,* 3, identifies Hoefle as an American convert (to Islam), but Khalifa's followers say that she was not Muslim.

10. Lisa Spray, *Jesus,* 123.

11. Martin Gardener, "Mathematical Games."

12. Khalifa, *Quran: The Final Scripture,* 471.

13. *Akher Sa'a* (January 24, 1973, November 28, 1973, December 31, 1975); cited in Spray, *Jesus,* 126.

14. Khalifa, *Quran, Hadith, and Islam,* 13, 19, 25, 29.

15. Ibid., 52.

16. Khalifa, *The Computer Speaks,* 2.

17. See, for example, similar denunciations of Sunna and Hadith in Khalifa's commentary on Suras 3:111, 4:48–51, 6:113, 7:30, 17:101–6, and 24:1–2, in which he refers to these traditions as Satanic, followed only by the half educated, false sources of jurisprudence, and serving a function similar to that played by the Mishnah and Gemarah in the Jewish tradition.

18. This is affirmed in many place in Khalifa's writings; see, for example, *Quran: Visual Presentation,* 4.

19. Khalifa, *Quran: The Final Scripture,* 499.

20. In *Quran: The Final Scripture,* however, Khalifa lists sixteen "simple facts" in appendix 1, 472–73, after which he goes on to what he calls "the intricate facts." *The Computer Speaks* lists fifty-two of these "physical facts," each with pages of tables and words and verses from the Qur'an.

21. See, as an example, Khalifa's commentary on the letters "A.L.R." prefixing Sura 10, in *Quran: The Final Scripture:* "These letters participate in the Quran's miraculous numerical code that remained a divinely guarded secret for 14 centuries, pending the preparation of this translation. . . . Thus, we find the total frequency of occurrence of these three letters a multiple of 19 in every single sura that is initialed with them.

This sura contains 2527 of the Arabic letter A, L, and R; sura 11 contains the same total of A, L, and R; sura 12 contains 2413; sura 14 contains 1216; and the last A.L.R.-initialed sura, namely sura 15, contains 931. Each of these totals is a multiple of 19. This miraculously flawless numerical code explains the expression, 'These letters constitute the miracle of Qur'an.' "

22. Khalifa, *The Computer Speaks,* 200; compare Khalifa, *Quran: The Final Scripture,* 2, 138, 165, 206, 321, 334, 407.

23. The charge has been laid against Khalifa by his critics that he has manipulated the letters and words of the Qur'an to make them fit his system. In *Quran: Visual Presentation* (p. 11) he presents the words of the first revelation within hexagon-shaped boxes so that the reader can see clearly that they are nineteen in number. One box, however, contains both "ma" and "lam," which could easily be argued are two Arabic words and not one, bringing the total of the words in the revelation to twenty.

24. These appendices are almost identical with the appendices in *The Computer Speaks.*

25. Khalifa, *Quran:The Final Scripture,* 484–85.

26. Ibid., 486–87.

27. Khalifa cites Suras 2:259, 6:60, 10:45, 16:21, 18:11, 19:25, and 30:55; *Quran: The Final Scripture,* 505.

28. See Smith and Haddad, *The Islamic Understanding of Death and Resurrection,* 67–70.

29. Khalifa, *Quran: The Final Scripture,* 503.

30. See Khalifa's commentary on Suras 5:92, 5:99, 6:21–24, 7:172–73, and 36:74–75 as examples of his insistence that neither Muhammad nor other figures such as Jesus, Mary, or the saints have the power to help or to harm.

31. Khalifa, *Quran: The Final Scripture,* 492.

32. Ibid., 488.

33. Ibid., 497.

34. Khalifa's certainty on this matter is not shared by many scholars, Muslim and non-Muslim.

35. Khalifa, *Quran: The Final Scripture,* 493.

36. Khalifa, *Quran, Hadith, and Islam,* 37.

37. Khalifa, *Quran: The Final Scripture,* 512–21.

38. According to Islamic doctrine, the original Torah and Gospel were revealed by God but were drastically changed either through carelessness or by intention by members of the Jewish and Christian communities.

39. Muslims traditionally have used this same explanation to identify biblical references attesting to the coming of Muhammad.

40. See Khalifa, *Quran: The Final Testament,* xii.

41. *Muslim Perspective* (March 1985).

42. Busool, "A Refutation," makes a scathing attack on Khalifa's interpretation, accusing him of completely misreading (or purposely misrepresenting) the historical facts he cites in support of his theory. "This writer congratulates Mr. Khalifah for his wild imagination and his ability to falsify history," writes Busool. "I challenge Mr. Khalifah to bring forth his historical source for the scholars of the Muslim Ummah to examine, as we are going to do with the sources to which he referred in his talk about the two verses supposedly added to Surat al-Tawbah" (p. 13).

43. The governments involved are in Afghanistan, Algeria, Bahrain, Egypt, Indonesia, Iran, Iraq, Jordan, Kuwait, Lebanon, Libya, Malaysia, Morocco, Nigeria, Oman, Pakistan, Qatar, Saudi Arabia, Somalia, Sudan, Syria, Tunisia, Turkey, Uganda, and the United Arab Emirates.

44. Gog and Magog are a recognized part of Middle Eastern mythology. According to Islamic tradition their appearance will be one of the signs of the coming of the last days, when they will sweep down as a scourge on the earth. Smith and Haddad, *The Islamic Understanding of Death and Resurrection*, 67–70.

45. *Muslim Perspective* (September 1985).

46. *Muslim Perspective* (September 1987).

47. Busool, "A Refutation," calls Khalifa the new "Musailimah" in reference to the false prophet Musailimah who appeared during the last years of the Prophet Muhammad in the Arabian peninsula.

48. This is an international umbrella organization, operating out of Saudi Arabia, that acts as a defender of Islamic interests.

49. *Muslim Perspective* (December 1987).

50. "Al-Azhar Leads the Muhammadan World to Utter Destruction," read the headline. "Specifically, the inevitable consequences are: 1. Egypt will die by the year 1990. 2. Egypt will take with her the rest of the Arab world. 3. Pakistan and the rest of the Muhammadan world will die around the same time." *Muslim Perspective* (March 1988).

51. *Muslim Perspective* (December 1987); (October 1988).

52. Khalifa sued the Islamic Society of North America for one million dollars for defamation of character, a suit he did not win. Muzammil Siddiqi, interview with the authors, March 21, 1991.

53. Speculation on the numerical values of letters has been important to some Sufi movements and has played a role in some esoteric Shi'i writings. Numerology has generally been disavowed, however, by Sunni Muslims.

54. Abdul Quddus Hashimi, "The 'Miracle' of 19," *Impact International* (October 9–22, 1981): 15.

55. See, for example, Abbas Amanat, *Resurrection and Renewal*, 94ff, for a discussion of numerological influences on the Bab.

56. See, for example, Twahir A. Mohammed and Saida Coulombe's contribution to "Reader's Response" in *Islamic Horizons* (January-February

1987): 5. Mohammed and Coulombe also accuse Khalifa's group of slandering the late Ismail Faruqi by saying he was condemned to hell because he added "Muhammad Rasoolullah" (Muhammad is the messenger of God) to the shahadah or confession of God's oneness. Members of the Sunni mosque in Tucson, in an interview with the authors conducted on May 5, 1991, expressed their concern that the whole mathematical theory plays off the ignorance of people who do not know enough Arabic to study the Qur'an for themselves.

57. Busool, "A Refutation," goes Philips one farther: "Congratulations to the New World on receiving this new imposter [Khalifah] who added his name to the long list of imposters who have infested the New World in recent years, for example, Jim Jones, who poisoned close to 900 of his followers; Oral Roberts, who extorted ten million dollars from the poor, the needy . . . ; Jimmy Swaggart, who preached morality day and night while he had a shameful relationship with hookers; James Bakker who committed adultery with his secretary; and La Baron, who killed some of his followers while he was living. It seems the god of the New World communicates with corrupt souls only" (p. 19).

58. Philips, *The Qur'an's Numerical Miracle*, 4.

59. Siddiqi, telephone interview with the authors, March 1991, said that since Khalifa's death the movement has dwindled significantly; he continues to give no credence to any of Khalifa's ideas. The reason why Khalifa was able to attract a following, he said, is because many young people in this country have no Islamic background and do not understand the real meaning of the Qur'an and the Sunna and thus find Khalifa's interpretations appealing. Siddiqi lamented the fact that there are so few Imams in North America who are able to help people interpret Islam accurately.

60. *Muslim Perspective* (January 1988).

61. It is interesting that Isa Muhammad of the Ansaru Allah also said that he was born in 1935.

62. *Muslim Perspective* (August 1988).

63. In the Qur'an the word *God* occurs 2,698 times ($19 \times 142$). The verse numbers where the word *God* occurs add up to 118,123 ($19 \times 6,217$).

64. Khalifa, *Quran: The Final Testament*, 637.

65. "Lo, I am sending my messenger to prepare the way before me; and suddenly there will come to the temple the Lord whom you seek and the messenger of the covenant whom you desire." Hebrew Bible scholars, it should be noted, are divided on the question of whether the messenger should be understood to be the same as, or other than, the Lord mentioned in this verse.

66. Khalifa, *Quran: The Final Testament*, 627.

67. Ibid., 642.

68. Ibid., 639.

69. Khalifa, *Quran: The Final Testament*, 703.

70. Ibid., 697.

71. Ibid., 667.

72. Other responsibilities, in addition to proclaiming the Qur'an's mathematical code and removing the two false verses, are explaining the purpose of our lives, proclaiming one religion for all people, proclaiming that Zakat (obligatory charity) is a prerequisite for redemption, unveiling the end of the world, explaining why most believers in God do not go to Heaven, proclaiming that God never ordered Abraham to kill his son, proclaiming the secret of perfect happiness, and establishing a criminal justice system. Ibid., 647.

73. *Submission Perspective* (October 1989).

74. *Muslim Perspective* (June 1989).

75. *Muslim Perspective* (July 1989).

76. *Submission Perspective* (October 1989). Yuksel cited March 19 as the date on which Muslim ʿulama in Saudi Arabia condemned both Rushdie and Khalifa, and also noted that the international organization campaigning in defense of Rushdie called itself "Article 19," the article of the Human Rights Charter of the United Nations that guarantees freedom of expression.

77. "God does not terminate the life of His messengers until they deliver their message and serve their function in this world. . . . "God reassures us with the example of Jesus that Dr. Rashad Khalifa's soul was raised before the disbelievers struck: 'For certain, they never killed him. Instead, God raised him to Him; God is almighty, Most Wise' (4:157–58; 3:55)." "They think they killed him," one of his followers is reported to have said, "but they were only messing with his body. They did the same thing to Jesus. They thought they were crucifying Jesus, but his soul was with God." *Arizona Daily Star*, March 4, 1990, p. 4A.

78. "Gulf War Continues: Hell Is Surrounding the Rejectors," *Submitters Perspective* (February 1991).

79. "The Contact Prayers [Salat]" (Tucson, Ariz., n.d.), 5.

80. "The Contact Prayers [Salat]," 1.

81. The reason for this seems to be because they do not want to distinguish among the prophets, and thus do not celebrate the ʿId of the Prophet Muhammad's birthday; they eschew all such forms of celebration.

82. "O you who believe, when you get up to perform the Salat prayers you shall wash your faces, your hands up to the elbows, wipe your heads, and wash your feet."

83. Khalifa, *Quran, Hadith, and Islam*, 78.

84. Ibid., 80.

85. "When you observe your Salat prayers, your voice shall not be too loud, nor too low; you shall maintain an intermediate tone."

86. Khalifa, *Quran, Hadith, and Islam*, 79.

87. In "Submission Song," for example, children sing about the five pillars. The affirmation that messengership is, on one level, the responsibility of all those who profess God's oneness is underscored in the chorus to a song entitled "Messengers": "You're a messenger, I'm a messenger, all of us are messengers, when we teach the word of God." Susan Erisen and Donna Arik, (Tucson, Ariz., 1990).

88. Khalifa could not, however, be accused of being liberal in his interpretation of verses in the Qur'an having to do with matters of personal modesty. In dealing with Suras 23:5–6, 24:30, 33:35, and 70:29–30, for example, he stressed the virtues of virginity and chastity as essential to countering the moral breakdown of today's society. *Quran: The Final Testament*, 706.

89. When asked how they identify themselves individually by filling out forms requesting religious affiliation, they responded, "Believer/Submitter to God Alone."

90. Edip Yuksel confessed that his own enthusiasm for Khalifa and excitement over the numerological analysis of the Qur'an was badly shaken over the matter of the two verses, and he accused Khalifa of having gone too far. Later, he says, he realized the validity of the analysis. Accepting an "alteration" in the Qur'an as he had always known it constituted what he called "the biggest spiritual problem I ever had."

91. Yuksel has written a pamphlet entitled "19 Questions for 'Muslim Scholars' " (Tuscon, Ariz.: Renaissance Institute, n.d.), in which he continues Khalifa's sharp critique of Hadith and Sunna. He cites Hadith that make the Prophet look vicious, cruel, and inconsistent, saying that they contradict the Qur'an and should be seen not as sanctioned by God but as the "manufactured" products of men in the second century of Islam.

92. See Aziz Ahmad, *Islamic Modernism in India and Pakistan*, 120–22. Compare the writings of the leader of the group, Abd-Allah Chakralawi, *Isha'at al-Qur'an*.

93. Khalifa, *Quran, Hadith, and Islam*, 76.

94. Translations from Khalifa, *Quran: The Final Testament*.

# Selected Bibliography

Abd-Allah, Umar F. *The Islamic Struggle in Syria.* Berkeley: Mizan Press, 1983.

Abu-Izzeddin, Nejla M. *The Druzes: A New Study of Their History, Faith and Society.* Leiden, Neth.: E. J. Brill, 1984.

Adamson, Iain. *Mirza Ghulam Ahmad of Qadian.* Surrey: Elite International Publications Ltd., 1989.

Afnan, Ruhi Muhsin. *The Revelation of Baha'u'llah and the Bab.* New York: Philosophical Society, 1970.

Ahmad, Aziz. *Islamic Modernism in India and Pakistan, 1857–1964.* London: Oxford University Press, 1967.

Ahmad, Hazrat Mirza Bashir-ud-Din Mahmud. *The Ahmadiyya Movement in Islam.* N.p., n.d.

———. *Ahmadiyyat or the True Islam.* Qadian, India: Tahrik-i-Jadid, 1937.

———. *Introduction to the Study of the Holy Quran.* London: Mubarak A. Saqi, 1985.

———. *Invitation to Ahmadiyyat.* London: Routledge & Kegan Paul, 1980.

Ahmad, Hazrat Mirza Ghulam. *The Essence of Islam: Extracts from the Writings of the Promised Messiah.* Vol. 1. Translated by Muhammad Zafrullah Khan. London: Ahmadiyya Centenary Publications, 1978.

———. *Message of Peace.* Lahore, India: Anjuman Ahmadiyya, 1936.

———. *Objectives Explained.* Lahore, India: Lahore Art Press, n.d.

———. *The Philosophy of the Teachings of Islam.* London: Ahmadiyya Centenary Publications, 1979.

———. *Tadhkirah.* Translated by Khan. London: Saffron Books, 1976.

Ahmad, Hazrat Mirza Taher. *Murder in the Name of Allah.* London: Butterworth, 1989.

————. *An Open Invitation to the Mubahala*. Washington, D.C.: Ahmadiyya Movement in India, 1988.

Ahmad, S. N. *The Anti-Ahmadiyya Stance*. Zurich: Published by the author, n. d.

————. *The Anti-Islamic Ordinance*. N.p.: Ahmadiyya Movement, n.d.

ʿAli, Maulawi Sher, ed. and trans. *The Holy Qurʾan*. Rabwah, Pakistan: Oriental and Religious Publishing Co., n.d.

ʿAli, Muhammad. *The Ahmadiyyah Movement*. Lahore, India: Ahmadiyyah Anjuman Ishaʿat Islam, 1973.

Ali, Noble Drew. *The Holy Koran of the Moorish Science Temple of America*. Chesapeake, Va.: Distributed by ECA Associates, n.d.

Amanat, Abbas. *Resurrection and Renewal: The Making of the Babi Movement in Iran, 1844–1850*. Ithaca, N.Y.: Cornell University Press, 1989.

ʿAmira, Abd al-Rahman. *Al-Madhahib al-Muʿasira wa-Mawqif al-Islam Minha*. Riyadh: Dar al-Liwaʾ, 1982.

"A New Islam in America." *Moslem World* (25 January 1935): 78–79.

Ashʿari, Abuʾl-Hasan ʿAli ibn Ismaʿil. *Maqalat al-Islamiyin*. Edited by Helmut Ritter. Cairo: Muhammad Muhyi al-Din ʿAbd al-Hamid, 1954.

ʿAta, Abd al-Qadir. *Al-Mahdi al-Muntazar: Bayn al-Haqiqa waʾl- Khurafa*. Cairo: Dar al-ʿUlum li al-Tibaʿa, 1980.

Austin, Allan D. *African Muslims in Antebellum America: A Sourcebook*. New York: Garland, 1984.

ʿAwf, Ahmad Muhammad. *Al-Qadyaniyya: al-Khatar Alladhi Yuhaddid al-Islam*. Cairo: Dar al-Nahda al-ʿArabiyya, 1967.

Baghdadi, ʿAbd al-Qahir. *Al-Farq bain al-Firaq*. Cairo: Muhammad Muhyi al-Din ʿAbd al-Hamid, n.d.

al-Baihaqi, ʿAli ibn Zaid Zahir al-Din. *Tarikh Hukamaʾ al-Islam*. Edited by Muhammad Kurd ʿAli. Damascus, 1946.

Balyuzi, H. M. *The Bab: The Herald of the Day of Days*. Oxford: George Ronald, 1973.

————.*Bahaʾuʾllah: The King of Glory*. Oxford: George Ronald, 1980.

Betts, Robert Brenton. *The Druze*. New Haven, Conn.: Yale University Press, 1988.

Beynon, E. D. "The Near East in Flint, Michigan: Assyrians and Druze and their Antecedents." *Geographical Review* 24, no. 2 (1944): 239–74.

Bijlefeld, Willem A. "A Prophet and More Than a Prophet." *Muslim World* 59, no. 1 (January 1969): 1–28.

Birge, John Kingsley. *The Bektashi Order of Dervishes*. London: Luzac, 1937.

Bontemps, Arna. *The Harlem Renaissance Remembered*. New York: Dodd, Mead, 1972.

————, and Jack Conroy. *Anyplace but Here*. New York: Hill & Wang, 1966.

Bousquet, G. H. "Moslem Religious Influences in the United States." *Moslem World* (25 January 1935): 40–44.

Braden, Charles S. "Islam in America." *International Review of Missions* 48 (1959): 309–17.

———. "Moslem Missionaries in America." *Religion in Life* 28, no. 3 (Summer 1959): 331–43.

Bromley, David, and Phillip Hammond. *The Future of New Religious Movements.* Macon, Ga.: Mercer University Press, 1987.

Burney, Mohammed Elias. *Qadiani Movement: An Exposition of So-Called Ahmadiyyat.* Durban, South Africa: Makki Publications, 1955.

Calverly, E. E. "Negro Muslims in Hartford." *Muslim World* 55, no. 1 (January 1965): 340–45.

Chakralawi, Abd-Allah. *Isha'at al-Qur'an.* Lahore, India, 1902.

Chaudhri, Rashid Ahmad. *A Book of Religious Knowledge.* London: Ascot Press, 1977.

———, and Shamim Ahmad. *Persecution of Ahmadi Muslims and their Response.* London: Press & Publication Desk, Ahmadiyya Muslim Association, n.d.

Cushmere, Bernard. *This Is the One: Messenger Muhammad: We Need Not Look for Another.* Phoenix, Ariz., 1971.

Dana, Nissim. *The Druze: A Religious Community in Transition.* Jerusalem: Turtledove Publications, 1980.

Da'ud, Abu. *Mishkat Kitabul Ulum.* Vol. 2. Cairo, n.d.

Deedat, Ahmed. *Al-Qur'an the Ultimate Miracle.* Durban, South Africa: Islamic Propagation Center, 1979.

Ellwood, Robert S., and Harry B. Partin. *Religious and Spiritual Groups in Modern America.* Englewood Cliffs, N.J.: Prentice-Hall, 1988.

Epps, Archie, ed. *The Speeches of Malcolm X at Harvard.* New York: Morrow, 1968.

Essien-Udom, E. U. *Black Nationalism: A Search for an Identity in America.* New York: Dell, 1962.

al-Faruqi, Isma'il Raji. *Tawhid: Its Implications for Thought and Life.* Kuala Lumpur, Malaysia: International Institute of Islamic Thought, 1982.

Faruqi, N. A. *Ahmadiyyat: In the Service of Islam.* Lahore, India: Ahmadiyya Anjuman Isha'at Islam, 1983.

Fauset, Arthur H. *Black Gods of the Metropolis.* Philadelphia: University of Pennsylvania Press, 1971.

Fisher, Humphrey J. *Ahmadiyya.* London: Oxford University Press, 1963.

Fisher, Michael M. J., and Mehdi Abedi. *Debating Muslims: Cultural Dialogues in Postmodernity and Tradition.* Madison: University of Wisconsin Press, 1990.

Fuda, Farag. *Qabl al-Suqut.* Cairo, 1985.

Galanter, Marc, ed. *Cults and New Religious Movements*. Washington, D.C.: American Psychiatric Association, 1989.

Gardener, Martin. "Mathmatical Games." *Scientific American* 234 (September 1980): 22–24.

Haddad, Yvonne Yazbeck, ed. *The Muslims of America*. New York: Oxford University Press, 1991.

———, and Adair T. Lummis. *Islamic Values in the United States*. New York: Oxford University Press, 1987.

Hatcher, William S., and J. Douglas Martin. *The Baha'i Faith: The Emerging Global Religion*. San Francisco: Harper & Row, 1984.

Hiskett, Mervyn. "Material Relating to the State of Learning among the Fulani before Their *Jihad*." *Bulletin of the Society of African Studies* 19 (1957).

Hitti, Philip K. *The Origins of the Druze People and Religion*. New York: Columbia University Press, 1928.

Hodgson, Marshall S. G. *The Venture of Islam*. Vol. 1 Chicago: University of Chicago Press, 1974.

Hollister, John Norman. *The Shi'a of India*. London: Luzac, 1953.

Holmes, Mary Caroline. "Islam in America." *Moslem World* 16 (1926): 262–66.

Holt, P. M. *The Mahdist State in the Sudan*. Oxford: Oxford University Press, 1971.

Hudson, Winthrop S. *Religion in America*. New York: Scribners, 1981.

Husayn, Muhammad al-Khadr. *Al-Qadyaniyya*. Cairo: Majma' al-Buhuth al-Islamiyya, 1970.

al-Husayni, 'Abd Allah. *Al-Judhur al-Tarikhiyya li al-Nusayriyya al-'Alawiyya*. Dubai, 1980.

Iqbal, Muhammad. *Islam and Ahmadism*. Lucknow, India: Islamic Research and Publications, 1974.

Isfara'ini, Shahfur ibn Tahir. *Al-Tabsir fi'l-Din wa Tamyiz al-Firqa al-Najiya 'an al-Firaq al-Halikin*. Cairo, 1940.

Jafri, Husain M. *Origins and Early Development of Shi'a Islam*. London: Longman, 1979.

Jones, Oliver, Jr. "The Black Muslim Movement and the American Constitutional System." *Journal of Black Studies* 13, no. 4 (June 1983): 417–37.

Khalifa, Rashad. *The Computer Speaks: God's Message to the World*. Tucson, Ariz.: Renaissance Productions, 1981.

———. *Miracle of the Quran: Significance of the Mysterious Alphabets*. St. Louis, Mo.: Islamic Productions International, 1973.

———. *Quran, Hadith, and Islam*. Tucson, Ariz.: Islamic Productions International, 1982.

———. *Quran: The Final Scripture*. Tucson, Ariz.: Islamic Productions International, 1981.

————. *Quran: The Final Testament*. Tucson, Ariz.: Islamic Productions International, 1989.

————. *Quran: Visual Presentation of the Miracle*. Tucson, Ariz.: Islamic Productions International, 1982.

al-Khalily, Ahmed ibn Hamed. *Who are the Ibadis?* Zanzibar, Tanzania: Al-Khayria Press Limited, n.d.

Khan, Muhammad Zafrullah. *Ahmadiyyat: The Renaissance of Islam*. London: Tabshir Publications, 1978.

————. *The Message of Islam*. Washington D.C.: Ahmadiyya Movement in Islam, n.d.

al-Khayyat, 'Abd al-Rahim Muhammad. *Kitab al-Intisar wa'l-Radd 'ala Ibn al-Rawandi al-Mulhid*. Edited by H. S. Nyberg. Cairo, 1925.

Lavan, Spencer. *The Ahmadiyah Movement*. New Delhi: Manohar Book Service, 1947.

————. "Polemics and Conflicts in Muslim History." *Muslim World* 62, no. 4 (October 1972): 283–303.

*Lessons on Islam, Book IV*. Rabwah, Pakistan: Majlis Atfalu-Ahmadiyya, 1966.

Lincoln, Eric C. "The American Muslim Mission in the Context of American Social History." In *The Muslim Community in North America*. Edited by Earl Waugh, Baha Abu Laban, and Regula B. Qureshi. Edmonton: University of Alberta Press, 1983, pp. 215–33.

————. *The Black Muslims in America*. Revised edition. Boston: Beacon Press, 1973.

Lyde, Samuel. *The Asian Mystery: Ansaireeh or Nusairis of Syria*. London: Longman, Green, Longman & Roberts, 1860.

Maesen, William A. "Watchtower Influences on Black Muslim Eschatology: An Exploratory Story." *Journal for the Scientific Study of Religion* 9, no. 4 (1970): 321–25.

al-Mahdi, Sayyid Isa al Haadi [Isa Muhammad]. *The Ansaar Cult. The Truth about the Ansaarullah Community in America. Truth Is Truth. Rebuttal to the Slanderers*. N.p., 1989.

Makarem, Sami Nasib. *The Druze Faith*. Delmar, N.Y.: Caravan Books, 1974.

Malcolm X. "God's Judgment of White America." In *The End of White World Supremacy*. Edited by Benjamin Goodman. New York: Merlin House, 1971.

Mamiya, Lawrence H. "From Black Muslim to Bilalian: The Evolution of a Movement." *Journal for the Scientific Study of Religion* 21, no. 2 (June 1982): 138–52.

————. "Minister Louis Farrakhan and the Final Call: Schism in the Muslim Movement." In *The Muslim Community in North America*. Edited by Waugh, Laban, and Qureshi. Edmonton: University of Alberta Press, 1983, pp. 234–55.

The Marcus Garvey and Universal Negro Improvement Association Papers. Vol. 5 (September 1922-August 1924). Edited by Robert Hill. Berkeley & Los Angeles: University of California Press, 1986.

Margoliouth, D. S. "On Mahdis and Mahdism." *Proceedings of the British Academy* 7 (1915–16).

Marsh, Clifton E. *From Black Muslims to Muslims: The Transition from Separatism to Islam, 1930–1980.* Metuchen, N.J.: Scarecrow Press, 1984.

Martin, B. G. *Muslim Brotherhood in Nineteenth-Century Africa.* Cambridge: Cambridge University Press, 1976.

Martin, Tony. *Race First.* Westport, Conn.: Greenwood Press, 1976.

Massignon, L. "La mubahala de Medine et l'hyperdulie de Fatima." *Opera Minora* (1963): 550.

Massoud, Muhammad Said. *I Fought as I Believed.* Montreal: Ateliers des Sourds, 1976.

Maududi, S. Abul A'la. *The Qadiani Problem.* Lahore, India: Islamic Publications, 1979.

Melton, J. Gordon, ed. *The Encyclopedia of American Religions.* Wilmington, N.C.: McGrath, 1978.

Memon, Naeem Osman. *Ahmadiyyat or Qadianism! Islam or Apostasy.* Islamabad: Islam International Publications Ltd., 1989.

Miller, William McElwee. *The Baha'i Faith: Its History and Teachings.* Pasadena, Cal.: William Carey Library, 1974.

Momen, Moojan. *Studies in Babi and Baha'i History.* Los Angeles: Kalimat Press, 1982.

Moosa, Matti. *Extremist Shiites: The Ghulat Sects.* Syracuse: Syracuse University Press, 1988.

Muhammad, Elijah. *The Fall of America.* Chicago, 1973.

———. *Messenger to the Blackman.* Philadelphia, 1965.

———. *Our Savior Has Arrived.* Chicago, 1974.

Muhammad, Isa. "Al Imam Isa Visits Egypt 1981." Brooklyn, N.Y.: Ansaru Allah Community, n.d.

———. "Al Imam Isa Visits the City of Brotherly Love." Brooklyn, N.Y.: Ansaru Allah Community, 1979.

———. *Al-Qur'an al-Muqaddasa; Al Wasiyya Al-Akhirah.* Brooklyn, N.Y.: Ansaru Allah Community, 1977.

———. *The Ansar Cult.* Brooklyn, N.Y.: Ansaru Allah Community, 1988.

———. "Are the Ansars (in the West) a Self-Made Sect?" Brooklyn, N.Y.: Ansaru Allah Community, n.d.

———. *The Book of Laam.* Brooklyn, N.Y.: Nubian Islamic Hebrews, n.d.

———. "Childhood and Reproduction." Brooklyn, N.Y.: Ansaru Allah Community, n.d.

———. "Christ Is the Answer." Brooklyn, N.Y.: Ansaru Allah Community, n.d.

———. "Disco Music: The Universal Language of Good or Evil?" Brooklyn, N.Y.: Ansaru Allah Community, n.d.

———. "The Dog." Brooklyn, N.Y.: Ansaru Allah Community, n.d.

———. "Four Horsemen of the Apocalypse: Can the Holy Qu'ran Solve It?" Brooklyn, N.Y.: Ansaru Allah Community, n.d.

———. "Hadrat Faatimah." Brooklyn, N.Y.: Ansaru Allah Community, n.d.

———. *The Holy Qu'ran: The Last Testament.* N.p.: Published by the author, 1977.

———. "Islamic Beauty Aids and Customs." Brooklyn, N.Y.: Ansaru Allah Community, n.d.

———. "Islamic Cookery." Brooklyn, N.Y.: Ansaru Allah Community, n.d.

———. "Islamic Marriage Ceremony and Polygamy." Brooklyn, N.Y.: Ansaru Allah Community, 1977.

———. "Men Who Dress in Women's Clothes." Brooklyn, N.Y.: Ansaru Allah Community, n.d.

———. "Menstruation." Brooklyn, N.Y.: Ansaru Allah Community, n.d.

———. "The Muslim Woman." Brooklyn, N.Y.: Ansaru Allah Community, n.d.

———. "The Night of the 100 Raka'aat." Brooklyn, N.Y.: Ansaru Allah Community, n.d.

———. "The Paleman." Brooklyn, N.Y.: Ansaru Allah Community, n.d.

———. "Racism in Islam." Brooklyn, N.Y.: Ansaru Allah Community, n.d.

———. "The Sex Life of a Muslim." Brooklyn, N.Y.: Ansaru Allah Community, n.d.

———. "Sons of Canaan." Brooklyn, N.Y.: Ansaru Allah Community, n.d.

———. "Sons of the Green Light." Brooklyn, N.Y.: Ansaru Allah Community, n.d.

———. "Thoughts of Muslim Women in Poetry." Brooklyn, N.Y.: Ansaru Allah Community, n.d.

———. "What and Where Is Hell?" Brooklyn, N.Y.: Ansaru Allah Community, n.d.

———. "Why Allah Should Not Be Called God." Brooklyn, N.Y.: Ansaru Allah Community, n.d.

———. "Why the Beard?" Brooklyn, N.Y.: Ansaru Allah Community, n.d.

———. "Why the Nosering?" Brooklyn, N.Y.: Ansaru Allah Community, n.d.

———. "Why the Veil?" Brooklyn, N.Y.: Ansaru Allah Community, n.d.

———. "Your Body." Brooklyn, N.Y.: Ansaru Allah Community, n.d.

Muhammad, Tynetta. *The Comer by Night.* Chicago: Masjid No. 2, 1986.

Muhammad, Warith D. *Challenges That Face Man Today.* New York: Published by the author, 1985.

———. *Focus on Al-Islam.* Chicago: Published by the author, 1988.

al-Murtada, Ahmad ibn Yahya. *Kitab Tabaqat al-Muʿtazila.* Beirut, 1961.

al-Nadawi, Abu al-Hassan ʿAli. *Al-Qadyani wa-al-Qadyaniyya.* Jidda, Saudi Arabia: Al-Dar al-Suʿudiyya li-al-Nashr, 1967.

al-Nadawi, Muhammad Ismaʿil. *Al-Qadyaniyya, ʿArd wa-Tahlil.* Cairo: al-Majlis al-Aʿla liʾl-Shuʾun al-Islamiyya, 1390H.

Naff, Alixa. *Becoming American: The Early Arab Immigrant Experience.* Carbondale: Southern Illinois University Press, 1985.

Najjar, Abdallah. *The Druze.* Translated by Fred I. Massey. N.p.: American Druze Society, 1973.

———. *The Druze: Millennium Scrolls Revealed.* Translated by Massey. N.p.: American Druze Society, n.d.

———. *The Tawhid Faith.* Vol. 2. N.p.: American Druze Society, 1985.

Nasr, Seyyed Hossein. *Traditional Islam in the Modern World.* London: Routledge & Kegan Paul, 1987.

———, Hamid Dabashi, and Seyyed Vali Reza Nasr, *Expectation of the Millennium: Shiʿism in History.* Albany: State University of New York Press, 1989.

*National Spiritual Assembly of the Bahaʾis of the United States and Canada.* Wilmette, Ill.: Bahaʾi Publishing Committee, 1944.

Perillier, Louis. *Les Druze.* Paris: Editions Publisud, 1986.

Philips, Abu Ameenah Bilal. *The Ansar Cult in America.* Riyadh, Saudi Arabia: Tawheed Publications, 1988.

———. *The Qurʾan's Numerical Miracle: Hoax and Heresy.* Riyadh, Saudi Arabia: Al-Furqan Publications, 1987.

Pritchard, E. E. Evans. *The Sanusi of Cyrenaica.* Oxford: Oxford University Press, 1949.

Rafiq, B. A. *Truth about Ahmadiyyat.* London: London Mosque, 1978.

Ritter, Helmut. "Philologia III: Mohammedanische Haresiographen." *Der Islam* 18 (1929): 34–55.

Rizvi, Saiyid Athar Abbas. *A Socio-Intellectual History of the Isna ʿAshari Shiʿis in India.* 2 vols. Canberra, Aust.: Maʿrifat Publishing House, 1973.

Robbins, Thomas, and Dick Anthony, eds. *In Gods We Trust: New Patterns of Religious Pluralism in America.* New Bruswick, N.J.: Transaction, 1981.

Rushdie, Salman. *The Satanic Verses.* New York: Viking, 1989.

Sachedina, Abdulaziz Abdulhussein. *Islamic Messianism.* Albany: State University of New York Press, 1981.

al-Safadi, Salah al-Din Khalil ibn Aibak. *Kitab al-Wafi biʾl-Wafayat.* Istanbul: Biblioteca Islamica, 1931.

Salman, Tawfiq. *Adwaʾ ʿAla Madhhab al-Tawhid.* Beirut: Published by the author, 1963.

al-Shahrastani, Muhammad ibn ʿAbd al-Karim. *Kitab Nihayat al-Iqdam fi ʿIlm al-Kalam.* Edited by Alfred Guillaume. London: Oxford University Press, 1934.

————. "Muslim Sects and Divisions." In *Kitab al-Milal wa'l-Nihal.* Translated by A. K. Kazi and J. G. Flynn. London: Kegan Paul International, 1971.

*Shorter Encyclopaedia of Islam.* Edited by H. A. Gibb and J. H. Kramers. Ithaca, N.Y.: Cornell University Press, 1957.

Simpson, Frank T. "The Moorish Science Temple and Its 'Koran.' " *Muslim World* 39, nos. 1 & 2 (January-April 1947): 56–57.

Simpson, George Eaton. *Black Religions in the New World.* New York: Columbia University Press, 1978.

Smith, Jane Idleman, and Yvonne Yazbeck Haddad. *The Islamic Understanding of Death and Resurrection.* Albany: State University of New York Press, 1981.

Spray, Lisa. *Jesus.* Tucson, Ariz.: Masjid Tucson, 1987.

al-Subki, ʿAbd al-Wahhab ibn. *Tabaqat al-Shafiʿiya al-Kubra.* Edited by Mahmud Muhammad al-Tanahi ʿAbd al-Fattah Muhammad al-Helu. Cairo, 1964.

al-Tabatabai, Muhammad Husayn. *Shiite Islam.* Translated and edited by Nasr. London: Allen & Unwin, 1975.

Taliʿ, Amin Muhammad. *Asl al Muwahhidin al-Druze wa-Usuluhum.* Beirut: Dar al-Andalus, 1961.

Toftbek, E. "A Shorter Druze Catechism." *Muslim World* 44 (1955): 38–42.

Turner, Richard B. "The Ahmadiyya Mission to Blacks in the United States in the 1920's." *Journal of Religious Thought* 40, no. 1 (1983).

————. "Islam in the United States in the 1920's: The Quest for a New Vision of Afro-American Religion." Ph.D. diss., Princeton University, 1986.

Vincent, Theodore G. *Black Power and the Garvey Movement.* Berkeley: Rampart Press, 1971.

Wallis, Roy, ed. *Sectarianism: Analysis of Religious and Non-Religious Sects.* London: Peter Owen, 1975.

Washington, Joseph R., Jr., *Black Sects and Cults.* Garden City, N.Y.: Doubleday, 1973.

Waugh, Earle H., Baha Abu-Laban, and Regula B. Qureshi, eds. *The Muslim Community in North America.* Edmonton: University of Alberta Press, 1983.

Waugh, Sharon McIrvin Abu-Laban, and Qureshi. *Muslim Families in North America.* Edmonton: University of Alberta Press, 1991.

White, Abbie. "Christian Elements in Negro American Muslim Religious Beliefs." *Phylon* (Winter 1964): 382–88.

Williams, Raymond Brady. *Religion of Immigrants from India and Pakistan.* Cambridge: Cambridge University Press, 1988.

Wilmore, Gayraud. *Black Religion and Black Radicalism.* Maryknoll, N.Y.: Orbis Books, 1983.

al-Zahir, Hassan 'Issa 'Abd. *Al-Qadyaniyya: Nash'atuha wa-Tatawwuruha.* Cairo: Al-Hay'a al-'Amma li-Shu'un al-Matabi' al-Amiriyya, 1973.

# Index

Abortion, 71
Aboulhosn, Malhim Salloum, 33
Abraham, 109, 136, 148
Abu Bakr al-Siddiq, 3, 126
Ackley, Sam, 40
Adam, 109, 113, 130, 132
Afghanistan, 7
Africa, 7, 9, 20, 32, 49, 79, 80, 82, 85, 96
African Americans, xi, 9, 10, 11, 19, 20, 49, 61, 62, 71, 76, 79, 81, 82, 83, 84, 85, 92, 93, 96, 98, 102–9, 111, 114, 115, 123, 126, 162
Ahmad, Hazrat Mirza Bashir-ud-Din Mahmoud, 33, 54, 58, 66
Ahmad, Hazrat Mirza Ghulam, x, 3, 51–60, 66, 69, 72, 117, 155
Ahmad, Hazrat Mirza Nasir, 53
Ahmad, Hazrat Mirza Tahir, 53, 67, 70
Ahmad, Kassim, 153
Ahmad, Mirza Monawar, 63
Ahmad, Mubasher, 67, 68
Ahmad, Muhammad, 110
Ahmad, Shaikh Mubarak, 73

Ahmadiyya, x, 9, 15, 49–78, 94, 107, 117, 125, 155, 162; annual conventions of, 63; associations of, 64; bans on, 54; education of, 70, 71, 75; founder of, 51, 59; international headquarters of, 64; Lahore Jamaat, 9, 19, 53; leadership within, 68; membership policy of, 50; mission of, 9, 50, 53, 56, 58, 59, 60, 61, 62, 63, 65, 68, 69, 70, 76; mosques of, 49, 64, 68; organizations of, 72–73; persecution of, 67–68; publications of, 54, 69; Qadianis, 9, 19, 51, 53, 54, 64, 155; women's roles within, 50, 70, 72–75; worldwide Ahmadiyya movement, 67
'Alawis, 7
Algeria, 8
'Ali ibn Abi Talib, 3, 4, 7, 126, 134
Ali, Muhammad, 41 (illus.)
Ali, Noble Drew, x, 10, 79, 80, 81 (illus.), 82–91, 93–106, 115, 124
Allah, 107, 113, 114, 127, 128, 131, 157; curse of, 57, 60, 67

American Muslim Mission, 20
Amir al-Mu'minin, 3
Amorites, 112, 113, 116
Ansaru Allah, xi, 10, 15, 105, 106, 107, 109, 110, 116, 117, 120–25, 127, 134, 136; communalism and, 110; community and, 128–33; marriage and, 113, 130; mosque's of, 133; national headquarters of, 110; pledge, 111; prayer, 133; unity and, 128; women's roles within, 130–33
Antichrist, 16, 56
Apocalypse, 115–17, 118
Arab Americans, 23, 39, 41, 42, 125; organizations of, 40
Arab-Israeli Conflict, 39, 40
Argentina, 58
al-ʿAskari, Imam Hasan, 7, 152
al-Atrash, Sultan Pasha, 36
Australia, 32

Babis, 9, 19
Baha'ism, 9, 19, 20, 154
Bahrain, 7
Bangladesh, 7
al-Banna, Hassan, 18
Bedouins, 3
Bektashis, 8, 19, 20
Bengalee, Mutiur Rahman, 63
Bey, C. Kirkman, 91, 99
Bey, F. Nelson, 99
Bey, Ira Johnson, 91
Bey, J. Blakely, 99
Bey, Sandra Weaver, 104
Bey, Sheikh Randy, 98 (*illus.*)
Bey, Sister R. Jones, 91
Bhutto, Zulfikar Ali, 67
Brazil, 58
Buddha, 87, 98, 160
Buddhism, 70, 158

Caliphate, 3, 8, 26; Fatimid, 24; Ottoman, 8, 21, 36

Canada, 49, 58, 64, 70
Christianity, 16, 43–46, 50, 57, 59, 65, 72, 79, 82, 85, 92, 95, 96, 103, 106, 107, 114, 126, 144
Christians, 32, 70, 153; Greek Catholic, 32; Greek Orthodox, 32; Maronite, 32, 39; missionary activity of, 54, 55, 56, 57, 70, 123
Colonialism, 8, 9, 36, 85
Confucius, 87, 98
Council of Masajid of North America, 67

Daoud, Sheikh, 108
Deedat, Ahmad, 138
Deen, Warith. *See* Muhammad, Warith Deen
DePriest, Oscar, 88
Dowie, John A., 59
Druids, 46
Druze, x, 12, 17, 23–48; American Druze Society, 24, 35, 36, 37, 39, 40, 41, 42, 45, 47; archives of, 43; community of, 31, 38; covenant of, 45, 169; cultural center of, 42 (*illus.*), 43; Epistles of Wisdom, 26, 38, 45; faith and, 24, 38; Foundation for Social Welfare, 42; founder of, 45; heritage of, 46; identity of, 39, 43–44; immigration and, 32, 33, 38; leadership among, 28, 29, 30; Majlis, 30; marriage and, 23, 29, 31, 34; mission of, 25; organizations of, 34, 35, 36, 37, 42; origins of, 24; reform and, 45; Shaykhs al-ʿAql, 28, 29, 37, 39, 44, 45; texts of, 26; traditions of, 25, 26, 38; wills of, 29; women's roles within, 30, 31, 34, 47

Darul Islam, 10
Dubai, 7

Egypt, 25, 49, 82, 108, 110, 115,
  124, 129, 132, 139, 154, 167
El, John Givens, 91
El, Robert Love, 99
El, William Gravitt, 91
Eschatology, 16, 59, 147

Farrakhan, Louis, 103, 121, 124
Father Divine's Peace
  Mission, 106
Fatimids, 17, 25, 126, 135
"Five Percenters," 10, 108, 116

Garvey, Marcus, xi, 62, 79, 81,
  85, 87, 95, 103
Ghana, 76
Ghani, Selma, 73
al-Ghazzali, Abu Hamid, 18
God, 8, 11, 12, 13, 27, 44, 51, 52,
  54, 55, 60, 68, 94, 96, 97, 99,
  102, 106, 146, 158, 160, 166;
  incarnation of, 46; oneness of,
  11, 12, 26, 27, 28, 45; submis-
  sion to, 160, 161, 162
Gravitt-El, William. See El,
  William Gravitt
Great Britain, 57
Green, Sheik Claude, 90
Guided One. See Mahdi
Gulf Crisis (1991), 71

Hadith, xi, 15, 18, 68, 71, 119,
  136, 140, 141, 143, 144, 148,
  149, 153, 162, 166, 167
Hakim, Amatul, 73
al-Hakim, Caliph, 25, 26
al-Hakim bi-Amr Allah, x, 24, 45
Halabi, Mohammed Khodr, 46
Hamid, Muzafaruddin, 10
Hammalists, 9

Hamza ibn 'Ali, 26, 27, 28, 45
al-Hanafiyya, Muhammad ibn, 51
Hassan II, King of Morocco, 86
Heaven, 95, 148, 159
HeLal, Samah, 47
Hermeticism, 26
Hinduism, 26; Arya Samaj, 55
Hindus, 70, 153, 158
Husayn ibn 'Ali, 25
Hussein, Saddam, 71, 161

Ibadis, 8
Ibn Abdullah, Muhammad Ah-
  mad, 108
Ibn Hanbal, Ahmad, 144
Ibn Khaldun, 18
Ibn Rushd, 18
Ibn Taymiyya, 18
Imam, 4, 25, 28, 50, 66, 135, 140,
  151, 161
Imamis. See Shi'ites, Imami
India, 7, 9, 49, 51, 54, 56, 59, 66,
  94, 153
Indians, American. See Native
  Americans
Indonesia, 49, 144
Iqbal, Muhammad, 66
Iran, 4, 7, 9, 19, 25, 49, 126, 134,
  144, 153
Iraq, 7, 20, 144, 153
Islam: attack on, 125, 148; faith
  of, 11, 12, 89; and law, 125, 129,
  153; leadership roles within, 12;
  lines of descent, 126; messen-
  gers of, 148; naming children,
  76–77, pillars of, 11, 157–58,
  162–64; reform within, 9, 18,
  52, 58, 120, 158, 166; revival-
  ism and, 24
Islamic Center International, 138
Islamic Society of North America, 67
Isma'il, Muhammad ibn, 25

Isma'ilis. *See* Shi'ites, Isma'ilis
Israel, 32, 38, 40, 166
Ithna 'Asharis. *See* Shi'ites,
  Imami

Jackson, Rev. Jesse, 41 (*illus.*),
  42, 103
Jama'ati Islami, 18, 58, 66,
  68, 167
Jaylani, Sheikh, 10
Jesus, 17, 52, 54, 55, 56, 85, 86,
  87, 94, 95, 96, 97, 109, 117, 119,
  143, 149, 160, 161; crucifixion
  of, 56, 159; intercession of, 147;
  journey to India of, 94, 96; return of, 15, 16, 67, 95, 117, 135;
  tomb of, 56
Jews. *See* Judaism
Jihad, 9, 58, 67
John the Baptist, 85, 95
Jordan, 32, 127
Judaism, 16, 32, 33, 46, 50, 54,
  70, 72, 95, 158; Jewish holidays, 76
Judgment, Day of, 147, 160

Kaleem, Alhaj Ata Ullah, 50
Kasem, Casey, 41 (*illus.*), 42
Kasem, Jean, 41 (*illus.*)
Khalifa, Rashad, xi, 11, 13, 107,
  137, 138, 139–68
Khalis, Hammas Khalifa
  Abdul, 10
Khan, Muhammad Zafrulla, 50,
  52, 66
Kharijites, 8
al-Khattab, 'Umar ibn, 3
al-Khidr, 110
Khoi, Imam, 20
Khomeini, Ayatollah, 18, 126, 166
King, Martin Luther, Jr., 103
Kuwait, 7, 71, 144

Lebanon, x, 4, 7, 24, 28, 31, 33,
  35, 38, 39, 40, 42, 43, 45
Libya, 139
Lord of the Age, 16

Mahdi, 12, 15, 16, 17, 25, 26, 108,
  110, 121, 125, 135
al-Mahdi, As Sayyid Abdur Rah-
  man, 108
Al-Mahdi, Imam Muhammad Ah-
  mad, 120, 125
al-Mahdi, Saadiq, 110, 113
Mahdiyya, 9
Makarem, Sami Nasib, 27, 37
Malaysia, 127
Malcolm X, 10, 79, 105, 121, 124
Manichaeanism, 46
Mansour, Ahmad Sobhy, 154, 165
Marston, Virginia, 138–39
Masih. *See* Messiah
Masih, Hazrat Khalifat-ul, 45
  (*illus.*)
Massoud, Muhammad Said, 32
al-Maududi, Abu al-A'la, 18, 58,
  66, 67
Mecca, 97, 100, 149, 151, 162
Medina, 2, 3, 149, 151
Mehdi, Mohammed T., 137
Messengers, 12, 13, 14, 148, 156,
  157, 158, 159, 160, 165
Messiah, 12, 15, 16, 25, 26, 50, 52,
  54, 55, 59, 111, 117, 119
Middle East, 29, 31, 34, 49
Millenarian movements, 17
Moorish Americans, x, 15, 83–93,
  95–98, 100–103; organizations
  of, 89, 99; scripture of, 93, 95,
  97, 100; symbology of, 100;
  temples of, 98, 99; worship of,
  99, 100
Moorish Manufacturing Coopera-
  tion, 88
Moorish National Convention, 88

Moorish Science Temple of America, x, 10, 79, 80, 84, 85, 87, 90, 91, 92, 96, 98, 100, 102–5, 108; doctrines of, 96, 97; economic independence of, 88, 102; goals and purposes of, 87–88; Grand Sheikh, 93, 99, 100, 101; heritage of, 80, 82, 83, 96; identity of, 96; leadership among, 93, 98, 99; management among, 99; marriage and, 101, membership within, 87, 98, 99
Morocco, 82, 85, 86, 96, 103, 115; flag of, 86, 96
Moses, 54, 109
Mu'awiya, Caliph, 4
Mubahala. See Allah, curse of
Muhammad, Elijah, 9, 10, 92, 103, 105, 106, 108, 110, 111, 116, 120, 121, 124, 155
Muhammad, Fard, 9, 92, 121
Muhammad, Isa, xi, 10, 80, 105–36
Muhammad, The Prophet, xi, 1, 2, 7, 11, 12, 13, 14, 15, 17, 27, 52, 53, 54, 55, 59, 68, 81, 84, 87, 97, 98, 111, 114, 122, 126, 127, 135, 138, 141, 142, 143, 144, 147, 148, 149, 152, 156, 158, 159, 160, 161, 163, 167
Muhammad, Warith Deen, 10, 20, 103, 120, 121, 123, 124
Mujaddid, 12, 17, 52, 53, 120, 121, 122, 135
al-Muntazar, Muhammad, 7
Murids, 9
Muslim Brotherhood, 12, 18, 58, 167
Muslim World League, 57, 66, 67, 109, 127, 154, 155; ban on Qadianis, 67; Council of Masajid of North America, 67

Nabi. See Prophet
al-Nadwi, Hassan, 67
Najjar, Abdallah E., 24, 36, 37, 42, 45, 47, 48
Najjar, Nada, 31
Nasir, Khalid, 63
Nation of Islam, xi, 62, 92, 103, 105, 108, 110, 120, 121, 124, 155
National Council of Islamic Affairs, 137
Native Americans, 84
Neoplatonism, 26, 46
Noah, 109
Nur-ud-Din, Maulawi, 53
Nuri, Mirza Husayn 'Ali, 20
Nusayr, Abu Shu'ayb Muhammad ibn, 7

Oman, 8, 20
Ottoman. See Caliphate, Ottoman

Pakistan, 7, 8, 21, 49, 64, 65, 66, 67, 68, 70, 71, 154
Palestine, x, 35, 49, 56
Paraklete, 149
Philips, Abu Ameenah Bilal, 109, 117, 118, 119, 120, 121, 128, 130, 135, 155
Pilgrimage. See Islam, pillars of
Prejudice. See Racism
Prophet, 12, 13, 14, 24, 53, 54, 56, 80, 96, 98, 103, 109, 121, 129, 135, 144, 148
Purdah, 73, 74, 75

Qadianis. See Ahmadiyya, Qadianis
Qur'an, 11, 14, 16, 17, 24, 51, 52, 55, 56, 57, 60, 63, 69, 71, 76, 81, 82, 83, 93, 95, 97, 103, 105, 106, 107, 110, 115, 119, 122, 123, 124, 128, 129, 130, 133,

137, 138, 140, 141, 144, 145,
147, 148, 149, 150, 121, 152,
156, 162, 163, 166, 167, 168;
miraculous nature of, xi, 137,
138, 141, 143, 156; numeric key
of, 11, 137, 138, 141, 145, 146,
147, 150, 152, 154, 168; translation of, 50, 60, 65, 67, 141, 157
Qaddhafi, Mu'ammar, 139
Quraysh, 3, 8
Qutb, Sayyid, 58

Racism, x, 61, 63, 65, 84, 106,
110, 111, 112, 113, 114, 124,
126, 134
Reformer. *See* Mujaddid
Reincarnation, 26, 44, 91, 92, 101
Resurrection, 7
Rushdie, Salman, 161

Salman al-Farisi, 7
Sadiq, Mufti Muhammad, 60, 61,
62, 63
Satan, 97, 107, 109, 113, 127, 132,
138, 144, 147, 153, 154, 161, 163
Saud, Sultan Abdul Aziz Ibn, 82
Saudi Arabia, xi, 7, 8, 12, 66, 109,
144, 154
Shahada, 12
Shari'a. *See* Islam, law
Shaykhs (Elders). *See* Druze, lead-
ership among
Shi'ites, 3, 45, 125, 134, 153;
'Alawis, 19, 20; Bektashis, 8,
19, 20; Ibadis, 19, 20; Imamis/
Ithna'Asharis ("Twelvers") 5, 7,
16, 19–20, Isma'ilis ("Seveners"),
4, 5, 19, 23–25; Zaidis ("Fivers"),
4, 5, 19–20
Shirk, 12
Siddiqi, Muzammil, 155, 156
Sikhs, 70, 153, 158
Smith, Clarence Jowars, 10

Soviet Union, 7, 49, 151
State Street Mosque, 108
Sudan, 9, 80, 108, 110, 111, 114,
120, 121, 123, 124, 125, 154;
Mahdist movement in, 111
Sunna, x, xi, 2, 11, 136, 140, 141,
143, 144, 148, 149, 153, 156,
162, 166, 167
Sunni, 1, 3, 7, 10, 12, 13, 17, 21,
22, 45, 50, 54, 59, 61, 103, 109,
119, 120, 125, 126, 130, 134,
152, 153, 155, 162
Syria, x, 4, 7, 20, 31, 33, 35, 49

Taha, Mahmoud Mahomed, 167
Tajikistan, 7
Tanzania, 8
Tawhid. *See* God, oneness of
Trinity, 8
Truth, Sojourner, 103
Turkey, 20
Tunisia, 154

Umar ibn al-Khattab, 126
Unitarian. *See* Druze
United Islamic Nation, 151, 152
United States, 9, 18–20, 23, 31,
33, 34, 35, 37, 38, 39, 40, 44,
45, 47, 49, 53, 58, 59, 60, 61,
62, 63, 65, 67, 68, 69, 70, 76,
84, 85, 86, 92, 110, 122, 123,
125, 126, 128, 139, 151
United Submitters International,
xi, 11, 107, 137–68; attack on,
154; community of, 162, 164,
165, 168; creed, 170–72; doctrines of, 146–48; pillars of,
162–64; postmodernism and,
168; universalism among, 160;
utopian view of, 168; women
in, 164–65
Universal Negro Improvement
Association, xi, 62, 84–85, 103

Union of Soviet Socialist Republics. *See* Soviet Union
Uthman ibn 'Affan, 126

Wahhabis, 12, 18, 109, 125, 134, 147
Webb, Alexander Russell, 9, 59
West Indies, 110
World Association of Muslim
Youth, 138

Yasin, Ghulam, 63
Yemen, 4, 20, 127, 152, 154
Yuksel, Edip, 165

Zaid ibn 'Ali, 4
Zaidis. *See* Shi'ites, Zaidi
Zia ul-Haqq Regime, 67
Zionism, 40
Zoroastrianism, 26